I10650038

THE
POWER
to
CHANGE
TODAY

THE POWER
to
CHANGE
TODAY

SIMPLE SECRETS TO THE
SATISFIED LIFE

Gregory Dickow

New York   Boston   Nashville

Scriptures are primarily taken from the King James Version as well as the New American Standard Bible.

The New American Standard Bible.
Copyright © 1960, 1962, 1963, 1968, 1971, 1972, 1973, 1975, 1977, 1995 by The Lockman Foundation.

Scriptures were taken from the New International Version.
Copyright © 1973, 1978, 1984 by International Bible Society.

Scriptures were taken from the New Living Translation Holy Bible.
New Living Translation copyright © 1996, 2004 by Tyndale Charitable Trust.
Used by permission of Tyndale House Publishers.

Scriptures were taken from the New King James Version.
Copyright © 1982 by Thomas Nelson, Inc.

Copyright © 2009 Gregory Dickow
All rights reserved. Except as permitted under the U.S. Copyright Act of 1976, no part of this publication may be reproduced, distributed, or transmitted in any form or by any means, or stored in a database or retrieval system, without the prior written permission of the publisher.

FaithWords
Hachette Book Group
237 Park Avenue
New York, NY 10017

Visit our Web site at www.faithwords.com.

Printed in the United States of America

First Edition: April 2009
10 9 8 7 6 5 4 3 2

FaithWords is a division of Hachette Book Group, Inc.
The FaithWords name and logo are trademarks of Hachette Book Group, Inc.

Library of Congress Cataloging-in-Publication Data

Dickow, Gregory.
  The power to change today : simple secrets to the satisfied life /
Gregory Dickow. — 1st ed.
    p. cm.
  ISBN 978-0-446-50414-0
  1. God (Christianity)—Love.   2. Love—Religious aspects—Christianity.
3. Spirituality.   4. Christian life.   I. Title.
  BT140.D53 2009
  248.4—dc22
                                                           2008038114

Contents

Foreword

We all want to be happy.

And in our vision of happiness, most of us want to feel loved, secure, and fulfilled. We want to have gratifying relationships, good health, financial security, and, most of all, a reason to get up in the morning—the end result being the *satisfied* life that God has always intended for us.

But how many of us go through our days feeling *dissatisfied*?

Perhaps money, time, or love seem to be in short supply. Maybe we don't have the body we'd like, the job of our dreams, the ideal mate, or the perfect circle of friends.

Or perhaps we're facing a serious health challenge, a family crisis, or battling demons of the past.

Sometimes we're so consumed by all this that our days are filled with worry, stress, frustration, or even despair.

The telling words of Mick Jagger echo the feelings of countless people: "I can't get no satisfaction—though I try, and I try, and I try..."

This book is all about ending that dissatisfaction, once and for all—and creating the life you truly deserve. And it isn't going to take forever. Our title has a promise built into it: **you have the power to change *today***—not next month, not in two years, and not after twenty years of counseling!

Remember, everything you see in this world was created in six days. Clearly, God is in the business of getting things done, and getting them done fast! So we can *expect* His help *today*.

After nearly two decades of pastoring and counseling people with every imaginable challenge, I've discovered that there are certain key principles that unlock the doors to inward contentment. These are the *sixteen secrets* that you're going to read about in the pages that follow, keys to creating an invincible spirit and a satisfied life.

What do I mean by *invincible*? This is our ability to *overcome* and to *conquer*. And at its heart, this book is all about conquering negativity and achieving breakthroughs toward gratifying relationships, vibrant health, creative purpose, and a deep connection with God.

I don't personally believe that the obstacle to a satisfied life lies in *external* conditions. Still, many people insist that "if only" they had the perfect job or spouse, or enough money, *then* they'd be happy. Yet, in a study of lottery winners, the overwhelming majority was no happier than before. (Just ask Hugo from the TV show *Lost*!) The "right" promotion, marriage, or bank account will not guarantee a satisfied life.

The only pathway to true contentment is from the inside out—not from the outside in. I can tell you that our success or failure in life will be determined by how we *think*—not by what we *have*. And so, the real battle we face has little to do with outside conditions. It's the battle raging between our ears! As you'll see in the chapters ahead, *what you think and the way you think will determine the quality of your life*.

So as we begin this journey together, we're going to go on a *fast*. (Don't worry, you can still eat what you want.) This kind of fast is all about abstaining from wrong ways of *thinking*. You're going to read about how to eliminate what I call the *mentalities of failure* and replace them with *mentalities of success*.

As you'll see, each of the sixteen secrets ahead provides a crucial blueprint for living the satisfied life. First you're going learn about the power of *being loved* and *believing*—and about how your world can change when you're *expectant*. You'll find true comfort in the chapters on *being healed* and *being still*.

Next you'll learn the value of *knowing* and *loving* yourself, and you'll discover the freedom in *forgiveness* and *falling out of love* with feelings that no longer serve you. You're also going to receive the secret to unlocking *the greatness in you*—and you'll be inspired by others who have done the same.

Then you're going to see the transformative powers of *planting a seed*: how every action has a reaction and that sowing wisely brings the harvest you want. You'll see the connection between *conquering* your greatest challenge and *finding your true calling*, and the value of *living on the giving side*, which when tapped into will be like putting Miracle-Gro on the garden of your life.

Finally you're going to learn how to *smile at the future* by no longer being *afraid of the dark* and by learning how to *live in the moment*, rather than the future or the past. And not least important, you'll see the wisdom of *leaving the country* of your previous limitations.

In each of these chapters, I'm going to give you a specific recipe—the *ingredients*, and the instructions, so to speak—that will allow you to get the results God wants you to have.

I compare it to making a cake. If I held up a Duncan Hines chocolate-cake box, you'd admire the mouthwatering picture on the front. However, no matter how long you feasted your eyes, you would never get to *taste* the cake if you didn't open the box, gather the ingredients, and follow the simple instructions on the back.

Folks, we all know that there are many inspirational self-help books that are good at showing you the picture on the front of the box. What makes this book different is that it's about actually making and enjoying the cake, not just admiring it. As you'll see, in each chapter there are specific steps that are going to help you to master the theme at hand.

So let's fire up the oven, mix up these powerful ingredients, and begin. As we set off on this journey together, I can promise you that you're going to be liberated from the old way of thinking—and discover a brand-new way of living that will make you both invincible and truly satisfied.

—*Gregory Dickow*
April 2009

Acknowledgments

Albert Einstein once said, "You don't really understand something unless you can communicate it in a simple way." Yet, the feelings and beliefs in our hearts are often deep and complex. For me, to get them out of my heart and onto the written pages of this book could not have been accomplished without the incredible people that joined me on this journey. Each of them helped me to draw out these secret treasures and present them with profound meaning and substance in a simple way. They have given me a gift and helped to reinforce the guiding principles of my life.

My deepest thanks to Glenn Plaskin—who is a brilliant artist, literary whiz and most importantly, a true friend. His passion for excellence and meaningful insight was inspiring and unrivaled. His skill, efficiency, and sense of humor were altogether indispensable in the production of this book!

I want to thank Harry Helm and the entire team at Hachette Publishers, who believed in this project, valued the precious truths in the book, and committed themselves to making it a far-reaching success.

I am incredibly grateful to Jan Miller, my literary agent, who believed in me and saw what this book could become. Special thanks to Nena Madonia, Shannon Marven, and all the gang at Dupree/Miller, who worked diligently to make this a reality.

Thanks to the outstanding editorial contributors—Ed Friedel and Daniel Johnson. Ed's insight was superb. Daniel's heartfelt contribution was exceptional. Thanks to Thea Jeanne and Brooke Venegas for organizing and compiling much of my material.

Immense thanks to the staff and leadership team of Life Changers International Church—whose commitment, sacrifice and dedicated efforts, enabled me to focus the needed attention to writing this book. Special thanks to Darrell Law and Jeff Goliszewski for their vital contributions to the technical, graphic and video aspects of the production, as well.

This book is dedicated to every precious soul that has ever desired to experience the power that lies within to change virtually anything. Many of us have been disappointed by the failure of 'organized religion' to bring real meaningful change in our lives. May the truths in this book free you—from the inside out—as they have me, and give you the power to be changed forever, and to truly live—happily ever after!

Introduction

GATEWAY TO THE SATISFIED LIFE

"It takes a lot of courage to release the familiar and seemingly secure, to embrace the new. But there is no real security in what is no longer meaningful. There is more security in the adventurous and exciting, for in movement there is life, and in change there is power."

—ALAN COHEN

No doubt, you've heard the story of the doctor who was deeply worried about his patient.

"You're in terrible shape," he told him, "and you've got to *do* something about it.

"First, because of your high blood pressure and cholesterol, your wife is going to have to cook you healthier meals.

"Second, you're going to have to stop working so hard.

"Next, you're going to make a budget and she has to stick to it.

"Finally, she should make love to you anytime you want.

"And," he concluded, "unless these changes are made, you're going to be dead in thirty days."

"Doc," the man answered with a smile, "could you please tell my wife all this—because coming from you, it will sound much more official."

The man returned home, looking forward to the good life he was about to enjoy. When he walked in the door, his wife rushed up to him and said: "Oh, honey. Your doctor told me the news. I'm so sorry. You poor thing. I'm really going to miss you!"

So much for hoping someone *else* will change.

Doesn't it seem sometimes that our happiness and well-being is dependent on what someone else does?

We tell ourselves, "If my spouse would only see it my way, if my boss would only promote me, if my children would only straighten out—*then* I'd finally be happy."

In my own experience, I've often been most *dissatisfied* when I expected someone else to make me feel better, only to be left frustrated and unfulfilled. And even if we could get everyone to do exactly what we wanted them to do, we *still* wouldn't be happy.

Why not? Because, **the keys to a satisfied life and the power to change lie within *us*.**

It reminds me of the story of a Zen master who was visiting New York City, and stopped by a hot dog vendor for what was, to him, a rare treat. He handed the vendor a $20 bill for his hot dog, expecting change. When the vendor put the $20 into his cash box and closed it up, the Zen master sharply challenged him: "What about my change?"

The vendor smiled, and in what seemed to be a reversal in roles, philosophically retorted, "You know better than I, O great master—that change must come from WITHIN!"

Yet how often do we feel that improving our lives is an insurmountable challenge? We tell ourselves:

"I'm too old. It's too late. I don't have the background or resources, the right education or experience."

Our excuses and rationalizations, combined with the vain hope that others might change, are all stumbling blocks that hold us back. Yet, every January so many of us start the New Year with a list of well-intentioned resolutions. We vow to exercise and lose weight, to be a better spouse, to turn over a new leaf in one way or another, only to find ourselves right back to our old habits in no time. One woman wrote me after watching my television program. She told me she had tried to quit smoking for over 50 years! She had tried every method and plan available, to no avail— that is until she followed some of the simple steps that I will outline in this book. Today she is finally free.

So what's stopping us from having the life we deserve? What's the force that always seems to get in our way? It can be summed up in a word: FEAR. This fear is about so many things—fear of the unknown, fear of failing, fear of rejection, fear it's too late, fear we won't be loved, you name it.

In fact, sometimes we would rather keep things the same *old* way because our old habits give us a sense of security and comfort. Sure, we may not be happy, but we know what to expect—and at least it's familiar. We just grow accustomed to the way things are and give up hope. We cope, procrastinate, and complain. We stress out and get sick. We stay stuck—and we settle. Things don't get significantly better and neither do we. The end result is that we're in pain.

> ◟ Nothing says it better than Proverbs 23:7: "As a man thinks within, so is he."

For some of us, in fact, changing would be an admission of failure or weakness, when, in reality, admitting our need to change or improve is really a sign of life and of strength.

God told the apostle Paul, "My grace is sufficient for you. My power is perfected in your weakness."

So too in our lives, God's power begins where our strength ends. When we become dependent upon Him, and acknowledge our need, His power shows up.

And armed with that power you'll find that you have *the ability to change anything you want to.*

To accomplish this, however, we have to surrender the old way of thinking by changing the direction of our *thoughts*—those mental habits that determine how we feel and what we do.

I always say that **what you think and the way you think will determine the quality of your life. Your mind-set frames your attitudes, which determine your decisions, lead to your actions, and establish your habits, your character, and ultimately your destiny.**

And that's why the battle for happiness is not in the heavens, but in our heads.

So if you're feeling frustrated, discouraged, or unsatisfied—rather than peaceful, content, and invincible—you need to turn to a better *diet* of thinking.

I can tell you that creating a happier life begins by winning the battle of the mind.

So just as the children of Israel left Egypt—the bondage of their past—*we must release the pain and old ways of thinking* in order to emerge from the wilderness.

You might ask, "How long is all this going to take?" Not long. Remember, though it took the children of Israel forty years to get from the wilderness to the promised land, it was only meant to be an eleven-day journey!

Why, then, did it take so long? It was because of their wrong thinking—and because, they didn't, at that point, have faith in the love of God.

Aren't you ready to turn your "forty-year" delay into an eleven-day journey?

I can promise that you already have within the **power to fulfill your greatest potential.** You just have to remember that . . .

THE CUPBOARD IS FULL . . .
The Secret Is Knowing It

So true satisfaction is an *inside* job. Sure, we all need material possessions, but we sometimes forget that the greatest "thing" we possess is inside *ourselves*.

So let's start with what you already have within YOU. It's like making a meal when you may not have a lot of money for groceries. Before you begin to worry, just look inside your cupboard to see what you already have.

In 2 Kings 4, there is a woman whose husband had died, and the creditors were coming to take away her sons as slaves for payment.

She cries out to the prophet Elisha for help, and his response has become legend: *"What do you have in your house?"*

All she had in the cupboard was a little oil—but when she took it and put it in the hands of God, a miracle happened, and her needs were met.

The miracle was that as she poured the oil <u>out</u>, *it kept on flowing* to fill up many vessels—and so she could use this to repay the debt.

As a pastor, I am amazed by some of the single mothers who raise their kids, hold full-time jobs, living paycheck to paycheck, serve in church, and never complain. Somehow, they make something out of nothing. They take a little bread, peanut butter, eggs and butter, and make them stretch, feeding their families for weeks. They're not looking on the outside for the missing ingredient. They have opened up their cupboard and remembered what's already inside! It happens all the time.

Friends, **the key to a satisfied life is to *remember*, with gratitude, what you already have in your cupboard.** Your cupboard is NOT bare! You have an amazing mind, a soul that is deep and passionate. You have gifts and talents that God has placed in you. Made in His image, you possess creativity and energy—the powers of faith, hope and love.

As it says in Philemon, verse 6, "That your faith becomes effective by the acknowledging of every good thing which is IN YOU..."

THE ANTIDOTE TO DISSATISFACTION

Knowing this—that the secret to our satisfaction lies within—comes as a great relief because we don't have to do anything to "get" it on the outside, or "earn" it from somebody else.

Why not? It's because the satisfied life is not about how we act, how we look, or what we have.

Yet so often, we attempt to find our fulfillment or measure our worth by the pursuit of things or the approval of people. Still, after all our efforts, dissatisfaction seems to quickly return.

But, as we'll see in the pages ahead, as we take control of our life, from the inside out, everything begins to change, and no matter how full our cupboard, there is always room for improvement, right?!

Indeed, everyone **has *something* in their life that they would like to see changed, improved, or turned around.**

Maybe you're struggling financially. You may want to improve or repair your marriage or another important relationship. Maybe you just want to stop hurting somewhere—in your body, mind or heart.

I can tell you this: **If you're not completely satisfied with your life, you're not alone.** A January 2007 Gallup poll found that 46% of Americans are either *barely satisfied* or *actively dissatisfied* with the way things are going in their personal lives.

What makes half of a nation feel like this? I believe it's a shared sense of *powerlessness.* **Powerlessness is the root cause of all negative feelings and emotions. When we feel powerless to change the past, we feel *guilt*; when we feel powerless to change our present, we feel *depressed*; and when we feel powerless to change our futures, we feel *afraid*.**

I had a call on my radio program recently from Jim who was frustrated by the lack of joy and purpose in his life. "Pastor, I've tried everything," he said. "I've prayed, fasted, studied the Bible, gone to counseling, you name it. But I can't seem to shake this feeling. **I'm just not happy.** What am I missing?"

I told Jim that the secret to gaining power over our lives and being truly satisfied was: *understanding.* The Bible says in Hosea 4:6: "My people are destroyed and fail, because of lack of understanding."

Notice, God didn't say, "a lack of money" or a "lack of time" or a "lack of friends."

What Jim lacked was: understanding some simple keys to happiness. I told him:

1. Stop comparing yourself to others.
2. Stop beating yourself up for what's wrong in your life.
3. Find a way to bring joy to someone else, and you'll reap the harvest of joy in your own life as well.

When he saw how simple it was, his thinking changed. His attitude immediately improved. And he was well on his way to the satisfied life!

"Understanding" provides the energy that turns information into results. And this book is all about giving you understanding—thereby freeing you from feeling powerless and putting you back in control of your life.

> ⌒ Expect things to get better in your life, beginning today.

MIRACLES IN TROUBLED WATERS

Taking control of your life, of course, isn't always *comfortable*. Anything new has a learning curve.

When I first started playing golf, it was incredibly frustrating, just as life can be. I asked a golf pro if he would help me improve my game. So he took me out to a driving range, and after observing me, said: "Not bad. There are only three things that you need to fix—*your stance, your grip and your swing.*" I quickly realized that these were the only three fundamentals of golf—and I was bad at all of them!

Troubled at first, by the challenge to change, I knew there was only one way OUT—and that was to jump all the way IN. (When I did, a "miracle" happened—I got pretty good!) But "trouble"—is usually the last thing we want to face in life. Most of us would do anything to avoid the trials and storms of life. But we are going to have them, regardless. And, while God promises that we will have trouble in this life, He also promises a way out...

Step into the troubled water. That's where your miracle is waiting.

It reminds me of one of my favorite stories from John 5 when Jesus comes upon the Bethesda pool in Jerusalem, where miracles would happen. Amazingly, an angel would come and *stir* the waters every so often. Whoever got into the pool first, *when the waters were troubled*, would be healed from whatever their affliction was. Jesus came upon a lame man who had been lying by that pool for *thirty-eight years*, languishing in the same condition.

How many of *us* have languished by that same "pool," stuck, bored, and unchallenged, or trapped in old habits and negative attitudes?

Think about it: ***Only the person who got into the troubled waters would receive their miracle.*** I've read this a hundred times, but it really jumped out at me recently. If we want to see a turnaround in our lives we can't wait for the waters to calm. So often we wait for all the conditions to become just right — and they seldom do. Our miracle is waiting in the ***troubled*** water. If we avoid it, ignore it or procrastinate, things won't get better. We need to face the trouble, jump in it and, as Larry The Cable Guy puts it, "Git-R-Done!'

If we don't, we may end up stuck on the sideline of our miracle for thirty-eight years, without ever experiencing it.

The goal of knowledge is ACTION. So, jump in the waters of the pages to follow, look your trouble in the eye and trust God with all your heart. You will not be disappointed.

Throughout my life, there have been a lot of "troubled" waters swirling around me. As you'll read in the coming pages, I grew up in a home void of much love or affection. And I sure didn't come from a family of preachers and never went to a seminary. But God ultimately touched me in a special way, rescuing me from a very dark life. I knew that if He could reach me, He could reach just about *anybody*.

Along the way, I've seen countless storms — the pain and suffering that people bring, the betrayals and disappointments we all face, and the daily responsibilities of being a pastor, a counselor, a husband, and a father of five.

But I don't think anything could be as troubling as the awareness of my own shortcomings and mistakes. So many times, I've felt the dark hand of despair in reflecting upon my past and weaknesses — coupled with the storms in other people's lives, for whom I have responsibility.

But like the sweeping stroke of an eraser over a marked-up blackboard, all of that despair disappears at the thought of one thing that fills my soul. It's the knowledge that God loves me *no matter what* I'm going through, no matter what I've done. It's this knowledge that trumps all other powers, obstacles, and trouble.

It's secret #1 to the satisfied life — the everlasting truth that *you are loved*.

THE
POWER
to
CHANGE
TODAY

Part I

EXPERIENCE THE SOURCE OF TRUE POWER

Secret #1

Be Loved

A REASON TO LIVE

The supreme happiness in life is the assurance that we are loved.
—Victor Hugo

When I was a little boy, I decided to run away from home.

I guess every kid daydreams from time to time about escaping, but in my case, I *needed* to get away. Why? Because the sadness I felt inside was just too much for me to bear. I didn't know what to do with that pain. And I was only eight years old.

To say that tempers flew high at our house, that there was little laughter or love, is an understatement. The fighting was *intense*. I felt like I was trapped in an emotional storm. Anger erupted like thunder, and fear chilled my heart. There was little physical tenderness or affection. In fact, I can hardly remember ever being embraced by my parents. Hugging, kissing, and the words "I love you" were as foreign to our house as Russian or Chinese. And I really can't explain this lack of affection, though I know how much I desperately longed for it.

How many of us have felt cut off from our own families—the very people we thought we needed most—not physically alone but trapped in an angry house with no ally? For me, the depth of loneliness was an aching sense of being *shut out* from love.

So although I started out as a tenderhearted little boy, I learned very quickly that I needed to protect myself. I built a shell around me that nothing could penetrate. In contrast to the emotional outbursts around me, I became unemotional, shy, and detached. I was timid, almost invisible, disappearing into the background. I was feeling so much pain, so much negative emotion, but I pushed it all down.

I realize that there are people out there who experience far worse—childhood sexual abuse, physical illness, total abandonment, you name it. Yet growing up **with the absence of love** is its own form of suffering. It brings to mind the words of Mother Teresa, that "loneliness and the feeling of being unwanted is the most terrible poverty."

How many of us have felt this loneliness or love deficit? **Perhaps you've felt the absence of love, but pushed it down or learned to tolerate it.** That's exactly what I did until the day I decided to run away.

> Growing up in an atmosphere devoid of love is its own form of suffering.

My plan was to jump out the bedroom window and leap ten feet to the ground, figuring I could absorb the impact and make my escape. Sure, I had no money or knowledge of life beyond our subdivision in Detroit, but I didn't care. I felt like a stranger in my own house, so why *not* run away?

Then something stung my heart—the obvious. As I packed my little bag with a couple of T-shirts and underwear, I suddenly realized... *I had nowhere to go.*

Have you ever felt like that?

You wanted to escape... but didn't know what to do. Maybe you, too, have felt unloved, rejected, or totally alone. Perhaps you believed that you would never find the romantic love of your life, or that the person you *had* found was a mistake. Even now, you might feel trapped in an unhappy relationship, or find yourself being mistreated or manipulated. Yet you hold on anyway, believing that any relationship is better than being all alone.

No matter what the circumstance, your heart may be hurting. When I was a young boy, mine sure was. And it took me years to find the comfort and love that were missing.

Likewise, maybe someone you know is feeling empty right at this moment, wondering to themselves "What's the point?" as they sadly pull on their clothes for school or work.

We live in a world that longs for love. Whether you're young or old, single or married, rich or poor, urban or suburban, *everyone, everywhere*, wants to be loved. We need to know that people care about us, that they value and cherish us — that we matter. This fundamental need is at the very core of our being.

And it starts right at the cradle. Just watch a baby being held by his mother. Inseparable, both mother and child are blissfully content. The bond between them is unbreakable, just as it was in the womb when the baby was attached to the mother by the umbilical cord. In fact, one of the words for "love" in Hebrew is "*ahav.*" It means "to be attached to." This profound attachment to the mother is a nurturing balm to every child with this meaning: *I won't let you go. I will supply your every need. We will always be one.*

Likewise, when you hear the words "God loves you," this means that *He* attaches Himself to *you.* He will never let you go. He will supply your every need. Everything He has is yours. And He will never leave you alone.

But how often are we so stressed or discontented that we forget that God is right there beside us, offering His love? We may feel inadequate, lonely, or discouraged, and lose this knowledge that we *are* loved.

As we see in Deuteronomy 1:27, the children of Israel had the conviction that they were *unloved*, which is the number one reason why they failed to enter into the Promised Land. "Because the Lord hates us, He has left us to die in the wilderness." Of course, God did not hate them at all, but their mistaken belief led them astray. They failed to *be loved* — to *be* who God created them to be. As a result, they failed to do what God intended.

THE SEARCH FOR LOVE

Consider for a moment that we are called human "beings," not human "doings." In other words, just "being" is enough to deserve God's love. We don't have to *do* something to get it. Each of us is *entitled* to it.

This means that *no matter what you achieve, no matter what you look like, no matter if you're single or married, no matter how much or little money you have, no matter what your education,* **YOU ARE LOVED**—accepted, **approved of, and treasured by God.**

> As it says in 1 John 4:10: "In this is love, not that we loved God, but that He loved us, and gave His son as the payment for our sins."

This is the good news, the gospel, the heart and soul of all sixteen secrets to a satisfied life. You are an original. You are valuable. And you don't have to *try* to find love.

So rather than searching for love and approval on the *outside*, all we have to do is look on the *inside*, discovering what is, in fact, already there, built right into us.

We are the beloved of God. So often, we hear the word "beloved" used in the context of a funeral or a wedding, e.g., "Dearly *beloved*, we are gathered today..."

But in the context of this chapter, **"beloved" is understood as a term of *endearment* that God uses about us. God is saying to us, "You are mine. You are special to Me."** This love has no conditions attached to it. Love is His unbreakable promise. It means: "I will never break My promise. I will never bring up your sins again. And I will never leave you or forsake you."

Yet it often seems that *everything* people do is motivated by the idea of gaining somebody's love—in the form of approval or attention. Especially in our search for romance, we try to buy love, earn it, trade for it, or seduce it—going to any lengths to win it with gifts, money, or promises. We'll even advertise for it online, though it may still elude our grasp.

Others already in intimate relationships may still be yearning for love anyway. A woman I read about put it this way: "I've only been married six months, but I feel completely alone—that I don't matter, like a puppy sitting under the table begging for scraps, looking for some sign that he still loves me. I know I am pathetic to need this, and hate it."

What would make a woman feel so empty and worthless? It's that desperate craving for love, so strong, that, like the song, states we're sometimes "lookin' for love in all the wrong places."

A church member recently confided that she had been involved with a married man for seven years. "I knew it was wrong," she said "but I couldn't break away. I rationalized our relationship as being okay because we 'loved' each other."

Many who are married but *dissatisfied* wind up in such affairs, searching for love instead of repairing the relationship they already have. Others are faithful physically but lose themselves in pornography. And then there's our population of teenagers! More "mature" than ever before, and always hyper-romantic, our teens today are actively searching for love, not only at school but on their computers.

How many of these kids are surfing the Web, making dates instead of doing their homework? In the absence of finding romantic love, a teen may even join a gang in order to feel a deep sense of belonging to *something* or *someone*.

And beyond the search for romantic relationships, one of the most common ways to feel loved is to *gain the approval of others*. So often we feel we must perform well in order to attain validation. How many well-intentioned parents put undue pressure on their children, pushing them to be *the best* and to win? Kids begin to think that they can only get the love they deserve by excelling at something.

> We live in a performance-oriented society where people are constantly vying for attention and approval. Why else do teenage girls lose their virginity so easily? They long for validation and the affection of a man—who tells them that they're beautiful and loved—even if the guy doesn't mean it. You are loved unconditionally because God calls you His child. Until you know that, the search for affirmation is a winding, endless road leading you far from your true home.

Precocious six-year-old girls compete in "little" beauty contests, flirtatiously wearing adult clothes and makeup. Other parents push their children to be straight-A students, or great athletes, or to excel at debating, ballet, and the piano, too—sometimes all of the above!

It may sometimes appear to kids that they'll only get the love and attention they crave by becoming *superachievers*. So they do somersaults—literally and figuratively—to get the validation they need.

And we're not much different as adults. Many think that getting a better job or earning more money is going to earn them love. Or they'll set out to *change something* about their physical selves in hopes that the object of their desire will choose them or love them more.

This year 11.5 million Americans are having cosmetic procedures—the most popular ones being Botox injections and liposuction. Why?

> God accepts us as we are, embracing us in His loving arms, and never letting go.

Because people feel that if they look younger and appear thinner, *then* they'll capture the love they need.

Let me be clear here: There's nothing wrong with tweaking our appearance a bit if there's something we'd like to improve. But let's make sure we are *approved* before we are *improved*.

When you know you have God's stamp of approval, you won't keep changing to get other people's approval. So if you're a young woman and you hear that a guy likes blondes, don't go running out to dye your hair. You're more valuable than that. Your acceptance comes from God. Besides, the day you bleach your dark hair blond will be the day he decides he likes brunettes! All this only proves that, so often, human love is the "love of the lovely." In the absence of recognizing God's love, we search for approval everywhere and expect others to do the same.

> Let's make sure we are approved before we are improved.

Indeed, every advertisement tells us we're nothing unless we look like a star and pose like a model, play like an athlete and spend like a CEO. That's why some professional athletes feel the need to surpass their own personal best, even if they have to take steroids to do it.

And when any of us fails to live up to *unrealistic physical* or *performance standards* set out before us, we sadly begin to dislike ourselves—feeling unworthy and inadequate, a subject we'll look more at later. Why does this happen? It's because we perceive that being loved is *conditional*—dependent on having a different body or résumé, or on others approving us—which only leaves us feeling all the more dissatisfied and alone.

IN THE ABSENCE OF LOVE

What happens when love is in short supply? We undoubtedly feel an emptiness inside, a space that must be filled with *something*. Although God designed it to be filled with love, in the absence of it, people will turn to a variety of habits, addictions, and distractions to temporarily fill the empty space.

Whether it's the pursuit of money, sex, drugs, food, extramarital affairs, smoking, gambling, or even mindless television, none of these things can satisfy our need for love. They never do.

One cigarette leads to another. One empty affair ends; another begins. We always come up empty trying to fill in

> Make no mistake about it: love is the number one need in everyone's life.

that emotional void with anything but genuine love. In fact, most of the time, we end up feeling worse, right? But that doesn't stop us.

The path to feeling whole again begins with knowing that you *are* loved by your friends and family—but especially by your Creator.

And so it is that **the secret to being *beloved* is being connected to the love and life of God.** This, as we'll see in a few moments, really *is* enough to satisfy us.

I was thinking recently that so many people are trying to live holy and clean lives, abstaining from all that is wrong, struggling to detach themselves from the bad. **However, the miracle is that when we are attached to the *right* thing—the love of God—we easily detach from the**

wrong things. We let go of those habits and distractions that only push us further away from love. It no longer becomes a choice of morality or strength of will, but rather a natural result of *being* loved.

One reason this subject of *being loved* is so compelling to me is that I felt absolutely unloved as a kid. By the time I was a teenager, I *hated* myself—beginning with my looks. I had no front teeth during most of the time I was growing up. It started in the third grade, when one of them was knocked out on a teeter-totter. I was taken to an incompetent orthodontist, who ended up extracting the wrong tooth, leaving a gap in the middle of my mouth, which remained until I graduated from high school! (And by then, it didn't matter anymore.)

There I was, a dark-skinned Middle Eastern kid in an "all-white" school in Detroit with no front teeth, a prominent nose, and big lips. I can tell you that I was anything but "lovely." To say I had no self-worth is an understatement. All of my flaws, though minor, were magnified by my own sense of insecurity and self-consciousness.

Folks, it's an unfortunate reality that we do derive some of our value from how we look and perform. Years later I would teach about the difference between human and divine love. As we've seen, human love is often only about the outside: the more beautiful you are, the more desirable. **But divine love is God's love—bestowing value and beauty *no matter how you look or act.***

Sometimes, though, it seems we can't escape our looks. In my case, I was in high school in 1980, at the time of the Iranian hostage crisis, and because of our family's ethnic background, we were lumped together in people's minds with *terrorists*! Although I was Iraqi rather than Iranian, nobody distinguished between the two. I was painfully aware of the stares and whispers; and as a fearful, skinny kid, I was easily picked on and often threatened. Rejection was something I experienced on a daily basis. I was often the last person picked on the baseball or football team. And I was the last guy any girl liked.

So let's just say I *despised* myself. And I'm sure I am not alone. I felt there was something innately wrong with me, which is a horrible thing for anyone to feel.

Young lives, in particular, can be profoundly damaged because of our failure to experience the love that God has in store for us. Young teenage girls starve themselves, becoming anorexic, so that they can emulate the Hollywood stars on magazine covers. Why? Because they want to be popular and noticed (translation: they want to be loved).

As the father of four teenagers, I can tell you that my wife and I still pour affection onto them. We kiss and embrace them all the time, showering them with adoration. Kids need meaningful touches and kisses and words of affirmation. I tell them how beautiful they are, how gifted and capable, and how much I believe in them.

Instead of pressuring our children, we *affirm* them, and as a result, they do well in school and, more important, *in life*. They know they're beloved by their parents—and by God.

As we all know, when this knowledge is absent, girls will give up their innocence in hopes that a boy will love them, which is why one out of three teenage girls today has had sex by the time they're sixteen years old, two out of three by the time they're eighteen.

> Teenagers may feel worthless if they believe they are unpopular or unloved.

Many wonder, *If I don't have sex with him, will he break up with me or sleep with someone else?*

Most tragic, teenagers may feel *worthless* if they believe they are unpopular or rejected. In 2007, we read about the tragic case of Megan Meier, a thirteen-year-old who committed suicide after being spurned by the person she thought was her online boyfriend. Her need for love was so intense that the idea of losing it led her to feeling she might as well not live at all.

Friends, when you realize you are God's beloved—with the deepest conviction—your life is going to change in even more concrete ways. Studies show that increased doses of love decrease stress levels, elevate overall emotional contentment, and improve physical health.

Some years ago, Dr. Karl Menninger, noted physician and psychologist, was seeking the cause of many of his patients' ills. He told his staff that all patients were to be given large quantities of loving care and attention with absolutely no negativity allowed. At the end of six months, the time spent by patients in his clinic was cut in half.

That's how important our need for love can be.

Whew! As we've seen, when people feel unloved, they'll do almost *anything* to escape the pain. In my own case, the anguish and humiliation I felt in school began expressing itself in anger, cruelty, and harshness to others. I was seething inside and gravitated toward the "troublemakers," other outcasts like me. We'd escape down to the creek near our house and smoke, drink, and taunt the neighbors with curses and vulgarity—just to prove we were cool.

Then, in the ninth grade, I started experimenting with drugs—mostly marijuana and alcohol. Marijuana became *the* great escape from all the pain, fear, and insecurity I'd felt. It was a high that seemed to last forever, and it was also one of my only ways of making friends.

By the time I was a junior in high school, I was what many would consider an alcoholic. I was drinking daily, blacking out, and coming home at lunchtime just to get drunk. I was into dark and psychedelic music of the '60s and '70s—Black Sabbath, the Who, Led Zeppelin, and the Beatles' *White Album*—drug music. I'd blast the sound way up and could get high just *listening* to "Revolution 9"—as if I had smoked three or four joints. That's how susceptible I was to the spiritual world of mysticism and to mind-altering states.

At this point I was definitely scraping rock bottom. In the following chapter you'll find out what happened to me next.

But for now, if you're hurting or doubting God's love—first and foremost—here's how to turn it around.

1. *Dispel the Myth of an "Angry God."* As I mentioned earlier, the first generation of the children of Israel believed that God was mad at them, even hated them. So as a result of their skepticism and negative beliefs, they failed to experience the fulfillment of His promise.

In our own lives, we sometimes mistakenly view God as punishing us for our mistakes and flaws rather than as an all-forgiving, all-loving presence in our lives. I tell people all the time: God is not mad *at* you, He's mad *about* you. He *is* love. Love gives. Love understands. Love never fails. That's the kind of God I'm talking about!

2. *Talk to God.* Pour your heart out to God, telling Him all that is in you, until there is nothing left to tell. Nothing you tell Him is going to knock Him off the throne! He is patient, compassionate, and understanding—the greatest shoulder to cry on, and the mightiest counselor! *And* He doesn't charge $150 per hour for His therapy! So hide nothing. Bare your soul to the One who will not judge or reject you. He knows your greatest fears and human failings, and no matter what you say, you remain His beloved. You will feel His love washing over you, like the gentle refreshing waves of the sea.

3. *Give Up Perfectionism.* Let go of the pursuit—altogether. Be loved the way you are. You don't have to have it "all together" to be loved. Nobody does. We all have things about ourselves that we'd like to change or improve, that we're dissatisfied with. But you don't have to fix everything wrong in your life in order to be loved. You can make gradual improvements knowing that you have the safety net of His love beneath you. So realize that God doesn't change you to love you. He loves you—and His unconditional acceptance is the catalyst for positive change in your life. So relax...for works of art take time. When you accept this truth, follow it up by being patient with yourself. I like the poem that goes: "It took God a week to make the earth and stars, the sun, the moon, Jupiter and Mars. How very special I must be—'cause He's still workin' on me!"

continued

4. *Banish the Voices of Rejection.* Look in the mirror and tell yourself that you are chosen by God. See the good in your reflection — your strengths, your special qualities, the energy in your eyes, the beauty in your presence. Remember: you are the crown of His creation — His beloved. As such, you were made with a unique purpose that no one can fulfill but you. For this reason, you are important to God and to His world. What others may reject or turn away, God accepts and embraces.

5. *Ask God to Heal You.* Many of us have suffered the wounds of rejection, abandonment, abuse, or mistreatment. Left behind are wounds and scars. We all have them. Perhaps you've been through a difficult divorce or have experienced some sort of betrayal. Maybe you feel consumed with worry and guilt. Ask God to let you know *His* love; to let you see the wonders of all that He has for you. Ask Him to heal you from the memories preventing you from believing in His love. Perhaps pray a simple prayer like this:

Lord, I want to feel Your love and Your warm embrace. Heal me from the memories that have blocked my ability to experience Your love. Set me free to know I am Your beloved. Amen.

In this rather personal chapter, which began with the story of my wanting to run away from home, I hope you might recognize something precious and vulnerable inside you — your own version of that little child who needed love and had nowhere to go.

He saw no refuge or hope, not until the day he found the love of God, which had always surrounded and protected him, even though he didn't know it then.

In the next chapter I'll tell you about the event that finally led me to discover the truth that I was not only beloved, but I could love others, too.

But for now, remember that you are accepted, approved of, and treasured by God.

And as we've seen, you are entitled to *unconditional* love regardless of what you accomplish or look like. And therefore the belief that we are unloved (or that we have to find love from others at any cost) is a lie.

Remember that when Jesus was baptized, God spoke to Him from Heaven, and said: "You are my beloved son and in you I am well pleased." What an amazing statement. Here we see that *before* Jesus even performed a miracle, or preached a sermon, or made the ultimate sacrifice by dying for our sins, He already had God's approval and love in His pocket.

From that moment forward, Jesus never needed anyone's approval. He was *beloved* by His Father. This *freed* Him to do what God called Him to do—as a response to God's love, not as an attempt to earn it. This is when you really start living. This is when life has true meaning and purpose.

I think all human beings long to run into the arms of loving mothers or fathers and pour out their hearts, knowing that they won't be judged, rejected, or abandoned. And we find this total acceptance when we run into the arms of our Heavenly Father.

That's why I titled this chapter "Be Loved." The title has a double meaning. It's both a *description*—that you are beloved—and an *action*—be loved—something you can actively practice.

So in the spirit of the Nike mantra, "just do it!" *Embrace something that cannot be earned. Allow yourself to receive the unconditional love of God.*

And best of all, once you experience His love, you are free from *needing* other people to approve of you. Sure, it feels good to be loved by others—but it feels really bad to "need" their love in order to feel good about yourself. It's almost like you're using them as a crutch. The irony is that when you don't "need" love from others, you are empowered to give and receive it more freely. Why? Because you're confident in God's love toward you. You *are* His beloved.

> Each of us is valuable and precious, even if we don't accomplish any great feat. We're deserving of love just because we're a child of God.

Suddenly, with God's approval in *your* pocket, it will free you to be who He created you to be. You're going to be more confident to go out in the world and shine. You can handle your responsibilities better and achieve great things because you are supported with love. In fact, you're already the very thing that everybody is searching for and seeking to become. Your attitude toward yourself and others will change. Accomplishments are going to matter less. You're going to shake off the performance anxiety that drives you to stress, unrealistic comparisons, and self-condemnation.

Knowing the truth of this infinite circle of love that surrounds each one of us, folks, is the first secret to changing today. Confidence in God's unconditional love is what so often spells the difference between success and failure in life. I can tell you that *being loved* by Him is the secret to every good thing that has ever happened to me. When I discovered God's love, it set in motion the confidence and faith I needed to walk in His will. It became like a magnet that drew His blessings and purposes into my life. All I needed to do, as you'll see in the next chapter, was to . . . *believe.*

Secret #2

Believe

Without faith, a man can do nothing. With it, all things are possible.
— Sir William Osler

My friend, Adam was trained as a classical pianist. He went to a conservatory of music for nine years — practicing six hours a day and giving concerts, while also teaching in graduate school and earning a doctoral degree.

But at age twenty-six, despite all that long training, he dropped out of school. His friends and family were shocked, most of them disapproving.

Why would he quit? What would possess him to throw it all away? Adam later explained that he hated the isolation of a practice room and was always nervous performing in public. In fact, he experienced such a high level of stress that his arms were locked in muscle spasms and he wound up in the hospital suffering from an ulcer.

"That was it," he told me. "I was really burned out — tired of the whole thing. And even though my parents couldn't believe I'd walk away from the piano, I'd had enough. It wasn't my future, not anymore."

So Adam borrowed $300 from a friend and moved to New York, carrying with him a new dream. He'd write a book about a legendary artist whom he had always admired. This was very odd. After all, Adam had never written anything before, much less had he had anything published. But armed with his idea, and expecting to succeed, he just picked up the phone and started calling major publishing companies. Adam then engaged one of the top literary agents in New York and soon had landed a substantial book contract, while just six months earlier he'd been broke!

How did he do it? What drove him? What made this miracle possible? "Honestly, it was faith," he told me. "I literally *talked* myself into the reality of *being* an author. I visualized it. I'd fantasize and dream about it—and pray for it." He also ignored any skepticism that came into his path, sensing that his future depended on it. When Adam's book was published, it became a worldwide success. It was reviewed in every major U.S. newspaper and hailed as "masterfully" written.

TRUE BELIEVERS

My friends, if Adam could zoom to the top of a field with no training or experience—armed with only raw talent, determination, a dream, and a brave forecast for his future—what could YOU do to change your life today?

What would it take? What would be the first step? Your new path starts with one indispensable element. It's the *key* ingredient that made all the difference to Adam, and a resource that is within your reach.

> What could YOU do to change your life today? What would it take? Only one thing: it's the power of believing.

It's the power of *believing*. You see, Adam had faith in a *second chance*, *believing* that he could start over again. With God's help, so can you.

And it doesn't have to take twenty years. You don't have to go back to school (unless that is your dream) or make a thousand changes in your life first.

I can tell you that those who improve their lives or achieve great things always look beyond what they can see with their eyes to the unlimited possibilities of faith.

> If Columbus had turned back, no one would have blamed him. Of course, no one would have remembered him, either.

I can never forget the story of Angela Cavallo, of Lawrenceville, Georgia, who discovered that her teenage son, Tony, was pinned under a 1964

Chevy Impala. It had collapsed as the boy was changing a tire in April 1982. The terrified mother grabbed the side of the car with both hands and pulled it up four inches, enough to take the pressure off her son. And she kept the car propped up for *five* minutes! How did a five-foot-eight-inch woman in her late fifties hold up a 3,500-pound car for five minutes while neighbors reinserted the jack and dragged the boy out? She *believed* she could. She was determined to save her son's life, and she did.

So often, faith is evidence that cannot yet be seen, but it's an active resource inside each of us, just waiting to be tapped into.

In this sense, believing is giving yourself *the power of permission*. As it says in Mark 11:24: "Whatever you ask for in prayer, believe that you have received it, and it will be yours."

This doesn't mean your dream will fall into your lap. You'll still need patience, persistence, and courage. But believing gives you the strength to reach out and try. It's the "sight" of your soul—the source of your potential.

How else did Wilbur and Orville Wright, two bicycle-shop owners from Dayton, Ohio, manage to fly successfully in 1903? Through countless trial-and-error experiments, this duo managed to do what others before them never could. It wasn't only engineering smarts but dogged perseverance and persistence—the true essence of faith. After all, who would have *believed* that their flimsy-looking *Kitty Hawk Flyer* could lift off the ground and fly 120 feet? They believed.

And one of the most prolific inventors in history, Thomas Edison, experimented with thousands of different filaments before perfecting an incandescent light that could glow for 1,500 hours. Did you know that Edison failed *nine thousand* times before succeeding? How's that for *believing*? How many of us might have thrown

> Faith is like electricity. You can't see it, but you can see the light it creates.

in the proverbial towel after ten or twenty tries, or maybe one hundred? When a reporter asked him how it felt to fail thousands of times, he replied, "I was glad I found nine thousand ways *not* to invent the lightbulb!"

And I can't resist a final "finger-lickin' good" example: the story of Colonel Sanders. Broke at age sixty-five, the former Kentucky service station owner, who was an amateur chef, decided he was going to make his fortune on his "secret recipe" for fried chicken seasoned with eleven herbs and spices. He doggedly drove from town to town, sleeping in his car, pitching his recipe to anyone who would listen. Although he heard no — 1,009 times

> Believe it, and you will achieve it.

before he sold his first piece of chicken — his persistence and faith finally paid off. Though Sanders never revealed the secret recipe, he did discuss his recipe for his success: "Never quit. Always believe..."

The Wright brothers, Edison, and Colonel Sanders all had a few things in common — perseverance, patience, and *believing* in a dream.

God placed greatness inside each one of us — a subject we're going to visit in-depth in an upcoming chapter. To believe in yourself is to have *faith* in the treasure that God put into you!

MAKING THE IMPOSSIBLE POSSIBLE

There were two atheists on a fishing trip in Scotland, when one of the men hooked the Loch Ness Monster. Immediately his fishing pole bent over as the giant sea creature began dragging their little boat wildly across the loch. Hanging on for dear life, the man cried out, "Oh, God, help me!"

"Hey," the other man said, "we're atheists, remember! We don't believe in God."

"Sixty seconds ago," he responded, "I didn't believe in the Loch Ness Monster, either!"

Folks, what we *believe* has *everything* to do with our ultimate destiny. As it says in Job 3:25, "For what I fear comes upon me, and what I dread befalls me."

I'm reminded of the miracle of Peter walking on water and of the force that *stopped* him. As Peter climbed out of the boat, faith arose in his heart and the impossible had become possible. But the Bible says in Matthew 14:30, "when he saw the wind, he became frightened." His fear robbed his faith so he began to sink.

In our everyday lives, how often does fear rob us? Perhaps we even give up before we begin. We try something a few times, get discouraged, and return to our old routine. Why? Because the bar on our *expectations* of life, as you'll read in the next chapter, is set too low.

And what we believe will happen usually does. If, for example, you fearfully believe that you will never escape a bad relationship, or a mountain of debt, or a really boring job, what are the chances that any of this is going to change?

Fear stops God's miracle power and blocks the flow of good in life; conversely, faith allows us to rise victoriously in the midst of whatever we're facing. That's how faith triggers God's miracle action in our lives.

I'm intrigued by one of the root meanings of the world "believe", which is to *give permission* or to *allow*. What a relief. This means that just in the act of believing—of having faith and strong conviction—we can begin the process of changing our lives, *from the inside out*.

> Believing is the force that gets things done. It overpowers opposition. It allows us to succeed.

The impossible becomes possible. The naysayers are proved wrong. We give the object of our faith the permission to come to pass.

Rather than pushing or pulling or controlling, we allow God to lead the way, to work in our lives in a positive, active manner. We create from the depths of our thoughts and soul a force field that can conquer any obstacle. We *allow* something to happen that would otherwise not have happened. In this way faith *allows* us to see what is *invisible*.

Look at the great patriarch Abraham, who was a nomad, a scavenger, and childless. He was without "sight" in his soul—though he could see perfectly well with his eyes. In Genesis 15, when all hope seemed lost, God instructed Abraham to go outside: "Look up at the heavens and count the stars—if indeed you can count them." Then He said to him, "So shall your offspring be." This was God telling Abraham that as many stars as he could count would be the number of people who would call him their father! Today he is considered by billions the patriarch of their faith.

Was this luck or coincidence? Neither. Abraham believed. He "saw" God's plan. And his faith "allowed" it to happen.

We need the same vision, the same ability to see the stars in our lives today, especially when we're feeling dissatisfied. Whether it's a financial crisis, a career challenge, a relationship problem, or a physical illness, it's faith that can allow us to create something that did not exist before it. It all starts with a *vision*. **You have to see it on the inside, before it becomes a reality on the outside.**

Many times, of course, there are forces that thwart us, seemingly preventing us from achieving what we most desire. We want to find our ideal mate, repair our marriage, cure an illness, get that new job, strike out in a new direction, or get a second chance in life. But circumstances seem to prevent that "impossible" dream from coming true. Everybody says it can't be done. It's not *realistic*, right?

But in Mark 9:23, one of the greatest verses of the Bible, we read that "all things are possible to him who believes." And armed with this mighty force, you can withstand any setback, disappointment, or trial. This is God's promise.

When we believe God's promise, any dream can become a reality. In fact, did you know that there are over seven thousand promises in the Bible? That's seven thousand *chances* God is giving us to become the best we can be. All we have to do is believe. But so often we *don't*.

> Faith gives our life "permission" to get better, to prosper, and to overcome anything.

Have you ever heard the story of the man who fell off a cliff, but managed to grab onto a tree limb on the way down? Hanging from the branch, he yelled out in desperation, "Help! Is anyone up there?"

"I am here," the Lord replied out of Heaven. "Do you believe in me?"

"Yes, Lord, I believe. I really believe—but I can't hang on much longer."

"That's all right. If you really believe, you have nothing to worry about. I'll save you…just let go of the branch."

There was momentary silence.

Then the man yelled out again: "HELP! Is there anyone ELSE up there?"

How many of us know that sometimes we have to let go of the branch and trust?

Believing is not just something we need to do just when we're feeling good, or when we're on a roll, or optimistic, or when we're sitting in church on Sunday. Believing needs to be an act of trust.

I like telling the story about Joe, who prayed after finding himself bankrupt. "God, please help me. I'm going to lose my house if I don't win the lottery." But the lottery came and went, and someone else won it.

Then the next week Joe asked for the same thing and lost again, his faith waning. So he prayed again: "Lord, why have you forsaken me? I've lost my house, my business, and my car. I've asked for your help to win the lottery, and nothing has happened. What's the problem?"

Suddenly a blinding flash of light appears, the heavens open, and Joe is confronted by the voice of God Himself: "Joe, meet me halfway on this: BUY A TICKET!"

Now, I'm not telling you this to encourage gambling, but simply illustrating: believing means *to be so persuaded* that you *act* accordingly.

Do you want to live the satisfied life?

Armed with the determination of true conviction, you need to start taking action. You need to stop thinking and begin doing. **Believing is not a wish; it's a deep conviction that *something is possible*, though you don't see it or feel it at the time.**

Believing is when every fiber in your being is convinced of something that no one can talk you out of. Even when a doctor says that you'll never recover, you believe you will. Even when friends give up on you, you find a way not to give up on yourself.

And so it is that believing is a tool that we can use when we're feeling uncertain, insecure, confused, or discouraged. I can promise you this: **an active *belief* system will *attract* all the good that life can bring you.**

But in my own case, as a teenager, I never knew that. I had no faith. And I believed in nothing. Allow me to finish the story I began in the first chapter, for the life-changing lesson in it is the entire reason I'm writing this book today.

THE DARKEST DAY

By the time I was sixteen, I was a troublemaker, an alcoholic, a drug user, and a drug dealer. And those were my *good* points! I had zero confidence in myself and no knowledge of God's love. And although I was pretty lost in my soul, I always worked and earned money. That year I was working as a cook at a country club.

Then something horrific happened. It was a tragic event, so unexpected and brutal, that it led me to deep sadness and searching. But it was also a sign that things were about to change.

> When it is dark enough, you can see the stars.
> —CHARLES A. BEARD

On the first day of school of my junior year, when I was fifteen, I found out that one of my best friends, Randy, had committed suicide. He had shot himself and was found in a ditch with his father's shotgun by his side.

All my life I'd been such an unemotional person, but I felt Randy's death in the core of my being. I just wept. It was the first time I can remember having cried as a teenager. The grief I felt was beyond any pain I'd known.

I couldn't *understand* it. Here was this kid that seemed to have *everything*. He was handsome, popular, and athletic with a fantastic girlfriend. And here I was a lonely, rejected, dejected kid with nothing going for me at all. I figured if *he* could kill himself at fifteen, what would stop me from doing the same thing? That's how little I *believed* in anything—in myself or in the gift of life itself.

Randy's death set into motion a hunger inside me to find *something*... though I didn't know what it was. But I knew that there was something *missing* in my life that would give me a *purpose*. And I can see now that a seed had been planted, that Randy's death was a catalyst for an awakening in me.

The Bible says in John 12:24 that when a grain of wheat falls to the ground and dies, it brings forth much fruit.

But not right away. The next year was one long party to dull the pain—drinking and doing drugs, while trying to find friends, get girls, and be happy—anything to fill up the emptiness inside.

Then one night, just before my senior year, one of my coworkers at the country club, Rich, who was always talking about Jesus and being "born again," confronted me as we walked outside from the kitchen to the garbage Dumpster.

"Greg, what are you going to do when Jesus returns and you've got that joint in your hand?" And I thought, *What is his problem? He doesn't have to get all personal and mess with my mind!*

A few weeks later, Rich came up to me again and asked, "Man, why don't you come to a Bible study with me?"

I thought, *Which one of us is on drugs? Me or him?* But I was intrigued by the invitation, and had nothing to lose.

There were about twenty people sitting around in a cozy family room, many of them in their twenties, sharing Scriptures from the Bible and singing. They weren't phony or strange. In fact, they seemed humble yet confident that they had "met" Jesus Christ and had a real relationship with Him. I could see that they were genuine, kind, and warm—so different from anything I'd known in my world.

However, I didn't think this was for me and I wanted to get out of there as soon as I could. I needed a smoke!

I was just out the door as the host grabbed my hand and asked: "Son, are you saved?"

From what? I thought.

I didn't know what it meant to be saved. And he opened up the Bible, turned to 1 John 1:9 NASB, and said: "You see right here. It says: 'If we confess our sins, He is faithful and just to forgive us our sins, and to cleanse us from all unrighteousness.'"

And I was thinking, *I gotta go, man, I'm meeting my buddies for beer at the 7-Eleven. So, can you speed this up?*

But in reality, I told him, "You don't know who I am or what I do. I could *never* be cleansed from all my sins."

"Oh, yeah, you could. All you have to do is pray right now."

Suddenly my heart began to beat rapidly. I felt as if the world had stopped and all of Heaven and Hell were focused on me. I felt torn in two—one force pulling me forward to pray and open my heart to God, the other telling me: "Get to the 7-Eleven!"

I knew right then that this was a battle for my soul. Let's think: *7-Eleven or Heaven?*

I said to this man, "No, I really don't want to pray, because even if I accept Jesus into my life, I'll probably never be able to live up to it."

"You don't have to worry about that," he wisely responded. "Once you invite Him into your heart and into your life, ***He'll give you the power to change.***" He then took me by the hand and led me in prayer.

That was the night I received Jesus Christ into my life. Instantly and miraculously I was saved.

On my way out the door, one of the women actually gave me her Bible as a gift; "Here, I want you to have it." And it was the first Bible I'd ever owned.

I took it with me in the car that night as I headed over to the 7-Eleven to buy beer and meet my drinking buddies. (I guess not everything was going to change, yet.) "Hey, guess where *I* was tonight? You'll never believe it." I shocked them all when I pulled out the Bible and held it up. "I was at a Bible study! Tonight I got saved."

And drunk as I was about to get, it was on that night that I became an "evangelist." Of course, my life didn't change on the outside overnight, but something supernatural had happened on the *inside*.

A REASON TO LIVE

And that day, friends, was the beginning of my new life. Why? Because for the first time in my life, I found something to *believe* in, something greater than my *pain*, more compelling than my *past*, something that gave true comfort. As I prayed and talked with God, heard His voice, and caught the glimpse of God as love, I was captivated. He saw my flaws and shortcomings— and He *still* loved me.

> There is destiny in the heart of every person—waiting to be awakened.

As we saw in the "Be Loved" chapter, when you know you're loved, this *conviction* can pull you through *anything*, no matter how far you fall, no matter how many mistakes you've made, no matter what your upbringing.

It was this love that gave me a deep, abiding confidence that can never be shaken from me again. For the first time in my life, I felt that *love had broken through*, that I had finally found meaning and purpose in my life.

I felt like a little kid whose father makes him feel significant by taking off the entire day and spending it with him. I felt like I mattered to God, like His arms were wrapped around me, that His eyes were focused solely on me. It's like He cleared His entire schedule to fix my life and make me His. *That's* what changed me.

This was not a *mental* realization but a heartfelt conviction that *I was truly loved*. I soon noticed that rather than being self-absorbed, as I'd always been, I was now absorbed in *Him*. God's love set in motion the confidence and faith I needed to walk in His will. It was this love that began healing and changing me.

The Bible became my refuge—a retreat that I could escape to when I needed relief from my everyday life. Instead of filling up on beer, I was slowly filling up on God's word. And His words were powerfully comforting to me.

In fact, there's a Scripture in Proverbs that says the words of your lips will satisfy us. And it was true for me. I found that God's words actually brought me the satisfaction that drugs, alcohol, and people never did. The more that His words and promises got into my soul, the more they began to win over the battle between darkness and light in my life.

Nobody could have forced me into this faith. I had to be ready for it. My way of living changed because I now had a greater *cause*. I believe that some people live *be*cause and others *by* cause. *Be*cause is just existing. That was the old me. Yes, I was breathing. I was alive. But I was lost.

But now, I was starting to live *by* cause. I had a true connection to God and began to believe that I had *value*—that I was *worth* something. I'm not talking about being self-assured because you look good, or have advanced degrees, or money in the bank. I had none of those things. I'm talking about feeling a sense of genuine confidence and self-acceptance.

> I mistakenly thought I would first have to clean up my act, then serve God. But it's really the other way around. Once you surrender to Him, He changes you.

I didn't get that worth from my parents, friends, or school. It ultimately came from the love of GOD. And everything grew slowly from that inner conviction.

Of course, everything in my life didn't change at once. Not at all. But each night, after school and work, I just kept coming home—filling my heart up with the words of the Bible. Then one night I remember driving home with a beer in my hand, stopping the car in front of our house, and saying out loud, "Lord, this is the last drink I'm ever going to have. It's over."

Then I poured it out. And that was the last drink I ever took. I started going to church regularly and serving God, really living the Christian life that I had proclaimed.

I can now see that the transformation of my life on the *outside* was a total result of what was happening to me on the *inside*. So often, as I said, we believe that our happiness is dependent on changing external circumstances or changing someone *else*; but I learned that when *I* changed, on the inside, things began to change *around* me, including my relationships.

I became more tolerant of others, more forgiving of my parents and the people who had abused me in school, because I believed in something greater than my pain—though the memory of it faded very slowly.

The biggest hurdle I faced, in fact, was *conquering* the nagging sense of insecurity and rejection left over from childhood. So it's ironic that in all that pain, I eventually found my true calling, which was helping *other* people conquer their insecurities and rejection. I had found *my calling in my conquering,* a subject we'll return to later in the book. And as you'll read in the next chapter, I started my own church, because I *expected* that I could.

So, you might ask, was being invited to that Bible study fate, destiny, or coincidence? I'd say it was all three and more. It was the providential hand of God, divine intervention. And it was God's mercy, too, because many nights when I was driving home drunk, I could just as easily have crashed my car and died—or killed someone else.

Friends, if God could do all this in my life—give me something to BELIEVE in—He could do it in *anybody's* life. And it all started with the death of my friend Randy. The grief for him had, in a strange way, opened something up in my heart that had been previously shut tight. The pain had turned into a purpose. And without quite knowing it back then, I'd found something to *believe* in.

EVIDENCE THAT CAN'T BE SEEN

We all need something to believe in, just as we all know pain. It's part of the human condition, and a subject we'll talk more about later in the "Be Healed" chapter. But for now, armed with the power of *believing* in ourselves and in God's love, we know that *anything* is possible.

You truly have unlimited potential to create the life you want: if you *believe* you can and believe in God's power to help you do it. If you're underachieving, what needs to change? It's not other people or circumstances, of which we have no control.

It's our *belief system*—the principles that rule our daily lives, that govern our thoughts, words, and actions.

As we've seen, what we believe becomes our reality. So if you want to change something in your life today, *concentrate and focus on how you want it to be.*

I wanted to build a church. What do *you* want to build? What kind of relationship do you envision having with your spouse? What kinds of friends do you want? What kind of lifestyle do you want to enjoy? **Achieving anything starts with *believing something!***

As we said earlier, the only thing that's stopping you from fulfilling your goals are your negative thoughts from the past: *I'm too old. It's too late. I don't have enough education. I'm not good enough, smart enough, thin enough, rich enough.* These are harmful beliefs—and *false* ones! It's only fear talking.

It reminds me of one of those "invisible fences" that can be installed along the perimeter of your property line in order to protect your dog from running into the street. Although you don't *see* a fence, it's still there. When the dog is on the verge of running beyond the yard, a collar with two electrodes in it transmits a mild shock—not enough to hurt the dog, but sufficient to warn him.

Isn't this just like so many who never move *beyond* the restrictions of their own "backyard"? You can go only so far before finding yourself blocked by those invisible fences that keep you limited and unhappy. These negative voices keep you imprisoned in limitation, scarcity, fear, and regret rather than abundance and joy. A little opposition or rejection bounces people back into mere existence, prohibiting dynamic and successful lives.

But just like that invisible fence that holds us *back*, faith is **evidence that cannot yet be seen**—but it's a source that moves us *forward*, that frees us from past and present limitations to enable us to live the lives we were meant to have. Here's what we're going to do:

1. *Expose False Beliefs.* Ingrained beliefs that hold us back are the *DNA of failure*—the lie that you are defined by your *upbringing.* If you grew up poor, or with an abusive parent, or with a family of alcoholics—you may assume that you're going to wind up the same way. Not true! What we need is *the DNA of success.* Decide that your father is God, and that you get your DNA from *Him.* He succeeds at everything; therefore, so do you. Your history does not forecast your future. You determine your life. Your horizons are bright and limitless. Replace a false belief with a true one.

2. *Choose a New Destiny.* Don't be limited by the belief that *whatever* happens in life was meant to be. Sometimes we see ourselves as the victims of life's cruel (or kind) intentions, and utterly powerless to change them. We tell ourselves: "This always happens to me." "Things are never going to change." "It's my fate." Wrong! Regardless of your life situation, take ABSOLUTE RESPONSIBILITY for your life. *There are no victims—only volunteers.* Rather than making excuses about how other people are holding you back, or that you have "bad luck," or worried about the stock market or economy— believe that you will *find a solution.*

3. *Don't Settle.* To "settle" means to accept something that is less than adequate or desirable just because you believe it won't get any better. As I'll share with you in the next chapter, it's time to give up that mind-set, the one that accepts life the way it *is* rather than the way you want it to be. So often, people are convinced that their condition will not improve; that they will never be better off financially, physically, or relationally. That thinking, of course, will always keep us stuck. Get *desire* back into your life—the desire to improve, to get better, to make something great out of life. Then do something to improve it. Start with just one single action—anything

continued

that will move you an inch closer to your satisfied life. By doing so, you will overcome the belief that tells you: "This is all there is."

4. *Eliminate the "Faultfinding" Mentality.* We're often our own worst enemies—filled with self-criticism and judgment. We also criticize others, filled with complaint, blame, and dissatisfaction about our spouse, boss, mother-in-law, church, children, parents, right? We keep picking away at things. *We need to find the good in things. We need to be encouragers, not discouragers.* Make up your mind that whatever you say is going to be constructive. Perfect the art of the compliment. And give yourself a pat on the back when you need one.

5. *Cultivate Abundant Thinking.* So often, despite living in an infinitely abundant universe, people have the false belief that there is *never enough* to go around—not enough time, money, help, you name it. This leads to fear and selfishness. It's like having an oven full of pizza, but asking your kids to share just one last piece. We need to shift our focus from what we *don't* have onto what we *do* have—to a *more than enough* mentality. God doesn't want you to live in scarcity. He is a God of abundance, not lack. When He fed the multitudes, there was enough for everyone to be full *and* twelve baskets left over. Begin to believe that He will supply all your needs. Share as if there will always be enough, and there always will be. Everyone knows the promise from Jesus: give and it shall be given back to you—good measure, pressed down, shaken together, and running over. Give that way, and you'll live that way!

Know this: faith is an active source within you, just waiting to be unleashed. **So get pregnant with belief on the inside and it will be born.** Plant seeds and images in your heart that create a vision of your life as you wish it to be.

If you've been feeling discouraged or depressed, pessimistic or hope-less—you have the tool to turn it around: *believing*.

Remember: Abraham saw a nation that had not yet been born; Moses saw a free people that had only known slavery; David saw victory when faced with a giant; and Jesus saw a feast for thousands when there were only five loaves of bread and two fish.

This vision, this ability to believe, came from the inside and was real-ized on the outside. This is God's promise to you. *Believe* it.

Secret #3

Be Expectant

AN AWAKENING TO PURPOSE

Nobody succeeds beyond his or her wildest expectations unless he or she begins with some wild expectations.

—RALPH CHARELL

My spiritual journey, as you've seen, began the year before I graduated from high school. After that first Bible study experience, and all that followed, I was so changed by God's love and power that I wanted to share it with *everyone*. In fact, by the time I got to college, I decided to start a Bible study of my *own*.

Me?! The druggie from high school? Wasn't I the *least* likely to become a leader, much less a spiritual one?

True, my organizational skills and ability to communicate were nonexistent. I had little knowledge of the Bible. After all, I thought the "epistles" were the "apostles" wives. I literally thought that the book of "Job" was about finding a "job" and that Noah's wife was "Joan of Ark." I was pretty clueless!

But my faith was on fire—and fire can spread. I desperately wanted the people around me to experience what had happened to me.

I began zeroing in on specific promises from the Bible that I could latch onto—and was especially inspired by something God spoke to Abraham in the book of Genesis when He said, "I will make you a father of a multitude of nations, and your descendants will be like the stars of sky and the sands by the seashore."

Multitudes? Stars? Sands by the seashore? I had only managed to gather five or six "sands" at my first Bible study. Yet, something inside me knew I could turn that tiny group into a *church*. And I remember marching around the floor of my little apartment in Kalamazoo, Michigan, every day, declaring out loud, "*I am a father of multitudes!* My members are as numerous as the sands by the seashore. People want to come to my Bible study and my church!"

Unfortunately, the picture I was seeing on the inside was not quite developing the same way on the outside. After two years my "sands by the seashore" had grown to a whopping thirty! Ugh!

One time we got up to . . . *thirty-six*, but that's only because I counted a pregnant woman as two, plus four dogs that camped outside waiting for their owners!

Each Sunday I would look at my "multitude" of thirty, but on Monday I would go back in that room and declare myself the father of multitudes: "My descendants are as numerous as the sands by the seashore. I have thousands of people in my church!" I guess you could say that apartment was the "birthing room" of what would years later become Life Changers International Church. It was like my own "expectant mother's room." (Wait, did I just compare myself to an *expectant* mother!?)

I obviously didn't have the experience or resources to develop a successful and thriving church. In fact, whenever we'd have a "membership drive," it seemed I'd end up "driving" more people away. I was brash and overly aggressive. I didn't realize what I would later come to understand, that love and simple truth would draw people, not just zeal and dedication. After four years of trial and error, I eventually closed up shop in that town.

I was so young (twenty-five) and inexperienced, and though that little church didn't grow much, something inside of me did! There was a seed God planted that was growing within me, and I knew it would one day turn into a great harvest.

Through vision and faith that God's promise would work, my wife, Grace, and I moved to Chicago, determined to start a new church, though experts warned me not to do so. Armed with less than $100 in the bank, but *all* the promises of God, I decided to try again.

If the definition of insanity is to keep doing the same thing over and over again, while expecting different results, I was heading for padded walls! After all, if we couldn't make a go of it in Kalamazoo, why even attempt building a church in a much larger, more challenging city?

But we did it anyway, and on a cold January morning in 1992, we held our first meeting in a hotel in Schaumburg, Illinois. To my amazement, ninety-five people showed up — three times more than our best turnout in Kalamazoo. It was working! A year and a half later, we officially incorporated as a church. What I saw on the inside was finally beginning to show up on the outside.

I kept praying — and preaching — and within three years, our congregation had grown to almost five hundred. Before long, we doubled and then kept on growing. Now, fifteen years after starting with nothing but the seed of expectation, we have thousands of church members, with an audience of millions more watching our program on television and listening on radio.

How had this happened? After all, I was the guy who dropped classes in school when told he would have to speak in front of the class — someone who could hardly carry on a conversation with a friend, let alone a stranger!

Yet, I was also someone who, in his heart, had been touched by the love of God — and by the power of a force you're about to experience as well. And with that power, *anything* is possible.

EXPECT THE BEST

Friends, if I could create a church from nothing — armed with only a passion for the Bible and a dream — what could *you* do to change your life today?

What would it take? What would be the first step? Your new path starts with one indispensable element, the key ingredient that made all the difference to me.

> Something good is going to happen today. The question: is it going to happen to you?

It's the power of **expectation** — the ability to *envision the invisible*, the act of looking *forward* to something, which allows it to become a reality.

What you *anticipate* and *imagine* is an accurate predictor of what will likely happen to you in any twenty-four-hour period.

If you begin the day *expecting* to enjoy it, something good is *going* to happen.

But if you get out of bed feeling pessimistic, or filled with dread, anxiety, and fear, your day is ruined before it even begins. You'll misinterpret even the things that are sent to bless you.

Take the lady whose lazy husband decided, after twenty years, to take a shower at the gym *before* coming home. For the first time ever, he brought her flowers, walking in through the front door instead of through the garage. When he rang the doorbell, with a smile on his face and a gift in his hand, she opened it up and began to cry.

He asked her why she was so upset and she said: "Billy broke his leg at school, a pipe burst in the basement, your mother called and said she was coming over for a week, and if that's not bad enough, YOU HAD TO COME HOME DRUNK!"

Funny how when our expectations are low we interpret even good things as bad.

Seriously, folks, isn't it true that anticipating the worst often brings it on? Traffic on the freeway will be bumper to bumper (and we'll get stopped by a Deputy Barney Fife type, who will prove his authority by making an example of us). The bottom of the coffee cup is going to leak; we'll trip over the bath mat, lock ourselves out of the car, or watch the house flood on the day our insurance expires!

As the author Francis Crawford said, "To expect defeat is nine-tenths of defeat itself."

So don't get out of bed convinced the world is about to end, or praying your boss gets hit by a bus! That's not a good prayer. Tell yourself things are going to go *right*, not wrong, that you're going to begin the day with optimism, hope, and enthusiasm.

We can't *expect* somebody else to instill a positive outlook into us, though we sometimes do.

Have you ever sat in church thinking: *I hope the pastor can come up with something to excite me today—because I'm falling asleep! And what time is it anyway? I wish he'd hurry and get us out of here because my roast is in the oven!*

We want the preacher to do our *expecting* for us and our boss to do our *promoting* for us. Instead, we need to come into church with uplifted hands and walk into the office the same way. Think: *I'm going to expect the best to happen—it's as good as done!* Maybe we find a new way to approach our work so that things just click into place. Our rhythm and ability to get things done clicks into place. We feel calmer, more competent, and ready to face any challenge. Living like this, with God's grace, we find the *best* in each situation—and in ourselves. We *rise* to our potential.

EXPECT IT TO HAPPEN

In my case, when my church began, I was trying to rise from our congregation meeting in an elementary school gym to a church building of our own, where we could welcome thousands. This was my expectation—and dream. So I went to twenty-five banks trying to get a loan to build my church, but no bank would consider it. "Too high risk! You don't have enough wealthy donors, or a large enough congregation, and no track record!" I could have just given up and told myself: "It's not meant to be," but faith and expectation spurred me on.

And one day I met a banker doing business out of a trailer! I knew I'd found someone just like me, living his dream. He could see something *before it happened.* He, too, was pregnant with a vision. You can imagine the rest. He loaned me the money, my church got built in twelve months, and the loan was paid off in full in less than thirty-six months! Today that banker is my friend and has all our bank accounts. And you can be sure he is not in a trailer anymore, either.

Nowadays many of those banks that turned me down would gladly welcome our business. But those banks didn't expect that it could happen, that the impossible was possible. You have to surround yourself with people who believe in your expectations and dreams. And so it is that a *persistent expectation can be more powerful than any opposing force.*

Folks, the truth is that **our expectations determine our realities—while our lack of expectations abort them**.

We vigorously train for the marathon—determined to make it those twenty-six miles—and we cross the finish line. We studiously apply ourselves in graduate school, and we get the degree. We believe we're coming down with a cold, and we wind up in bed. For better or worse, **imagining how things will work out shapes the way we behave, and the way we make others (and the universe) behave *toward* us**.

So often, people who see themselves as victims are treated that way. They even look like they're about to take a beating! Others simply set themselves up for failure through negative expectations.

Take the legendary story of Job in the Bible. Most have heard of his many afflictions, but few have realized the amazing lesson he gives us about the power of expectation. Consumed with fear that his children will turn their backs on him and on God, he woke up every day worrying about it, continually fearing the worst.

Expectation is not a onetime feeling or fear. I believe what we continually expect will eventually show up in our lives—good or bad.

When the day came that Job's children did actually turn against God, as he had expected, Job, in 3:25, gives us these telling words of honest admission and warning: "For the thing I have greatly feared has come upon me..."

How many of us as parents have feared the worst might happen to our children? Not only does it affect your own peace of mind, but it *also* has energy to turn expectation into reality.

Some of us may be afraid that we'll be alone all our lives, or we'll never have enough money, or we'll die of some sickness or disease. We've probably all experienced these kinds of disaster-prone fears.

> If you think you can do it—it can be done. And if you're convinced it's never going to work out, it usually doesn't.

We know that thinking this way "works," meaning that negative thoughts can easily lead to negative results. So let's replace negative expectations with positive ones, and watch what will happen. Expect that you *will* meet the right person, hear the "good report" from the doctor, and have the money you need to meet your needs.

Folks, true miracles happen when we expect they can. Take the case of Buffalo Bills tight end Kevin Everett, a fantastic football player. Remember what happened? While making a tackle in the team's opening season game in Denver in September 2007, he was crushed on the field and wound up with a severe spinal cord injury!

Paralyzed from the neck down after the accident, doctors told the twenty-five-year-old that he would most likely never walk again. What a tragedy. But Kevin wasn't having any of that. Miraculously he later returned to the same stadium where the accident happened, munching on a candy cane and waving to fans from the stands, able to *walk* from his wheelchair to his car unassisted!

One of his teammates said: "I was speechless, on the verge of tears. He got out of his wheelchair and had a smile on his face. I remember the last time I saw him, he was out here on the field being carried into an ambulance, and we were all gathering around saying a prayer for him."

Consider those prayers answered.

How did he do it? What allowed him to recover so quickly despite the dire predictions? Simply this: He *expected* that he could and would walk again—no matter what his doctors said.

In each of our lives, miracles occur when God interrupts the status quo and makes something happen in our lives that would otherwise not have happened at all through our own power or ability. The impossible becomes possible. How? Because: **great things always happen in an atmosphere of expectation.**

It reminds me of the story about the eager, new insurance agent who was looking for prospects. A friend of his, successful in the same business, promised he would help him. So he handed the new salesman ten prospect cards and told him to call these hot leads immediately, and report back after he had finished.

One week later, when he reported back, he could hardly contain himself. He had sold policies to eight of the ten referrals, and was waiting to hear back from the other two. "Do you have any more referrals?" the young buck asked his friend. The shrewd businessman smiled and handed him a phone book. "Here," he said, "I randomly picked the first ten out of here — you find the next ten!"

It was this sense of expectation that turned cold leads into hot ones. It's this sense of expectation that will make anything possible in your life today!

Simply put: **expectation creates manifestation**.

Scientists have long known this. For example, in medical trials for chronic pain, patients are given a placebo instead of a real painkiller and yet they improve dramatically. A Harvard University study proved that 30 to 40 percent of patients obtained significant relief from pain, hypertension, and asthma from a fake pill! Why? It was because the patient *expected* relief. And expectation leads to a release of endorphins, the brain's natural painkillers, which contribute to a sensation of reward and well-being.

This only proves what people of faith have known for eons: faith works. What we *forecast* becomes a self-fulfilling prophecy.

Another landmark study proving the power of expectation was conducted four decades ago by researchers who went into the San Francisco school system, using a calculated piece of misinformation to prove a point. They told teachers that their classrooms were filled with gifted students — a total lie! The researchers discovered that if teachers were led to believe that their students were exemplary, the students (who were actually only average) performed far above average. In fact, their IQ scores rose 15 to 30 points in just one year. Why? It was because the teachers *expected* the students to excel.

This became known as "the Pygmalion effect," its meaning taken from the George Bernard Shaw play *Pygmalion*, the basis for the Broadway show *My Fair Lady*. As we all know, Eliza, a mere flower girl, is transformed into an elegant "lady" — because more is expected of her. And she succeeds in bettering her life because she expects more from *herself*, and works hard at turning her dream into a reality.

So can you.

ARE YOU SETTLING FOR LESS
THAN YOU DESERVE?

Remember some of the dreams you had when you were younger, when you hoped for great things to happen? Maybe you envisioned becoming a professional athlete, a dancer, a great actor, or an accomplished business-man, inventor, astronaut, or even president. When we're young, we dream *big*. And we don't consider the obstacles or the things that might go wrong. We're unafraid. We look forward with infinite hope and expectation.

But somewhere along the line, *doubt* crept in. So did *mediocrity*. High hopes surrendered to low self-expectations. Of course, few people would willingly admit that they've settled for an average or below-average life, but our expectations and resulting behaviors say otherwise. We drag our-selves along, with minimal effort, on automatic pilot, thinking: *What's the point?* We don't aspire toward being great—not anymore.

This kind of secure, safe, settled life may have even been reinforced by parents or teachers who encouraged us to second-guess our dreams: "Theater is nice—but why don't you find a more *practical* major."

Or we may have *lowered* our expectations because we dreaded failing and wanted to protect ourselves from disappointment. This self-protection is fear talking, which blocks us from expecting something better for our-selves.

So what happens? We slip into complacency, into jobs that don't chal-lenge us and relationships that don't serve us. We become realistic and practical, rationalizing that the status quo is "good enough."

Yet we would *never* tolerate mediocrity from others, especially those we chose to hire for a job.

Imagine if your doctor walked casually into the operating room where you were waiting on the table and told you, "I'm a little tired today, so I hope I can do this. I'll give it a shot." You'd be out the door. Forget your clothes...you'd be streaking to your car! Or if your contractor came into your house with a hangover and said, "It would be cool if I could install your cabinets correctly...I'll try." He'd be fired in a flash.

We wouldn't put up with such low expectations from others, yet we tolerate them in ourselves. We begin settling for second and third best. We become complacent and resigned to a mediocre existence. We become addicted to mindless TV instead of reading or learning something new. We let our hobbies go. We neglect reaching out to old friends or making new ones. We stop exercising, start eating fast food, and developing unhealthy habits. We settle for

> We're created to thrive, not just survive. When we do, it yields a powerful and satisfied life.

jobs (or relationships) that bore us, rationalizing, *Well, this is the best I can do; at least it's a job.* or: *I know my marriage doesn't have much passion in it, but at least I'm not alone.*

We've reduced ourselves to a life of *surviving rather than thriving.* The result is a *powerless* life—and an *unsatisfied* one. Yet, strangely, settling gives us a certain degree of comfort. We know what to expect. And in the back of our minds, we vaguely hope that we'll be rescued from it all: *Maybe things will improve. Maybe a new job will come along—or I'll win the lottery.* Legions line up daily in hopes of hitting the big jackpot, right? **But you deserve more than a 1-in-14-million chance at success!**

To change our lives today, we have to break out of our comfort zones and reverse our low expectations. We've got to leave behind those lazy, halfhearted resolutions—and *expect* the best from ourselves and others. Don't settle for "making it" through college; expect to graduate at the top of your class. Don't settle for surviving from paycheck to paycheck; expect abundance!

Sometimes we're resigned to make it *through.* We tell ourselves a prayer such as, *Lord, just get me through the day.*

Guess what's going to happen? You're going to *get* through the day. And guess what? That's all you're going to get. But just making it through isn't enough.

Coach yourself: *I won't just get through the day. I will* get *the day. I will maximize it. I will win it over and change it. I will overcome it. I will smile and praise God. And most of all, I will rejoice and be victorious no matter what's going on in my life!*

We've got to start dreaming and believing again—and expect-

ing miracles to happen. Tell yourself that the status quo is no longer good enough. You have to believe that you were created for something special, that you have incredible and unique gifts that only await your command. This is not conceit, arrogance, or pride. You really do have a positive future, no matter how old or young you are. To believe this is actually a sign of *humility*. You are accepting what God thinks about you, and rejecting anything less. God told Abraham, "I will make you great, and I will make your name great." This is not something to boast about, but something to *believe* with every fiber in your being. You are not average, and not designed for mediocrity. You are not an average mother, average wife, or average businessman. You are destined for greatness — start believing it, and it will begin to happen.

GREAT EXPECTATIONS...THE MAGIC OF ANTICIPATION

So let your imagination wander. Right now — at this moment in your life — what can you dream about? What can you believe in again? Is it a brand-new career, an exotic vacation, relief from illness or pain, a romantic relationship, or a vast improvement in your financial condition?

No matter *what* you're expecting, isn't it true that our entire lives light up when we begin to *hope* for something — and to *want* something?

So start thinking and talking with yourself about what you *really* want — and begin making plans to DO it.

1. *Create a Great Expectations List.* Begin a simple list of everything you'd like to change. Write down everything you can think of that you'd like to EXPECT from this day forward, the ingredients to a satisfied life. These are your new goals for your career, your relationships with family, friends, colleagues, your finances, your

health, and your spiritual life. Take the first step without worrying about where it might lead you.

2. *Start Praying.* Bless the day, beginning and ending it with great expectations. As it says in Ephesians 3:20: God "is able to do exceedingly abundantly above all that we ask or think." This means that **God can allow us to achieve things *beyond* our wildest expectations**—but we have to begin by *having* some wild expectations. So start your day by declaring: "Something good is going to happen to me today!" End your day by filling your mind with a vision of your future and drift off to sleep dreaming about it rather than worrying about your current condition. Expect the amazing career, the beautiful home, or the wonderful marriage. God is on *your* side! When you have confident expectation, anything can happen. As it says in Luke 1:37, "For with God nothing shall be impossible."

3. *Get Your Hopes UP!* It has been said that a man can live forty days without food, four days without water, four minutes without oxygen, but not four seconds without hope! Proverbs says that "hope deferred, makes the heart sick." Hope is the healer of the heart. Somehow we have bought the lie: "Don't get your hopes up." This is nonsense. Get them up and keep them up. (Hope is Viagra for the soul!) Have childlike faith that good is coming to your life. Don't worry if the thing you need hasn't happened yet. That's what *gives* hope a reason to exist. Breathe in hope today like oxygen. **To hope is to live!**

4. *Let Go of People's Expectations of You.* So often, people's opinions condition us to live up to—or down to—*their* expectations. Somebody tells us we shouldn't move beyond the limitations of our "comfort zone," and we don't! "You're right where you belong. You're lucky to have a job. You family didn't aspire toward anything like

continued

that—stick with what you have!" And then there are the below-the-belt slights: "You're not the sharpest knife in the drawer. For a homely girl, you've done the best that can be expected."

What *other* people think of us is none of *our* business! Yet, so often, we are prejudged by these outside, limiting critiques that shape the view of ourselves and our destinies.

Remember, *God* is your potter—not your parents, your past, or other people's opinions. Let Him shape your expectations. He never gives up on you. Jeremiah 18:4 says, "The clay was marred and damaged in the hand of the potter; so He made it again." Your flaws and limitations are not the final sentence on your life. He's making you new again!

5. *Associate with Greatness.* If we're going to witness miracles in our lives, we **need to associate ourselves with *others* who are equally expectant. *Surround yourself with* people of great expectation**—friends, family, and colleagues who will challenge and hold you accountable to a higher standard. These are the people who are most *supportive* of bringing out the *best* in you. They're optimistic, enthusiastic, and forward-thinking—and can inspire you to keep *up* with them. It's like playing tennis with someone a little better than you. You're motivated and driven to get better, and win.

And avoid the "*doom and gloomers*," people who are pessimistic, cynical, or skeptical of your high expectations. They poison your spirit and stop your momentum. Don't get me wrong. Of course, we love those who are still in pain and we must not stop believing in them. But our job is to believe in God first, people second. So raise your expectations of what God can do, and don't worry about what others can do for you. Instead, encourage them to be *expectant* themselves.

Friends, let's get "pregnant" with expectation—with the goals and dreams that are going to change our lives. When you imagine that dream as your reality and welcome it with an open heart—when you allow God to lead the way—*anything* is possible.

Answers are coming. God's blessings are on the way. He is not only *with* you—He is *in* you. 1 John 4:4 says: "Greater is He that is in you, than he that is in the world." This, my friends, is the promise that your miracle is going to show up.

THE MIRACLE IS WAITING

The skeptic in you may be asking, "But what if it doesn't work out? Won't I be even *more* disappointed than before?" No. Absolutely not.

No more looking *backward* at what went wrong. **No more looking** *down* in defeat at what is never going to happen. **No more looking** *around* at what's happening to somebody else. **Let's start looking** *UP*, expecting to receive something even greater. LOOK UP!

> Look up, expecting to receive something... —ACTS 3:5

In an amazing account of biblical miracles, Peter and John were on their way to the temple to pray when they came upon a lame man begging for money. Peter stopped and said, "Look *up* at us!"

This man, disabled from birth, with nothing to lose, looked up "*expecting* to receive something from them," and receive he did! Taking him by

> Expect brainstorms and breakthroughs, healing and epiphanies.

the hand, Peter said, "In the name of Jesus, rise and walk." Instantly the man's feet and ankles became strong. He jumped to his feet and began to walk for the first time in his life.

Your miracle is waiting for you, too. But as we've seen, many of us haven't been looking *up* enough lately. We haven't been expecting anything, so nothing much is happening.

But from this day forward, expect brainstorms and breakthroughs, healing and epiphanies.

If you have a resentment at work, expect forgiveness; if you have a health challenge, expect healing; if you're estranged from your mate, expect reconciliation; if you feel harshly toward your children, expect understanding; if you're in debt, expect relief.

Expect the answer. Expect the opportunity. Expect a smile. Expect love.

Sure, you may not fulfill every one of your dreams, but you'll come a lot closer than if you hadn't even tried. Remember, cynics view the world in terms of what *isn't*, or of what won't work. We're going to view the world in terms of what IS and what WILL work.

So instead of living our lives on the defense — doubting our potentials or waiting to be hurt or rejected, or convinced that sickness and tragedy are just around the corner — let's wake up in the morning *expecting* something good to happen.

Attack life with a smile. Attack it with joy. Attack it with praise.

Tell yourself: "God is on my side. He is for me, not *against* me. I'm going to run into the *right* people, not the *wrong* ones. Doors are going to *open*, not *close*. I'm going to be *happy*, not *depressed*. I'm going to *win*, not *lose*. I'm going to *hold* my temper, not *lose* it. I'm going *up* — not *down*. I'm *blessed*, not *cursed*. Everything I put my hand to will *succeed*, not *fail*. I have an *invincible* spirit today and a satisfied life — not a *defeated* one."

This is the day for your miracle, friends, if only you'll *expect* it.

Secret #4

Be Healed

RELIEVING THE PAIN THAT BINDS US

Many of us spend our whole lives running from feeling—with the mistaken belief that you cannot bear the pain. But you have already borne the pain. What you have not done is feel all you are beyond that pain.

—KAHLIL GIBRAN

Throughout the ages man has always suffered.

As human beings we can hardly escape the sorrow, affliction, and pain that comes with living.

But, friends, whether it's a broken leg, a broken heart, or far worse, God created us to bounce back, to mend, and to repair our bodies and our spirits. As you're about to discover, this ability to be healed is nothing short of miraculous.

No matter what the problem—physical, emotional, mental, or spiritual—we *can* be cured. And we *can* recover.

The Bible says in Exodus 15:26: "I AM the God that heals you." What I love about this verse is that He doesn't say, "I was." He *is*, right now, today, the God that heals. We may be sick and suffering—yes—but God can heal any part of us that is broken or hurt and we can become whole again.

Let's remember that Jesus said in Luke 4:18, "The Spirit of the Lord has anointed me to heal the brokenhearted, to bind up their wounds."

Why was Jesus called the prince of *peace*? It's because the true meaning of peace, taken from the Hebrew word "*shalom*," means to be made

> God can heal any part of us that is broken or hurt, and we can become whole again.

whole and complete, peaceful, calm, and sound. Nothing is missing and nothing is broken.

This is God's promise—to bring *shalom* into your life, to take the wound of your worries and your pain and restore you to the glory of glowing health.

But implied in our title—"Be Healed"—is the truth that there *is* undoubtedly something in our lives that needs to stop hurting, to get better, and to recover. There is something *broken* inside each of us, something aching and sore that needs mending, a wound that must be treated.

We all know it. We've all felt it. PAIN.

Whether it's the physical pain of sickness or injury, the emotional pain of losing someone we love, the mental pain of constant worry, or the spiritual pain of losing faith, pain is something we all experience—and *witness* in the lives of others.

Just open the newspaper or turn on the TV and you'll see that in every corner of the globe, there is an overflow of pain and suffering—enough to break your heart. Millions suffer from debilitating sickness and disease. A *billion* people have no access to clean drinking water, while 2 million people die each year (90 percent of them children) from waterborne diseases. Fifteen million kids have been orphaned by AIDS. The news is filled with incidents of violence, abuse, kidnappings, the horrors of war, heartbreak, and misery. It never seems to end.

Sometimes we need more than mere *help*—we need a miracle! And it's in those times of inexplicable tragedy that our faith in God can not only comfort, but heal.

> We each carry a burden of pain that weighs us down. And when we're weighed down, it's impossible to dance, run, or jump, much less to leap with joy. From this pain, we can and will be healed.

In our church, and in so many others, the number one prayer request is for healing some sort of pain. Bodies are hurting. People are grieving. Some are suffering financially. Others are unhappy in their marriages, or worried about their children, or wrestling with temptation or addiction.

So, yes, the world is suffering. **Pain is universal and inevitable. It's part of the human condition—and always has been.**

Obviously, no one wants to keep hurting. Yet, people sometimes try to deal with their suffering without God, even though we weren't designed that way. For example, when it comes to healing emotional pain, people so often turn to drugs, alcohol, adultery, overeating, smoking, gambling—or various other ways of temporarily *numbing* the pain.

Nowadays the most popular solution to relieving pain is picking up a prescription for it! There are 118 *million* prescriptions written each year for antidepressants. And that's just for treating *emotional* pain. There are over 86 million Americans suffering from chronic *physical* pain, with millions of prescriptions written for pain relievers, tranquilizers,

> He has borne our griefs and carried our sorrows...and with the stripes that wounded Him, we are healed and made whole. —Isa. 53:3–4

and sedatives. (All combined, that's about one prescription for every human being in America.) We'll do just about anything to dull the pain.

God understands this and has a much better solution. In the Bible there are, in fact, over one hundred specific mentions of the word "pain" and multiple other references to "suffering" and "hurt." He knows we suffer and He has an answer.

But we must have faith that others have suffered, too, and overcome, and that our suffering can, in the end, be relieved. I'll show you how shortly.

I'm reminded of Isaiah 53:3–5, referring to the hardship endured by Jesus. The Bible says: "He was despised and rejected of men, a man of sorrows and familiar with suffering...Surely He has borne our griefs, carried our sorrows...and with the stripes that wounded Him, we are healed and made whole."

Think about that: *we are healed and made whole*. That's why Jesus suffered, as he did—to bear our pain as a surrogate and become our Healer.

I asked my congregation the other day, "How many are dealing with some sort of pain or suffering right now?" Almost every hand went up. I joked with the few who didn't raise their hands by saying, "The rest of you must be in *too much* pain to even lift your hand!"

Is there an area of *your* life today that needs to be healed and made whole? Have you been wounded or hurt—or are you suffering right now? If so, you are obviously not alone. God wants to heal it, to free you from it.

A woman named Cindy recently wrote to me, saying, "I've had migraine headaches since I was young, and for the last seven years, I've suffered from epilepsy, too. I was having several episodes a day, including grand mal seizures."

To be a mother and a wife while working a full-time job has enough "pains" of its own. But to have to deal with physical suffering, too, is almost too much for anyone to bear.

In my church, one of the ways we experience healing is through the celebration of Communion. Most people have heard of Communion or Passover, where we remember the sacrifice God offered for our suffering, pain, and judgment. I believe when faith is released, miracles of healing can take place at the Communion table. That's what happened to Cindy.

After years of suffering from the migraines and epilepsy, Cindy heard me teaching about Communion on our TV show, and she decided enough was enough. So she wrote me a second time: "After listening to your teaching on Communion, the exercise of eating the bread and drinking the wine became more than just a ritual: it became an encounter with God. I literally felt a physical sensation in my head. As strange as it sounds, it was as though my brain was being warmly massaged, and immediately, I knew I had been touched by the Lord. I was healed! Since that time, the migraines are gone, the seizures are gone, and my epilepsy medication is gone."

As miraculous as it sounds, Cindy's healing is not an isolated incident.

In fact, in my years of being a pastor and praying for the sick, I could share hundreds of such stories, just like hers.

But more important, the Bible says that healing is a special gift that God *offers* to the hurting and suffering. (*The power of faith will restore the one who is sick*—James 5:15.) After all, what kind of loving God *wouldn't* provide relief to the children He so adores?

That's why, in addition to His miraculous acts of power, He has also given the world a host of medical breakthroughs, discoveries, and cures. And so it is that God's power to heal can never be underestimated.

We all understand *physical* pain, which can usually be relieved, lessened, or cured—thanks to all these gifts that God gives. That pain cries out for immediate attention—and usually gets it.

But *emotional* pain is more subtle, more easily ignored. It sometimes creeps up on us until we find ourselves feeling depressed or functioning at a fraction of our true potential. Sure, pills for emotional pain may offer temporary relief, but none of them can get to the true root of the problem and fix what's really broken and hurting.

More than 21 million people in the United States suffer from clinical depression today, thirty thousand of them commiting

> Prayer is a profoundly healing force that can erase both physical and emotional pain.

suicide each year. And how many others are undiagnosed, feeling just generally "down," a much trickier kind of pain to recognize, defuse, and heal? People get accustomed to their pain, comfortable and familiar with it. They even start believing that it's inevitable and will never end, so they tolerate it and simply learn to cope with it. This is not how God intended for us to live.

Others, of course, actively seek treatment for emotional pain—and there are many ways to do it. Some "check out," ignoring it by overworking or by using some form of distraction or addiction to escape the pain.

Others seek out therapy or pastoral counseling; while others find solace in intense physical exercise or a passionate hobby.

And as we'll see in the next chapter, *prayer* is the most powerful healing force at our disposal, easing and often erasing both physical and emotional pain. Prayer has undoubtedly contributed to the recovery of countless people. Jesus prayed for every sick person He ever came in contact with—and they were healed. He later told us to pray for the sick as well, laying hands on them, and trusting God to heal them.

The Bible continues, in James 5:16, by telling us that fervent prayer offered by any believing person accomplishes much. In fact, science has proven that there is an indisputable connection between the mind and body, between prayer and healing. What the faithful believe so often comes to pass.

I can tell you that prayer always changes things (as does gratitude and laughter). Prayer, gratitude, and laughter are, in fact, three of the essentials of the satisfied life that we'll look at more closely in chapters to come.

In addition to healing physical and emotional pain, there's also the challenge of healing our *mental pain*. Sometimes we just can't escape our nagging, incessant thoughts and worries: *What am I going to do about this? How am I going to handle that? Why didn't I do this? How could I have done that?*

Consumed with the past, worried about the future, we're seemingly incapable of enjoying the moment, a subject we'll also look at in depth later. For now, let's recognize that the pain of being prisoner in one's own mind is its own kind of torture.

> No matter what kind of pain we experience—physical, emotional, mental, or spiritual—there is relief and it can begin today.

How many people have trouble sleeping at night or concentrating during the day, because they simply can't stop *thinking* about their problems?

And beyond physical, emotional, and mental pain, sometimes we also have a nagging sense of being discontented or incomplete. Something is missing. We don't feel fulfilled. Our heart seems empty no matter how busy or successful we might be. This is *spiritual* pain—and I compare it to being lost in the woods or stranded in the desert with no compass. You're lost, disoriented. All sense of meaning and direction is gone, so you're subject to depression, hopelessness, and despair. You don't know where to walk or what to do because there's nothing *guiding* you.

As the Scripture says: "Without a vision (or purpose), people run aimlessly and confused."

So let's create that vision to heal the pain today. God doesn't want us to deny it, ignore it, or just cover it up.

When someone is shot with a gun, the wound isn't just closed up. First, the doctor has to remove the bullet and treat the infection, and then carefully sew up the wound.

We need to do that in our lives, too. We need to heal the wound properly—remove the bullets of betrayal, hurt, resentment, disappointment, and unforgiveness. We need to forget about what people have done to us. **It's time to heal it, not hold on to it**. Otherwise, your pain limits you and keeps you from the greatness that God has in mind for you.

So the first step in treating our wound is understanding what lies *behind* it and *how* to treat it.

HEALING THE NEGATIVE SPIRIT

Why are we suffering so? What's driving all this pain, specifically the mental and emotional kind? It's called *negative thinking*. Every thought we have is attached to an emotion—either a positive or a negative one. **Negative emotions equal pain. Positive emotions equal pleasure**.

I think we all know the power of negative emotions. These are the feelings that drag us down and torture us. These are the emotions that ruin friendships and marriages, that sabotage careers, that negatively influence our children's development, and that detract from our ability to enjoy life. I'm talking about emotions like guilt, blame, bitterness, regret, hatred, revenge, fear, hostility, and rage. (Are you getting depressed yet?!)

As we know too well, these negative emotions flood people's hearts and minds, producing a troubled world that desperately needs healing. Some people walk around with a Murphy's Law mentality—"whatever can go wrong, will go wrong," and it usually does!

How often do you hear negativity experts (pessimists) saying things like this: "The world is going to hell in a handbasket. Life is so unfair. Nothing ever works out for me. Nobody loves me. It's too late." I call these perspectives the *mentalities of failure*—negative ways of thinking that pollute our lives, defeatist statements that become self-fulfilling prophecies.

This barrage of negativity is served up by friends, colleagues, and relatives who bring us down. These are the faultfinders and naysayers in life who doubt and fear and undermine our value. They're always criticizing and complaining about their spouses, their bosses, their parents, their church. Things are never quite good enough.

> Mentalities of failure are negative ways of thinking that pollute our lives, defeatist statements that become self-fulfilling prophecies.

It's not much fun spending time with complainers, gossipers, and backbiters, is it? These people are irritating, for sure, and may drive us to the borders of insanity! And while we can have compassion for them and forgive them, we also have to detach from them. Otherwise, we become just as negative as they are, convinced that "this is the way life is."

Look, folks, I know it's sometimes difficult to get through the day without having a negative thought or two; but how often do we get into the *habit* of repeating hundreds of those thoughts until they become a fixed part of our thinking?

In order to change our lives, we have to change our thinking. We have to declare a *FAST* today—not a fast from food or fun—but a fast from negative thinking.

That's why last year I launched a new online program called "From the Inside Out—a Fast from Wrong Thinking." Instead of fasting from food,

I took people on a forty-day journey of fasting, or abstaining, from wrong thoughts and negative mind-sets. You know them well: *I can't. I don't have enough. I'm overwhelmed. I'm afraid something bad will happen. My life is not as good as others. I feel inferior. What's wrong with me? That's just the way I am. I'm not that smart. It's no use. I'll just have to settle.*

Within each of these statements is a lack of true awareness and appreciation for the gifts we have inside us. Isn't it true that we often don't give ourselves credit for being whole, worthy, and capable? Why is this? It's because people are thinking *backward*.

> Right thinking produces right living.

What do I mean? **Backward thinking is when we're concentrating on what we *don't* have instead of being thankful for what we *do* have.** That glass isn't half-empty. It's empty! The discontented person thinks that everything he does for God is too much—and everything God does for him is too little.

Perhaps you've heard the story of the conscientious wife who tried very hard to please her ultracritical husband, but she failed regularly to do so. He was always most cantankerous at breakfast. If the eggs were scrambled, he wanted them poached. If they were poached, he wanted them scrambled. One morning, with what she thought was a stroke of genius, his wife poached one egg and scrambled the other, placing the plate before her husband. Anxiously she awaited what surely would be his unqualified approval. He looked down at the plate and snorted: "Can't you do anything right, woman? You scrambled the wrong one!"

Backward thinkers are typically ungrateful, sullen, and sad—and living this way makes a person very un-Christlike. In fact, it's tragic when a soul can't see the positive because they're so focused on the negative.

And so it is that we become *addicted* to negative emotions, not realizing that we're consciously *choosing* them. We choose guilty, lonely, sad, and worried. We choose gossip, resentment, blame, and bitterness. We choose anger, impatience, revenge, and intolerance.

The result? **The more we use negative emotions, the more pain we feel**. And it's not only emotional pain. Scientists have proven that **negative emotion is detrimental to our physical well-being**. When we're angry, our bodies are flooded with stress chemicals—adrenaline, norepinephrine, and cortisol. Your heart pounds. Your blood pressure shoots up. And all that aggravation and rage can cause headaches, insomnia, anxiety, depression, high blood pressure, heart attack, and stroke.

> What we need in life are encouragers—not discouragers.

Friends, **in order to be healed, we need to replace mentalities of failure, eliminate negative thinking, and detach from negative relationships**. And we need to stop thinking backward.

As the Bible says in Psalm 34: "Who loves life and desires to see good days? Let him refrain his tongue from speaking evil. Let him refrain from thinking guile. Let him refrain from thinking the wrong thoughts and speaking the wrong way."

So pray: *Lord, let me stop focusing on what I don't have and start focusing on the good that You have already done. Give me the strength to surrender mentalities and failure—and cultivate a new way of living.*

HEALING COMES!

A man is but the product of his thoughts. What he thinks, he becomes.

—MAHATMA GANDHI

What you already have in life will pave the way for what you *don't* have. You see, when you think about what God has already done, you begin to grow in your faith for what He *can* do now.

Ten lepers were cleansed from their leprosy, but only one turned back to thank God for what He had done. The result? Jesus said to the one man who came back: "Where are the other nine? Didn't anyone come back to thank God except this one man?"

As you can see, first, the man's gratitude got God's attention! Second, his gratitude made him whole. Jesus said, "Your faith (expressed through thankfulness) has made you WHOLE." Indeed, not only did the leprosy heal, but all that was lost from his body and life through the diabolical disease was completely restored.

When you fill your mind with thankfulness and positive expectation, everything starts turning in your favor. You become a magnet of healing and contentment. You've already won the day, won the *Spiritual Super Bowl* before it even begins. You're blessed and favored by God. Your spirit is healed and calm.

And so it is that **the only escape route from mental and emotional pain is replacing negative emotions with positive ones**. These are emotions like love, tenderness, forgiveness, appreciation, faith, optimism, gratitude, and charity—the emotions of God. As it says in Proverbs 12:18: "While a reckless tongue wounds like a sword, there is healing power in thoughtful words."

> Mentalities of success are positive ways of thinking that enhance our lives, triumphant statements that become self-fulfilling prophecies.

Indeed, when we're driven by positive emotions and loving thoughts, everything in our lives gets better. Why? Because a positive attitude of faith conquers any challenge. In 2 Corinthians 1:20, the Bible says, "All the promises of God, in Him, are yes." Does that sound like a positive or a negative God?

Positive Emotions =

Pleasure, love, laughter, forgiveness, affection, tenderness, enthusiasm, humility, kindness, gratitude, passion, faith, compassion, empathy, trust, caring, integrity, commitment, determination, patience, optimism, persistence, loyalty, playfulness, creativity, generosity, grace, godliness, hope, intimacy, selflessness, enthusiasm, courtesy, charity, resolve, sensitivity, fidelity, gentleness, justice, perseverance, fearlessness, innovation, devotion, inquisitiveness.

A positive life of faith filled with a reservoir of healthy thoughts is a balm for every kind of pain. As the great apostle John wrote: "You'll have good health as your soul prospers."

And not only will your soul prosper—but it will know the joy of laughter, too, for as it says in Proverbs 17:22, "A merry heart doeth good like a medicine: but a broken spirit drieth the bones."

So no more dry bones! God wants you to be happy, healthy, and healed. So instead of being trapped in mentalities of failure, it's time to *cultivate mentalities of success*—positive ways of thinking that enhance your life, triumphant statements that become self-fulfilling prophecies. With this goal in mind, here are a few healing steps:

1. *Cultivate Positive Thoughts.* Beginning right now, anytime you catch yourself saying or thinking something negative, stop! Write down a list of the most common negative statements you tell yourself on a daily basis. Then, on the other side of the page, write down positive statements that will replace the negative ones. Practice saying them out loud. These are like prayers—drawing toward you everything good in life.

2. *Surround Yourself with Positive People.* Spend your time with friends, family, and colleagues who are encouraging and kind, compassionate and supportive. These are the people who love you and have your best interests at heart. We need to limit or avoid exposure to people who are undermining, critical, competitive, sarcastic, discouraging, manipulative, or judgmental. Pinpoint which relationships are corrupting the way you see yourself. As it says in 1 Corinthians 15:33: " 'Bad company corrupts good character.' " Instead, seek out people who celebrate you (rather than tolerate you). Just as misery loves company—so does joy!

3. *Redirect Your Focus.* What you focus on is what you feel. Focus on fear—you're anxious. Focus on resentment—you're angry. Focus on insecurity—you're doubtful. Instead of concentrating on what's *wrong*, focus on what's *right*.

Focus on faith—you will be confident. Focus on God's promises—you will be expectant. Focus on others—you will heal yourself. **Remember: freedom from pain often depends upon *charity* and love.**

4. *Take Good Care of Yourself.* Self-care is an act of love, and healing in every way. It's paying attention to your body and giving it what it needs—food, exercise, rest—you can rejuvenate yourself in a hundred different ways. So often we spread ourselves in a hundred different directions, diminishing our effectiveness, and tearing ourselves apart. Without enough sleep we become restless, cranky people. We tell ourselves we're "too busy" to get enough rest or to go to the gym or outside for a bike ride or a run. In truth, we can't afford *not* to do these things.

Sleep, of course, is a natural state observed in the animal kingdom. When, for example, was the last time you saw a dog staying up all night to clean up his doghouse? And have you ever heard of a cat with insomnia, staying up stressing over a relationship?

Rest is exactly what we need. As Jesus said: "Come to me all who are weary and heavy laden, and I will give you rest!" You've got to take care of your mind and body at least as well as a good mechanic takes care of your car!

What could you do to feel more vibrant, more energetic, and alive today? Get those feet rubbed. Stretch those muscles. Take a walk. **Remind yourself:** *I believe that God created me with value, so I'm going to take good care of myself.*

We all know by heart the speech given by flight attendants, telling

continued

us to "put your mask on first, then assist your child." Why? Because we can't be of service to our children, spouse, or friends until we take care of ourselves first. So heal yourself—*then* heal others.

5. *Have Some Fun.* Be *playful* and *carefree* and enjoy yourself and unwind with no other motive than the sheer pleasure of it. Whether it's taking your kids to the circus, playing a board game, building a snowman, hiking up a mountain, going to a movie, or taking a vacation—having fun is rejuvenating. You focus on pleasure, not responsibility.

So often, as adults, our capacity for fun is greatly diminished. All the things that we did when we were younger have fallen by the wayside. Whether it was finger painting, bowling, woodworking, Ping-Pong, kickball, playing the piano, singing, or racing bikes—what happened to it all? When did life become such drudgery—just work, sleep, and an occasional movie? I can tell you that if we don't deliberately plan healthy pleasures, we're going to find ourselves tempted by the unhealthy ones. This is how people get connected to the wrong people and the wrong substances.

Recapture your ability to be *lighthearted* again—to play—just as children do. Kids just *exist* to have fun. They giggle and squeal, skip and jump, leaping around with joy. The smallest things give them pleasure—throwing a ball, watching a butterfly, blowing bubbles, chasing a ball. They live to love and to be loved, to hug and to be hugged.

Even as I'm finishing this chapter, my three-year-old son, Roman, is laughing and playing, and wanting me to tickle him and throw him in the air. It's what he lives for. In fact, if it were up to him, play-

> How much fun do you have in life? *Most of the time I don't have much fun. The rest of the time, I don't have any fun at all!*
>
> —WOODY ALLEN

ing is all we would ever do. There's something really powerful about that. He keeps saying, "Mo, Dada, mo," meaning "more," of course. He instinctively knows that having fun is what he was born to do. It makes him happy, healthy, and satisfied.

In fact, the Hebrew word "*Eden*" is translated as "pleasure," a place with all the enjoyment that could be desired. That healing pleasure lives within you today. To rediscover it, all we have to do is remind ourselves *daily* that it's time for a FUN BREAK, a time out from all work and worry.

6. *Take Action!* As I've said many times, the goal of learning is not mere knowledge—but *action*. Don't wait for the finished product of healing to "show up" one day. Begin your healing right now. Don't wait for a reason to laugh—start laughing. Declare out loud the faithful affirmations we've just discussed. Go to my Web site [www.thinkingfast.org] and join the revolution, from *the inside out*. Sign up for my fast from wrong thinking, and expect things to begin to change. Remember, nothing just happens. The man at Bethesda was lame for forty years, but Jesus told him, "Pick up your pallet and WALK." He didn't tell him to sign up for a marathon, or to run around the block. He just said, take a step. That began the miracle action. So it will be for you.

Friends, when you cultivate mentalities of success in all these ways, your vision of life changes. You see the *good* in things. Little problems don't bother you as much. They begin to fade away. You see the big picture and you're grateful for it. All this is a recipe for healing in any and every area of your life.

Tell Yourself

I'm willing to do whatever it takes. I'll get over it, under it, or through it. I'm going to win my way through this situation. I'm going to stick with it and overcome this trial. I'm going to get up and pray. I'm going to trust and believe in God. I'm going to overcome sickness. I will recover. I'm the head, not the tail. I'm above, not beneath. God is for me, not against me.

I can tell you that I don't see the glass as half-empty; nor do I see it as half-full. **I see the glass *brimming* over, *overflowing*, just as it says in Psalm 23:5, "My cup runneth over."**

Say yes to that: *My life is abundant, running over. My cup will run over tomorrow, the next day, and every day. Every day I receive vast amounts of unexpected healing, health and vitality!*

How you see it is your choice. Instead of thinking that *everybody turns their back on me,* how about realizing there are a lot of people who *don't.*

> You deserve twice as much healing as pain, twice as much freedom as bondage, twice as much victory as defeat.

Look over the mountain, not under it. Look higher, not lower. Put out your hand to help, not to hinder. See the good in everything that God has provided.

Remember earlier when I mentioned that there are over one hundred references in the Bible with the word "pain" in it? Well, amazingly, there are over two hundred references to the phrase "Be healed." For example, in II Kings 20:5: "I have heard your prayer, I have seen your tears; surely I will heal you."

This means that for every pain in our lives, there are two healings; for every negative, two positives; for every sickness, two remedies; for

every mystery, two answers; for every puzzle, two solutions; for every sorrow, two doses of joy; for every dark hour, two hours of light.

Think about it. We sleep eight hours a night, which leaves us sixteen hours of light—twice as much light as darkness. This is God's blessing and promise. He has made provision for every malady, calamity, and ounce of pain you've ever faced, with twice as much wholeness, health, and deliverance awaiting you—if only you'll believe.

Every new day has folded into it a *promise* and an *opportunity* to heal every part of your life—and to bring healing to others. There's always something good to look *forward* to. There's always something to be *happy* about. There's always something to *smile* about. And there's always something to be *thankful* for.

So have some fun. Redirect your focus. Turn negatives into positives. Take care of yourself. Have faith in God's power and love. And be healed!

Secret #5

Be Still

THE MAGIC OF SILENCE

We need to find God and He cannot be found in noise and restlessness. God is the friend of silence. See how nature—trees, flowers, grass— grows in silence; see the stars, the moon and the sun, how they move in silence... We need silence to be able to touch souls."

—MOTHER TERESA

President Franklin Roosevelt had grown increasingly tired of the long receiving lines at White House functions. After more than a decade of such ceremonial duties, he complained to his aides that no one paid any attention to the words exchanged. No matter what he said, he would continually hear comments such as "Well done, Mr. President," "Congratulations, Mr. President," or "Good job, Mr. President."

So on one occasion, unable to endure the boredom of it any longer, he decided to have some fun with his guests. As each person passed by in the receiving line, shaking his hand, Roosevelt whispered, "I murdered my grandmother this morning!"

His guests responded with "Marvelous!" "Keep up the good work," or "God bless you, Mr. President."

It wasn't until the end of the receiving line, as the ambassador of Bolivia passed by, that the meaning of his words was finally heard. Unflustered, the ambassador leaned over to Roosevelt and responded: "I'm sure she had it coming, Mr. President."

THE ART OF LISTENING

How often in our lives are we *hearing* but not *listening*? Whether it's our spouse or children, our colleagues or friends, how much of what they're saying are we *missing*? And how many times has God spoken to us, though we didn't really hear Him? Yes, His wisdom and grace were whispered into our ears, but we blocked it out, too busy worrying and thinking about what *we* had to say or do. So we turned deaf ears to the message, unable to hear the still, small voice of victory in our heart.

Just as radio signals are always being broadcast, so it is that the voice of God is always speaking, though we're not always tuned in to it.

In school we're taught the communication skills of reading, writing, and speaking. Yet the most important secret to successful communication goes unmentioned.

What is it? It's the ability to *listen*.

> *The average person suffers from three delusions: (1) that he is a good driver, (2) that he has a good sense of humor, and (3) that he is a good listener.*
>
> —STEVEN SAMPLE

As King Solomon said in Ecclesiastes 5:1–2, "When you go to the house of God, draw near to listen, rather than to offer the words of fools."

Draw near. Slow down. And eliminate the interference and static all around you so that you can tune in to God. After all, He gave us two ears and one mouth, because He probably expects us to listen twice as much as we speak! But do we?

In our relationship with God, and with those closest to us, are we tuned *in* or tuned

> God gave us two ears and one mouth, because He probably expects us to listen twice as much as we speak!

out? Maybe we can't hear because there's too much interference on the "line." You know what I mean: Our own thoughts are furiously spinning. Our mouths are moving, but our ears are closed. So, typically, we end up in arguments because we're more interested in stating our *own* opinions and feelings than listening to somebody else. Or we hear only a fraction of the conversation.

Scientific research has, in fact, proven that immediately after we listen to someone, we only recall about 50 percent of what they said; while long-term, we only remember about 20 percent.

Listening, folks, is the ability to absorb what is happening around us — to truly hear what someone is communicating. **Listening is an act of generosity — a gift you can give your spouse, your children, and your friends. It demonstrates that you are genuinely interested in understanding what someone else is thinking, feeling, or wanting**.

Listening builds trust and respect, it reduces tension, and it creates a safe space for problem solving. Most important, **listening opens up our mind to grasp what God is telling us**.

THE WHITE NOISE IN OUR LIVES

There's a condition out there in the world that is working against us, an obstacle to peace of mind that prevents us from hearing the people around us — and the voice of God. It's a force field that's blocking our ability to be calm — to have the capacity for prayer, reflection, and appreciation. This disturbance is hovering around us, every single day. What is it?

It's called *distraction*. More than ever before, we live in a frantic, technology-saturated world filled with every kind of interruption, diversion, commotion, and amusement — *two hundred and seven million* cell phones ringing, pagers beeping, iPods blaring, e-mails flooding our mailboxes, text messages, and FedExes streaming into our offices, telemarketers pitching their products, six hundred

> If you refuse to be hurried and pressed, if you stay your soul on God, nothing can keep you from that clearness of spirit which is life and peace. In that stillness you will know what His will is.
>
> —AMY CARMICHAEL

television channels—not to mention movies, pop-up advertisements, Internet shopping, and all the junk streaming into our real and electronic mailboxes.

Our kids are particularly wired up for distraction, armed with electronic gadgets of their own that allow them to tune *us* out. I know a six-year-old boy who's so busy playing with his computer games at the dinner table that he has no time to talk to his own family. Mom and Dad don't mind because they're so distracted—they forgot they had a son!

And so, with our toys and devices vying for our attention, is it any wonder that we're *driven to distraction*? Our minds aren't just stimulated—they're *overstimulated* by a constant media and communications flood. Just as in Genesis 7:24, while the waters flooded the earth for 150 days, we're drowning year-round in a sea of distraction.

Psychiatrist Edward Hallowell, who wrote a great book titled *Delivered from Distraction*, says that "we have unwittingly become slaves to the miracles of technology—those labor-saving devices that supposedly made our lives easier. The result? *Nobody is in the now nowadays*!" This is a subject we'll return to later in the book.

Think about it. When you speak to someone, you frequently get the sense that they're somewhere else—pulled away by their e-mails, BlackBerries, voice mail, texting—giving you only a fraction of their attention.

The result is the disappearance of the "human moment" (face-to-face contact)—having dinner together, taking a walk, or sitting on the porch with friends or family. Such moments are very different from the "electronic moment," hours spent behind our computers and TV screens, which give us the illusion of connecting, but, in fact, make us feel more isolated and alone.

I often ask people, "When was the last time you saw one of your closest friends?" The answer is "A year ago." That's not a friend. It's a memory!

Isn't it ironic that the technology that was invented to *connect* us is actually *disconnecting* us. Instead of mastering it, we've allowed it to master us. We're always "on duty," never at rest. But even computers have to go to "sleep" sometimes, right? All this distraction swallows up our attention spans and eliminates our ability to reflect and ponder, to connect back to God—our true source of power.

God has to become our hard drive, the force running our entire system. And when this doesn't happen, you know what does. We're distracted even during the most intimate communication.

I recently read in the newspaper about a couple divorcing because the woman could no longer tolerate her husband's distracted attitude. Would you believe that even when they were in bed (and I don't mean sleeping) he'd keep his BlackBerry on a pillow nearby, and check it every minute. Talk about multitasking!

The other day I got into a taxi and the driver was counting his money, talking on the phone, listening to his radio, *and* eating a donut and coffee. And I'm still alive to tell about it!

Perhaps you, too, use multitasking as a way of getting through the day. I know many of us are guilty of giving our spouses or close friends just half an ear. People tell me that they can never "catch up," that there's so much coming at them from so many directions, that they can't even catch their *breath*.

In fact, did you know that some people are so intensely distracted that they almost forget to breathe? In the scientific community this is referred to as *shallow breathing*—taking in just the minimal amount of breath necessary to keep going. We're alive, yes, but we're not getting enough oxygen into our bodies to energize ourselves. Taking in rapid, shallow breaths, we become jittery and wind up feeling exhausted, depleted, and overwhelmed. And our stress level climbs.

If you've ever felt this way, you're not alone. In a recent survey it turned out that nearly *half* of all Americans believe that their stress has increased over the last five years, one-third of them reporting extreme levels of stress.

What's the good news? **We can take back control and become the masters of our own lives**. Instead of spinning like tops, we can slow down and end all this chaos. But how?

SIESTA OF THE SOUL

I know only one true solution: **we need to STOP and LISTEN to the most powerful voice there is — the soothing, peaceful voice of God**.

But in order to *hear* God's voice, we need to *be still* — to slow down and shift attention away from our incessant distractions. We need to find a calm place within — a place of inner contentment — where we can refuel and recharge ourselves, like recharging a battery instead of always draining it.

To put it another way: we need to *pull over to the side of the road* and take the time to rest and reflect — to exhale, to listen, and to pray.

It's just like when you're on a long road trip and feeling exhausted. Your eyes begin to get heavy and you start weaving on the highway, driving on automatic, almost asleep at the wheel. Rather than ending up in a ditch or worse, you pull the car over and shut the motor down. You close your eyes and go to sleep. You do this to survive.

It's exactly the same thing when you're depleted by the demands of a world filled with endless distraction. We need to take a "time-out." If we don't take a siesta of the soul, the engine of our minds overheats — and eventually we burn out.

Just as the navigational system of a car is designed to be set only while the car is stopped, we likewise can reset our course only if we allow ourselves to take a break. It might be inconvenient, but it can save your life!

So, in order for us to access the *power* to change today, we need to rest and recharge ourselves. God has, in fact, wired us to *stop and listen* for His direction and wisdom. By being still, we receive from Him a fresh supply of strength and clarity. But we can only do it by opening the space between our ears.

I'm reminded of the man who wanted to seek God in solitude, so he joined a monastery where the monks all took a vow of silence. Once every five years they were allowed to speak two words.

After the man's first five years had passed, he was invited to speak his two words. "Hard bed," he said. The head of the monastery assured him they would do what they could about his bed.

Five years later the man was invited to speak again. "Cold food," he said. Again, the head of the monastery assured him they'd do what they could.

Five more years passed and the man spoke again. This time he said, "I quit."

"I'm not surprised," the head of the monastery said. "For fifteen years you've done nothing but complain!"

There are many better ways to BE STILL—and to listen.

In our own family, one of the things my wife and I have done in raising our kids is to teach them to listen to God when we're together in the evening. At dinner I often ask them, "What have you heard from God today?"

Don't get me wrong. There are many moments of total silence around the table when I've asked that. But if they can't recall hearing anything that day, I lead them in prayer. We ask God to speak to us, and we *wait* for a moment to listen. It's amazing some of the things my kids have said they heard.

One time, when my son Joseph was nine, he prayed and heard this at the dinner table: *"When you don't know what to do, put yourself in your parents' shoes and think about what they would do."*

This was especially significant because two years before he had announced to his mom that he had officially changed his name. He wanted to be called "Gregory"! The following day she was calling and calling him, but he didn't answer. She finally found him in his room and said, "Joseph, I've been calling you for twenty minutes. Why didn't you answer?" He looked at her as serious as can be and said, "Who's Joseph?"

It was hilarious—because he meant it. He had changed his name, his identity, and had successfully put himself in my shoes!

But seriously, my children have developed the *habit* of listening, and it has shaped their lives, their conscience, and sensitivity to God and to others.

In your everyday life, there are many opportunities to listen and to be still. It can happen during a fifteen-minute nap, a hike in the woods, or a nice, long bath. I've "heard" many sermons in the shower (and yes, sometimes they've been all wet)! In fact, communing with God—whether on a bike path, a mountain, or just in your own backyard—is a great way to escape distraction and cultivate serenity.

Read a psalm, or even just one chapter of the Bible in a quiet place. It will have a miraculous effect. When discussing the key to overcoming worry, Jesus said, "Go outside and look at the birds, look at the fields, look at the lilies..."

He wasn't saying, *think* about it, but do it—GO OUTSIDE and look at how God takes care of His creation. Then He said, "You are much more important than they are." If your Heavenly Father knows how to take such good care of them, He will do even more for you. You'll be amazed at the peace, the energy, and the refreshment you're going to feel.

And, of course, throughout the ages, one of the proven ways of restoring faith and finding satisfaction is engaging in the power of PRAYER. I like what Acts 3:19 says, "Times of refreshing will come from the presence of the Lord."

Prayer is *communication* with God. It allows us to put aside self-interest and all distraction and connect with someone greater than ourselves. And it all begins with listening—with being *silent* and *still*.

Interestingly, the words "listen" and "silent" are composed of the same exact letters. Stillness, friends, is the source of all peace and contentment. It allows us to *hear* God, to receive His strength, guidance, and comfort while collecting our thoughts and taking control of our life.

I often explain prayer this way: like any living being, we inhale and exhale in order to survive. To maximize our spiritual lives, it's no different. Prayer is breathing *in* the presence of God so that we have something valuable to exhale—to give throughout our day.

In this way **prayer is an exchange with God.** As we listen to Him, we exchange our weaknesses, and He gives us His strength. We exchange our lack, and He gives us His sufficiency. We exchange our limitations, and He gives us His love and unlimited blessings.

When I was a little boy growing up in Detroit, we would visit our grandparents on Sunday afternoons. I'll never forget the memory of my grandfather, who spoke very little English. He would sit on the couch in the corner of the living room and just *listen* to everyone, hardly moving or saying a word. Even while we kids were playing and jumping, he'd BE STILL.

His silence kind of scared me as a kid. In fact, I can remember him frowning anytime one of us turned on the television. But you know what? I also sensed that he was always the one who seemed to be at peace. He was simply content when he was *still*.

And so it is in our relationship with God. In Psalm 46:10, God says, "Be still, and know that I am God." In fact, the phrase *be still* is actually translated as "let go, relax." Another translation says, "Cease striving."

I've always loved the story of the cowboy who was riding along and came upon the wise Indian lying flat on the ground with his ear pressed to the earth. The Indian said, "Wait. Wagon. Two miles off. Drawn by two horses. One black. The other gray. Four people on board: man in a red flannel shirt, his wife, and two kids."

The cowboy was very impressed. He said, "It's amazing you can tell all that just by listening to the earth."

The Indian said, "No. They ran over me thirty minutes ago. Go after them!"

Well, truthfully, you *can* tell a lot by listening with your knees to ground and your ears to heaven. To do this, all we have to do is get rid of the clutter that so occupies our heart. That's when we'll find rest and repose.

Whether you're being still in church or at home, whether you're standing, sitting, or kneeling, with eyes opened or closed, hands folded or upraised—the ability to be still and to pray is one great secret to living a satisfied, invincible life.

What a relief! No more living against the current of life. We're going to flow *with* it—reduce our stress and live longer, too.

Ever wonder how Methuselah lived to be almost one thousand years old? Maybe he had a good prayer life! As scientists have now proven, prayer has a powerfully healing effect on our bodies. It lowers blood pressure, reduces free radicals (a major factor in aging), and lessens the level of stress-related chemicals. Not bad for something we can do anytime—day or night.

So tap into the power of prayer, of being *still*, which means that you're going to give yourself permission to *let go of your anxieties and worries.*

Stop trying so hard to make life happen, and, instead, listen to God. He will make it happen and give you *the power to change today*—if only you'll *listen.*

THE SECRETS TO ACHIEVING STILLNESS

I know it's not always going to be easy to slow down long enough to get quiet and hear the voice of God. There are some obstacles we need to overcome. Let me mention a few:

1. *Turn Off Your Machines.* We need to create *technology boundaries* that prevent us from being *driven to distraction.* So turn those machines to "off," "silence," "mute" and "take a message."

I often say: *connect, but don't overconnect.* I can tell you that the off switch on our machines allows us the space to breathe and think.

So don't take any phone calls during dinner, at bedtime, at the movies, in the park, in church, or when you're talking to your spouse, playing with the kids, or meeting people you value. If you take those calls, you're telling the people you're closest to that you don't value them as much as the person calling. Don't worry that you're going to miss a sale, an invitation, an opportunity, or the latest gossip! God is going to give you something better. Time with Him can lead to success in business, but success in business will not lead you to intimacy

continued

with God. In church I've often joked with people that if I hear their phone ring during a service, I'm going to come over to their seat and answer it! When I do, I always ask the caller why they aren't in church, too!

2. *Turn Off Your Thoughts.* On average, according to scientists, each of us have fifty-five thousand thoughts a day! That means we're having 2,292 thoughts per hour, thirty-eight thoughts per minute. With all these ideas racing through our minds, no wonder we're so distracted, worried, and worn out. Massage therapists will tell you that one of the secrets to finding relief from tension and stress is taking deep breaths, letting go of all concerns—a subject we'll return to later in the book, in the "Live in the Moment" chapter.

This is your time-out, a rest period. And remember: you're a human *being*—not a human *doing*. Reflection is a necessity—not a luxury. So don't fall into the bondage of "the urgent." As the author Richard Carlson says: "Life isn't an emergency." We can't solve all our problems today, but taking time to be with God will certainly improve our chances. Attachment to Him, and detachment from all that is distracting is the source of our true satisfaction.

3. *Keep It Simple.* We need to unclutter and simplify our lives in every way possible. So choose your activities with care. I always say, "Honor your commitments, but only commit to the things you truly honor." So often, we've created a crammed calendar with every minute accounted for. Like an airline, we *overbook* ourselves. This does not allow us the space to be still. So create a reasonable schedule that fits the essentials in and keep to it rather than overextending yourself. Remember: overcommitment creates a tired mind. Commit, but don't overcommit.

4. *Keep a Soft Heart.* In order to be still and hear the voice of God, we need to keep a *soft heart.* A soft heart is one that is loving and kind. A soft heart is forgiving and compassionate. It's open and sensitive to others.

But so often, our heart becomes *hard,* resistant to prayer and faith. Maybe it's because of disappointments and setbacks we've endured. Rather than forgiving and forgetting, we hold on to our anger, past hurts, and resentments. We feel bitter, guilty, and regretful. We keep remembering the mistakes we've made and replaying the mistreatment we've felt at the hands of others. Our heart is in turmoil, not at rest.

Let go of all that pain that we've talked about. With a soft heart, in a state of stillness, our minds will be like fertile soil, ready to *receive* (rather than reject) the seeds of optimism and hope.

5. *Start the Day in Prayer.* Each morning, *choose* a silent, peaceful place and talk to God. Enjoy His company. Most people get derailed from trying this at all because they think praying is a major project. It isn't. Start with praying just five minutes a day. Greet God as you would a friend. "Good morning, Lord! I'm looking forward to spending the day with You." This creates an attitude of *expectancy* and confidence. As it says in Isaiah 50:4, "He awakens me morning by morning to listen. He has opened my ear."

Billy Graham was once asked which of his life experiences was the greatest—his fondest memory after sixty-five years of preaching. Was it counseling numerous presidents and heads of states or speaking before the largest audiences in the world?

"Forget about all those things," he answered. "The greatest experience I've ever had is the fellowship that I've had with Jesus Christ."

Now here's a man who has truly been *satisfied* in life—by *being still* in prayer with God.

Imagine it folks: the God of the universe has the interest and humility to spend time with *you*—to speak to *you*.

Who gets the better end of that deal? So let's take the time to get to know Him. I can promise you that being still and communing with Him puts you in a place of strength. The gift and strength of stillness is reflected in Exodus 14:14: "The LORD will fight for you; you need only to be still."

So let's get off the merry-go-round that is making us so dizzy. Shed the weight of those distractions and all those wondrous machines. Break free! Tune out—and tune in to God!

Folks, the life we long for is not in Hollywood or in the wealthy neighbor's house. It's in that quiet place with God.

As David said, "A day in your courts, Lord, is better than a thousand outside" (Ps. 84:10). David knew the dissatisfaction of *any* life without closeness with God.

Look forward to being still—for its promise is pure joy.

Part II

CHANGE FROM THE INSIDE OUT

Secret #6

Know Yourself

FROM THE INSIDE OUT

Knowing yourself is the beginning of all wisdom.

—ARISTOTLE

The great king of the forest, the lion, was proud of his mastery over the entire animal kingdom.

One day the lion decided to make sure all the other animals *knew* he was the king of the jungle. In fact, he was so supremely confident that he bypassed the smaller animals, who weren't even worth his time, and instead went straight to the great bear.

"*Who* is the king of the jungle?" the lion demanded, baring his teeth.

The bear quickly replied, "Why, *you* are, of course, Mr. Lion!"

The lion gave a mighty roar of approval and moved on.

Next he asked the tiger, "Who is the king of the jungle?"

And the tiger was equally agreeable, answering, "Everyone knows that *you* are, mighty lion."

Next on the list was the elephant, who stood still, towering over the lion, ignoring his question altogether. Then, the six-ton giant grabbed the lion with his trunk, whirled him around in the air six times, and slammed him into a tree! When the lion attempted to get up, the elephant pounded him onto the ground several times with his trunk, dunked him underwater in a nearby lake, and finally dumped him out onto the shore.

The lion—bruised, bloody, battered, and seemingly beaten—struggled to his feet, looked the elephant straight in the eye, and, without hesitation, said: "Look, just because you don't know the answer doesn't mean you have to get nasty about it!"

Friends, that lion *knew* who he was. And so must you.

You must *know* your true worth, your values, strengths, and weaknesses. You must know what *matters* to you and what you *believe* in. And even when you're disappointed, rejected, or seemingly beaten by life, you will live to fight another day, solid in your conviction that you can conquer any challenge.

And so, as we begin Part II of the book, I can tell you that **the secret to the satisfied life and true empowerment is, first and foremost, understanding *who* you really are —*from the inside out*— and not letting others define it for you.**

Yet today, it seems we live in a time when a whole new generation is trying so hard to "find" themselves. How did they get so *lost*?

I often think that with all the knowledge at our fingertips, **knowing ourselves is actually more difficult than ever**. Why?

The answer to this quest is so simple. But before I give it to you, allow me to make you a promise. When you come to *know* yourself, as I'll describe it in this chapter, you will become *invincible*, just like the mighty lion.

This book is all about creating that kind of unwavering spirit, one that cannot be defeated or beaten. You will become unshakable, indomitable, and incapable of being conquered or overcome.

Does the idea of becoming this powerful seem too far-fetched, or too good to be true? It isn't. For this is exactly what God has in mind for us.

Believe me, I don't have an exaggerated sense of my own power to change you, or to put something *in* you that you don't already have. My job is much easier than that. I'm not interested in talking about what you *need*, or what you *don't* have, or where you can go to *get* what you "ain't got"! **I'm here to uncover what you already *do* have, about what is already *true*, and about who you already *are*.**

Everyone knows that in order to know where you are going, you need to know a little bit about where you came from, right? Well, you didn't come from Brooklyn or Detroit or Compton or New Orleans. You didn't come from Italy or Mexico, Paris or Guam. You didn't come from the Smiths or the Hendersons, from Celeste or Chaniqua!

You came from God's Spirit. The Bible says in Genesis 1, "Let us make man in our image, after our likeness." When you recognize that you are made in the image of God, you will talk differently, walk differently and live with confidence, worrying little about what others say or do. Armed with this divine knowledge, you will never be defeated again.

Many of the great sculptors of the world have stated that they didn't so much "create" something, as uncover it. Yet this profound truth is what we frequently miss. Instead of seeking to become something, God simply wants us to discover who *He* already made us to be. It's right there inside us, waiting to be uncovered.

Yes, you might be knocked down, but you're not out. As Rocky Balboa said in the latest movie of the same name, "You, me, or nobody is gonna hit as hard as life. But it ain't about how hard you hit; it's about how hard you can get hit and keep moving forward." But you will get up again just as that lion did. Why? It's because you are truly invincible.

DISCOVERING WHO GOD INTENDED US TO BE

Remember the Who? They were the British rock band who used to sing a song that said: "Who are you? Who, who, who who?" That *is* the million-dollar question, though: *who are you?*

We're not talking about your occupation or last name, or where you went to college, or who your relatives are; we're talking about awakening to who God made you to be. I am convinced when you discover that (from the inside), you will never be the same.

Joy and peace will fill your life. Your search for significance and purpose will be over, while the enjoyment of your journey will only begin! The first step toward knowing yourself is to know where you came from.

If you knew you came from the Royal Family of England, you'd be in good shape no matter how much English muffins cost, wouldn't you? If you came from the Royal Family of Saudi Arabia, it wouldn't matter how much gas cost, would it?

On the other hand, if you thought you came from an ape (as one theory purports), you would probably have an insatiable desire for bananas and climbing to the top of a New York City skyscraper!

Maybe you heard about the man who was hired by a zoo to pretend to be a gorilla for a summer while their regular gorilla was on loan to another zoo. Every morning he would put on the gorilla suit and prowl around the enclosure while eating bananas and pounding his chest. There was a tire hanging on a rope in one corner and every so often he would swing on it. One day he was swinging on the tire and got a little overly enthusiastic—and managed to fling himself over the wall and then fell into the lion enclosure. A giant lion rushed over to where he lay.

"Help!" the gorilla screamed. "Somebody help me!"

"Quiet, you fool," the lion whispered, "or you'll get us both fired."

The truth is, you came from the very heart of God. He made you out of the stuff He's made of. And when you realize the stock you come from, you begin seeing yourself differently, talking differently, and living differently. When we surrender to God, we become a part of His royal bloodline.

I like to use the phrase "*Royalty destroys inferiority.*" What I mean is that when you discover your connection to God—and come to know Him as your Father and the Source of all you need—you begin to live differently. You realize you're a child of the King (not just of the forest, but of the universe)—and everything begins to change.

In *The Lion King*, young Simba runs away from home after the death of his father, Mufasa, and begins to associate with lower creatures in the animal kingdom, who teach him to eat slimy things and live a life of irresponsible pleasure-seeking. (It sounds like college!)

In a moment of truth, after the monkey, Rafiki, clobbers him over the head with his staff, Simba has a vision of his father saying, "You have forgotten who you are and so have forgotten me. Look inside yourself, Simba. You are more than what you have become. You must take your place in the circle of life."

Simba responds: "How can I go back? I'm not who I used to be!"

Mufasa answers: "Remember who you *are*. You are my son and the one true king."

Armed with that awakening, Simba begins the journey back to his true origin, and to his true place in life—as the king of Pride Rock, as the proud son of a legendary father, as one who will rise up to his great calling in life because he *knows* who he is, and accepts responsibility for his life.

BURN THE NEGATIVES

And so it is in our lives: *we are more than what we have become.* We, too, can take our rightful place in life and break out of our spiritual amnesia, remembering who we truly are—who God created us to be. All we need sometimes is a good knock on the head! Hopefully, that's what this book is providing.

We have to get our eyes on what God says. You may be reading this, and you've never really understood much of the Bible, or perhaps you are a believer and have never gotten your arms around this Christian life. Today you can start looking in this fascinating book—the Bible—in a whole new way: as a mirror, a reflection of the image of God, and the image of who you are.

The greatest part about the Bible is that it will always tell you the truth about the REAL you—the person on the inside who God created you to be.

What a contrast to the stark reality of how we see ourselves sometimes.

It reminds me of the sick man explaining his recent visit to the doctor. "He looked me over and asked what was bothering me," the sick man said. "I told him, 'When I look in the mirror every morning, I see thinning hair, sagging jowls, a bulging stomach, crooked teeth, and bloodshot eyes. I'm a mess. What is it, Doc?'"

The doctor replied, "I'm not sure, but the good news is that your eyesight is perfect!"

Aren't you glad that *God* doesn't look at us that way! He doesn't list all our mistakes and shortcomings, or focus on all that's "sagging" in our lives. He provides forgiveness and the power to change—which begins when you discover who you are from the inside out.

That's why **knowing yourself becomes possible when you know your value.**

Yet, as we know all too well, we often *devalue* ourselves—and, sadly, others as well. In Chicago, believe it or not, there is actually an "ugly law" on the books. It states, "No person who is deemed to be an unsightly or disgusting object is to be allowed in or on the public ways or other public places in this city. He shall therein expose himself to public view, under penalty of not less than $1 nor more than $50 for each offense."

No wonder people bundle up and cover their faces so much in Chicago. It's not the bitter cold winter weather; they just don't want to be fined!

All kidding aside, allow me to introduce you to the REAL you!

You are a masterpiece, a work of art. You're a chip off the old block! On the inside, you look like God—on the outside, we can all be quite a mess at times, but that's why God works from the inside out with us.

Often the image we have of God is a caricature of something stuffy religious people made up in their own minds, not a picture of what He is really like. What He's really like can be seen most accurately in the life of Jesus.

Jesus was the coolest man in the world. He was funny, warm, engaging, and never left someone in the same condition that He found them in. When He came in contact with the blind, He opened their eyes. He fed the poor. He healed the sick. He relieved and comforted the suffering. And He defended the defenseless.

When He came in contact with a storm, He calmed it; a mountain, He moved it; a temptation, He overcame it.

He hasn't changed, folks. The Scripture says, He is "the same—yesterday, today, and forever."

Why am I delving a little into this picture of God? Because when you know what God is like, you will have a more accurate picture of yourself, since you are made in His image.

In fact, one of the Ten Commandments says, "You shall not bow down to any graven images." This doesn't mean that God didn't want us to have statues or wear crosses. It means that God didn't want us to have an image of ourselves that was any less than the one He created us in.

So, from this day forward, we are not going to bow down to an image of failure within ourselves. We're not going to bow down to an image of inferiority, defeat, illness, or disease. We're not going to see ourselves, broke, busted, or disgusted! **We're going to stop "idolizing" a concept of ourselves that is not God-ordained. We'll bow down, only to the image of God**!

You see, whatever you "bow down" to is what you're going to be like. That's why God wants us to bow down to Him—not because He is narcissistic! But because He wants us to walk in the kind of power that comes from knowing who we truly are!

So, to *know* ourselves, we **must once and for all** *burn the negatives*. What do I mean?

In photographic terms, a negative is the reverse image of the picture you actually see in your camera's viewfinder. Light areas appear dark, and vice versa.

In our own minds the light of our true image is likewise cast in shadow. We see only flaws, the weaknesses, the things we did wrong, and our regrets.

Friends, we need to burn all the "negatives" of ourselves that reflect what is negative in life, those mentalities of failure that we described in the "Be Healed" chapter. This gives us the strength and confidence to prevail over any obstacle or challenge.

Remember, we think in pictures rather than words, conjuring images and associations in our minds, both positive and negative. For example, when I say the word "dog," you don't think *"d-o-g,"* but rather you see your pet, Fido, running around the house or that Doberman that nipped your behind when you were a kid!

Reggie Jackson, the great 1970s home run hitter for the New York Yankees, said about himself: "When I was a kid, I used to play in the backyard and *picture* myself hitting a home run to win the World Series."

Twenty years later, of course, that image of himself became a reality. Why? It's because that's how he saw himself. He never let go of that image. Neither should you.

The ancient Greek phrase "Know yourself," often ascribed to Socrates, was so profoundly important that it was inscribed in the stone of one of their temples. The message behind these two words? We can understand all human behavior, emotion, and thought by understanding ourselves, and most of all, by understanding that we are made in the image of God. This gives us incredible strength, courage, and resilience. In fact, in the epic military manual, *The Art of War*, the sixth-century B.C. Chinese author Sun Tzu reveals the three secrets to winning any battle: *Know yourself, know your enemy, and know your weapons.*

This is so true in winning the battles of life. Two of the most pivotal moments in history had to do with the truth of *knowing yourself.* In the Garden of Eden, God told Adam and Eve that He had created them in His image. It was there that they *knew* they were like God. But when the serpent comes to tempt Eve, he challenges this truth. "God doesn't want you to eat of the tree of knowledge of good and evil, because He knows that when you eat it, you will be like Him."

That was the lie they swallowed. The truth was, they *already* were like Him. But when they doubted it, they gave in to their tragic sin. The sin was not eating from the wrong tree. It was believing the wrong information about themselves. They doubted who they were. And therefore they lusted to *be* more and *have* more.

Secondly, when Jesus was fasting and being tempted in the wilderness, Satan offered the same bait. "If you're the Son of God, turn these stones into bread." Notice that he used the phrase: "*If you're the Son of God.*" But, because Jesus knew who He was, He overcame the temptation.

Likewise, when you know who you are, you can overcome whatever the temptation or challenge. I like what it says in Romans 8:37: "You are more than a conqueror, through Him that loved you!" And when you believe that you are God's child, rather than caving into how others may see you, you can tap into incredible resilience and incredible strength.

Make up your mind today—don't allow others to damage the image God placed in you. Burn the negatives.

CONFIDENCE

Recently I was talking to a lady in my church, Cheryl, who had been suffering for months from a series of illnesses that left her feeling anxious and discouraged. As her condition worsened, she lost her appetite and was hospitalized.

As I delved into her situation more deeply, I found out that she had been taking advice from a rather judgmental, critical relative who had made her feel worse. (Know anyone like that?) This person had "intellectually"assessed her condition and undermined her simple faith in God and His ability to heal her.

Cheryl felt beat because the words of her well-meaning relative were burying her in self-condemnation. She was seeing her weaknesses, rather than God's strength. Yet, in the midst of this self-doubt, she heard a still, small voice inside her say, "My daughter, you've taken your eyes off Me. You're trusting in what others are saying, rather than what I'm saying."

She heard the voice of God. She began to put her hope and trust in HIS POWER, and HIS STRENGTH, again. Her condition immediately began to improve. Psalm 118:8 KJV says, "It is better to trust in the LORD than to put confidence in man."

The next time she saw her relative, Cheryl gave him a warm hello, walked right on by, and with a victorious smile, declared: "I've got my confidence back!"

When I heard those words, something went off inside me: *That's the difference*, I thought,

> Therefore, do not throw away your confidence, which has a great reward.
>
> —HEBREWS 10:35

between victory and defeat, sickness and health, joy and sadness, between wealth and poverty. It's confidence — *a powerful force that can move mountains, change lives, and restore the vitality and enthusiasm of life that we were born to walk in.*

Now Cheryl is smiling at life — a victor, rather than a victim. She walked differently, she talked differently, she began treating herself better, and seeing others in a whole new light. She soon recovered from all that was ailing her! Why? What was the key to this miracle turnaround in her emotions, her health, and her relationships? Simple. She got her confidence back! And she did it because she, once again, knew who she really was!

Folks, when you truly *know* yourself in the ways we've discussed, you're going to feel in tune with your God-given nature. A new sense of confidence will emerge, and nothing will be able to defeat you.

You're going to have the conviction that you can accomplish anything. You will have less fear of the unknown. You can stand up for what you believe in. You have the courage to take risks and accept challenges. You can attempt anything. You can get up when you've fallen. You can still believe when others doubt. You can look in the face of opposition and even near ruin, and laugh in its face. What's the secret? Confidence.

SIX SIMPLE STEPS TO KNOWING YOURSELF

1. *Know Where You Came from.* As we've seen, you came from the very heart of God. You are His creation and made in His image. Remember that *royalty destroys inferiority* — so when you know you're part of God's family, fear and worry are going to disappear. *Knowing* where you come from is truly the gateway to discovering your God-given purpose in life, where the satisfied life is a guarantee!

2. *Know Your Value.* The other day in church, I held up a $100 bill to illustrate a point about the unquestioned value that each of us has. I asked people to raise their hands if they would like to have that $100 bill. Hands went up all over the audience. Then I crumpled up the bill in my hand, and asked again who wanted it. All the hands still went up. Then I threw it to the ground, stomping it under my foot, nearly ripping it apart. I asked *again* who wanted it, and all the hands went straight up! (In fact, one lady came running up the aisle waving her hand, yelling, "I'll take that, Pastor, give it to me!" She almost knocked me over trying to get that $100 bill!)

Why did I do this? I wanted to make the point that no matter how many times in life we've been thrown down, crumpled, or walked on—no matter how dirty we've ever gotten—God still views us as having the same value as when He created us. He believes in us with passion and promise. He still wants us, no matter what we have been through, no matter where we have been. That's true value!

But, as we discussed, we're quite often harsh on ourselves. We berate and downgrade our efforts or behavior, beating ourselves up about what's wrong with us.

Stop being your own worst enemy. Stop judging yourself for falling or sinning or making a mistake.

I can tell you that when we're overly self-critical and knock ourselves down, we have forgotten who we are and where we came from. Start acting *as if* you ARE what God says you are—valuable and precious.

You ARE forgiven. You ARE a success. You ARE intelligent. You ARE capable. You ARE beautiful. You ARE enough. You ARE victorious.

3. *Know Your Values.* This is your base—your moral and ethical compass—the standards and sense of responsibility that provide

continued

guidance and determine your character in life. Your actions in life will eventually match what you believe to be right.

Your true character is revealed by what you do when no one is looking. It's based upon an inner conviction of right and wrong. So you have to make up your mind to live by a set of values that don't bend with the wind. They are constant, even when keeping them hurts sometimes. Integrity, honor, humility, loyalty, and love should reign supreme at the core of your being. These types of values govern the choices you make, the people you surround yourself with, and the quality of life that you live.

4. *Know What's in You.* The moment we yield to the grace of God, He makes an eternal investment in us. He puts His very Spirit in us. Trust me when I tell you that you possess more talent and ability inside you than you have ever known or thought possible, a subject we'll turn to in more detail in the *Discover the Greatness in You* chapter. Your knowledge of this unlimited potential is what triggers God's power in your everyday life. As the Bible says in Philemon, verse 6, "your faith becomes effective by acknowledging every good thing that is *already* in you…"

5. *Know Your Weaknesses.* You can't change or improve your life if you're unaware of what's stopping you. We all have an Achilles' heel, a blind spot. Maybe you're incredibly impatient or you tend to judge others too quickly, or have a bad temper, or tend to procrastinate. Among other things I have the hardest time letting anyone drive when I'm in the car. If they do, I'm the worst backseat driver you can imagine. "Turn here. Get in that lane! Pass that slowpoke!" I tell you, you can tell a lot about a person by the way they act in a car! (That's why I wear dark glasses and a wig when I drive!)

Admitting your vulnerable points, though, is a sign of great strength. The Bible says in James 5:16: "Confess your weaknesses to one another and pray that you would be healed." The point of this verse is that we need some genuine relationships, a church—our spiritual family—where we can be honest, and get the encouragement we need to strengthen and cover our weak areas. We can be completely honest and confess our flaws, in all humility, to those we're closest to. There is power in this honest transparency that God promises will heal you.

6. *Know Your God.* It's been said in life that it's not *what* you know, but *who* you know! Well, that statement has never been more true than today, when it comes to knowing God. No religion, tradition, ritual, church, synagogue, mosque, or human being can give you the love and power that comes from knowing Him.

So if you don't know Him personally, allow me to introduce you: God is the divine artist who created mankind with the magnificent ability to enjoy all of the pleasures He placed in this world. He is love and He is a lover, who desires to be freely loved in return. His relationship with you is therefore not based upon guilt or punishment—the guilt of your not praying enough, or not doing enough, or living a holy enough life. It is based on love.

No matter what you've done or *haven't* done (or even if you've "blown it" in some way), run into His arms. Talk to Him. Lean on Him for strength. And rather than viewing the Bible as a rule book, see it as a love letter.

Remember: Every human being has a deep need for love, and this need comes directly from God. Without it, life spirals into despair, depression, and darkness. Indeed, scientists have proven that when infants are deprived of love, they sometimes even die, or grow into adults who hate themselves and others. As we get older, still deprived of love, we often turn against others and then ultimately against ourselves. But when you know

God, and love comes into your life, everything changes. Darkness turns to light, despair to hope, depression to joy, and death to life.

So resolve today that you will no longer yield to self-doubt, to second-guessing yourself—undermining your confidence and strength! This habit has kept us limited and weak. But when you know yourself, you become a treasure of power, wisdom, strength, and virtue.

Friends, the lion, at the beginning of our chapter—though bruised—*knew* who he was. Likewise, no matter how bruised you've ever been, when you know yourself and your value—you can get up, wipe the dirt and dust off your knees, look life straight in the eye, and say this: "Life, no matter what you have ever done to me, no matter how bad you think you've beaten me, I know who I am. I am a child of God. I will overcome you and I will not be defeated another day in my life. I'm immovable, unshakeable, and invincible!" That's what knowing yourself is all about.

That's change from the inside out! At last, you can stop striving to become something on the outside because you know who you are on the inside. Discovering our good in God is always the difference between success and failure in life, between victory and defeat.

So having faith that you have been made in the image of God, touched by His love, is more than enough to uncover the victorious life.

It's only a matter of time before the caterpillar turns into a butterfly. God's Word is the cocoon that insulates and surrounds us, feeding our minds and hearts, allowing us to truly be more than what we have become—to know ourselves, and to know God.

And when you know Him, you will love Him; and you will love yourself, in a healthy and powerful way—from the inside out.

Secret #7

Love Yourself
THE ROAD TO SELF-ACCEPTANCE

You must love yourself before you love another. By accepting yourself and fully being what you are, your simple presence can make others happy.

— JANE ROBERTS

One day, when my oldest daughter, Olivia, was twelve years old, I noticed that she was a little discouraged.

When I asked her what was wrong, she said, "Nothing," which, of course, is always "something," right?

So I probed a bit more, we talked about some of the things that she wanted out of life at her ripe old age. After beating around the bush for a while, I finally asked her: "Olivia, what is it you *really* want right now in your life?" And with little hesitation, she responded, "Daddy, I just want to know how to be *beautiful*."

I was really struck by this. Didn't she know how utterly beautiful she was, inside and out? But already, at such a young age, her heart and mind were filled with comparisons to fashion models and movie stars, images that are daily portrayed as "true beauty."

Olivia got me thinking. So I walked away, sat down with a pen and paper, and put together what I thought were some secrets to being truly beautiful—ideas you'll read about in the next few pages. What I said changed her life—as I hope it will change yours as well.

When I talked with Olivia a bit later, I told her that there is nothing wrong with wanting to be beautiful. We all have the innate drive to look and feel our best. Unfortunately, the only way most people ever *feel* their best is when they believe they *look* their best. But, as I told her, they've got it backward. No matter what your age or body type, when you're feeling happy, loving, and peaceful, people will tell you that you have a "glow." This is beauty that radiates *from the inside out*.

And the same is true when you're feeling bad about yourself, or when you're filled with negative emotions, or when you ignore the compliments you get and only zero in on what's wrong with you. If you feel lowly on the inside it will begin to show on the outside. So there's some truth to the old joke that "beauty is only skin-deep, but ugly goes all the way to the bone."

I told Olivia that people are able to acquire beauty in two ways—by putting it *on*, or by putting it *in*. And when you really know who you are as a child of God, His beauty is already *in* you. As Psalm 45:13 KJV declares, "The king's daughter is all glorious *within*." Indeed, no matter how critically others may view us, we need to ignore it and view ourselves the way God does—as a King's daughter or son.

TO LOVE OR TO HATE OURSELVES?

How many of us have experienced similar moments of low self-esteem or self-doubt—feeling insecure about *who we are* and *what we look like*. Not only do we not *love* ourselves—but, at times, we don't even *like* ourselves, right?

I can't tell you how many people ask for counseling because they don't feel *good enough* or because they're convinced that they don't *measure up*.

At times like these, when we're lacking healthy love for ourselves, we feel inadequate, defective, and flawed—"unacceptable" to ourselves and to others. In fact, when someone's esteem is at its lowest ebb, it may even turn to self-hatred or shame.

The challenge? To *love yourself*! It sounds a little strange, doesn't it? After all, doesn't loving ourselves sound self-absorbed? Does this mean we're conceited, or that we only put our own needs first? Aren't we supposed to be more concerned about expressing our love and care for *others*?

Well, loving yourself—taking care of yourself, appreciating your special gifts, valuing yourself—is actually the first step toward loving anyone *else*. For if you don't love yourself, you are not a reservoir of love from which others can drink. Your well is dried up instead of brimming over.

If the greatest commandment is to "love your neighbor as yourself," then it must be assumed that your ability to love your neighbor is in direct proportion to your ability to love yourself. Makes sense, doesn't it?

Now there is a vast difference between *self-love* (self-centeredness) and *loving yourself.* **Self-love is our attempt to preserve ourselves, to seek only what's good for us, to pursue only the things that make us feel good, even at the expense of others**. This is not what I'm talking about.

Loving yourself means respecting what God made when He created you. You take good care of His creation, appreciating your special gifts. I'm not saying we don't all have flaws and weaknesses, or that there aren't things about ourselves that we would like to change. Nobody could argue with that. But when we love ourselves, we acknowledge, with gratitude, the good in us and thank God for it.

Notice: **People who love themselves are *comfortable* with themselves. They usually look on the bright side, they see opportunity in adversity, their sense of well-being doesn't depend on performance, and they don't hold on to grievances and resentments.** Just being in their company makes you feel better. It's not what they do or what they think, but who they *are*.

Too many people, however, think poorly of themselves, degrade and deride themselves. It's called self-hatred.

Whether it's the overweight teen or the anorexic, the unathletic male or the so-called "goon," or the person with "too little" money or the super-rich guy who's never satisfied, people beat themselves up for what's "*wrong*" with them or for what they "*lack*."

I can tell you that **self-hatred is the archenemy of the satisfied life.** It produces eating disorders, depression, violence, perfectionism, criticism, obsessive behavior, and wars. And I believe it's the source of much of the failure we will ever experience. Getting rid of it—and learning to love ourselves God's way—will be the source of our true success.

You might ask: "How will I recognize this self-hatred?" It makes you feel like you're never good enough; you're constantly guilty for not measuring up; you feel tormented by a grievous sin or mistake from the past. You're always discontented until everything is perfect—which is never!

When people feel less than worthy, they not only denigrate themselves, but often lash out at others, too, becoming impatient, intolerant, or critical. It's as if their *dissatisfaction* within creates a restless spirit that can neither find love nor give it.

We can all recall some grouchy guy in the office—the one always backbiting and criticizing, right? It isn't too hard to imagine that deep down, he wasn't too happy with *himself.* In this state people continually punish themselves—never feeling good enough, no matter what they do.

And it all begins in childhood. According to a study at the University of Texas, childhood experiences that lead to low self-esteem include:

- being harshly criticized,
- being yelled at, or beaten,
- being ignored, ridiculed, or teased,
- being expected to be "perfect" all the time,
- experiencing failures in school or social interactions.

Hello!? Isn't that how we all grew up?

Here's the point that really hits home. **People with low self-regard feel that failure of *any* kind**—losing a game, getting a poor grade, being rejected for a date, not staying thin—**is a failure of their entire self.**

Feeling unworthy and fatally flawed, we may become perfectionists, demanding a standard that can never be attained, a subject we'll return to later in the book. So we wind up having a low opinion of ourselves and of our potential (yet often disguise this with grandiose boasts about what we will do one day, or what we've already accomplished).

In short, we feel *bad* about ourselves. And every one of our decisions is colored by this affliction.

No matter what the cause of it, when people don't feel loving toward themselves, they always find a strategy for coping with (or compensating for) that negative self-image. Some clam up and become introspective, as I did as a boy, and wind up depressed and isolated. Others become self-congratulatory in an attempt to feel superior and quell feelings of inadequacy and self-hatred. Others accumulate things, stay constantly busy, or overachieve. They may look happy and successful, but this only covers over the pain inside.

No matter how we cope, these defenses temporarily protect us from fear, rejection, loss, and emotional pain — though they can't entirely cover the reality that we don't feel good about ourselves on the *inside*, where it really counts.

So we continue to suffer, often numbing our pain with comfort food. Anyone feeling hungry? And what about smoking, alcohol, or any number of other addictive behaviors that we talked about in the "Be Healed" chapter?

You might ask: why is feeling negative toward ourselves so profoundly damaging? Well, it's one thing for someone *else* to criticize us: at least we can defend ourselves and fight back.

But when we criticize and attack *ourselves*, there is no one to stick up for us. There is no predictable outcome except defeat, suffering, and conflict. That's when people give up on themselves and become victims of life — denying their ability to grow, change, and contribute.

What's the answer to all this? And how, in a culture more plastic than ever, can we reconcile our profound feeling of discontent?

THE RIDDLE AND BURDEN OF "BEAUTY"

In the first chapter, I told you how inferior I felt in junior high school, ostracized by the "in crowd" because of my name, Middle Eastern background, and appearance. With no front teeth, a prominent nose, and big lips, I certainly didn't feel even close to *normal*! In fact, I can honestly say that I *despised* myself! I can remember looking into the mirror when I was in eighth grade, saying out loud, "I hate you!" as I'd hit myself across the face with my fist. How's that for self-hatred? So I know this subject pretty well.

But was I alone? Hardly. Did you know that 60 percent of American teenage girls wrongly believe that they weigh too much? And one out of every hundred girls in the United States between the ages of ten and twenty is starving or stuffing herself (sometimes to death), suffering from anorexia and bulimia nervosa.

And did you know that up until 1995, when Western TV was introduced to the Fiji Islands, only 3 percent of teenage girls had any eating disorders? But Western TV changed all that, and nowadays five times as many girls there complain about being "too big or fat." They, too, want to be stick thin.

Why is this? It's because our culture is inundating us with images of perfection — pictures of what we're supposed to look like and act like in order to be accepted and respected. So all we see are supertoned, lean, perfect bodies — which sends the message to our children that being beautiful (and thin) is the secret to being popular, loved, and happy.

What a lie! How many films stars — Marilyn Monroe, a legend among all — were idolized worldwide for their incredible beauty and talent? Yet, she once said, "All I ever wanted was to be loved." Sadly, even with all her gifts and beauty, she felt flawed, inadequate, and was, of course, prone to addiction and eventual suicide.

Still, the myth persists: you're not "enough" unless you're perfect. It's as if we're living in a society that has outlawed anyone *less* than the preordained perfect. So if you don't look like a Victoria's Secret model, then you're not a legitimate citizen and should go to a country where they accept fat people!

So millions are having plastic surgeries to "correct" themselves, requesting Cameron Diaz's nose or Nicole Kidman's cheekbones or Tom Cruise's smile.

Friends, **all this emphasis on looks only keeps us from valuing and loving ourselves the way God intended us**. We become discouraged, despondent, and less than confident in our potential. We feel guilty and *unforgiving* of ourselves for not measuring up. Instead of seeing what's *right* about us — we're always looking at what's *wrong*.

> Getting rid of self-hatred and learning to love ourselves—God's way—will be the source of our success.

We have to realize that **the "perfect image" we're being shown is a *false idol*, and bowing down to it is "idolatry"** as we learned in the last chapter.

Indeed, when we succumb to becoming enslaved to this false idol, we lose confidence and become anxious, and set ourselves up to have to "perform" for the self-respect that we long for.

And inevitably, when we realize we *can't* attain perfection, we lose hope, become despondent, and begin to let ourselves go.

The ultimate result is that we feel *worthless*, like something is innately *wrong* with us, that we're *unacceptable* and *unlovable*—just *not good enough* as we are. Skinny doesn't always mean healthy. And thin isn't always in!

Listen, could some of us stand to lose a few pounds? Maybe. But don't lose weight or exercise so you can start liking yourself. Do it because you already *value* yourself, because you want to take better care of your health and your God-given body that deserves the best.

Now, please understand, I'm not preaching for *being* fat, but I'm not preaching against it, either. **I'm preaching against self-hatred**. Sure, improve what you can. But if there is something you would like to change about your appearance, ask yourself these things: *Why? Is it worth it? What are the drawbacks?*

I promise you that if you don't like yourself *before* you make some radical changes, you will not like yourself *afterward*. Disdain for yourself is the wrong reason to change or improve anything about your appearance. We have to realize that attempting to create a perfect image on the outside is never going to spell satisfaction on the inside.

So in the end, what is real beauty? As I told Olivia, the source of it isn't to be found in Hollywood actresses, fashion models, or cosmetics experts. It's God. He is the most beautiful being in the universe and when you see His compassion, His power, and His wisdom—you're looking at the NEW YOU, the real you. As it says in 1 John 4:17, "...as he is, so are we in this world."

I can tell you that **when your reason for acquiring beauty is to develop your inner spirit, this motive will overshadow the shallow desire to attract attention and praise.** Instead, as the Bible says, people who are truly "desirable" are kind, loyal, generous, and have a full, thankful heart. Embodying these qualities, you will acquire beauty that is deep, real, and liberating.

And so it is that **beauty begins in the heart that has meditated on the Word of God and bathed in His love.** These hearts produce the most beautiful people. You can be 40, 50, 60, or older and still radiate a presence that is stunning. Why? Because you love yourself the way God intended... *You are valuable!*

YOU ARE VALUABLE!

About now, you might be thinking, *what's the big deal about loving myself anyway? I don't even think about it.*

Well, I can tell you that one of the top issues discussed in therapy, in counseling, on TV talk shows, in self-help books, is the fact that people *don't* love themselves. (As I said earlier, they often don't even *like* themselves!)

They call this LOW SELF-ESTEEM—it's a worn-out phrase for sure, but it hits the mark. If you don't esteem yourself—value and prize and cherish yourself—then it's very difficult to present a loving presence to the world.

You might ask, where does it come from and how do we stop it?

Everyone's heard of Cain and Abel—the first two sons of Adam and Eve? The Bible tells us that Cain commits the first murder by killing his brother, Abel. God had rejected Cain's offer to get the leftover fruit of the harvest, but accepted Abel's (the first and best lamb of the litter). This sad but amazing story reveals a lot about human nature and why we do what we do.

First, Cain shows disrespect toward God by giving Him what is left over. As a result, he loses respect for himself. He then has no regard or love for his brother, whom he views as the reason for his own discontentment. So feeling enraged by jealousy and self-hatred, Cain's method of coping is to transfer his feelings toward his brother and rid himself of the thing he thinks he hates. In truth, he hates himself even more after the murder, so the vicious cycle continues.

Have you ever wondered how you could change the way you treat others—giving them more kindness and consideration? This is how it works: **You put God first in your life and honor Him.** By giving respect to the Creator of the universe, you, in turn, feel respect for yourself. He puts that in your heart, and you begin to show it toward others. Anger, envy, and fear are replaced by love, acceptance, and courage.

But to have this kind of respect and love for yourself, you need to know how loved you are by God, which we discussed in our "Be Loved" chapter. To put it into proper perspective...

Imagine for a moment that you were married to the most perfect person in the universe. I'm talking about the ultimate mate—someone spiritually, emotionally, financially, and physically perfect.

Even when *you're* at your least attractive and respond with anger, they put their arms around you and say: "You're everything to me and there's nothing you can do that will stop me from loving you."

And even if you went out and sinned, they would forgive you: "It doesn't matter," they say, "My love for you is greater than that. I embrace you and welcome you back."

Would it be difficult to love someone like that?

I don't think so!

Well, that's exactly the kind of love that God has for *you*. He never mistreats or hurts you. He always forgives. It's His kind of unconditional love that we need to nurture in *ourselves*; and it's His blessing of love that we must bestow on ourselves.

If you really love yourself the way God intended you to (not in a self-absorbed or egotistical way), the natural result will be both self-respect and an outpouring of encouragement and love toward others. In fact, when you feel God's love for you (and, in turn, high regard for yourself), love will flow out of you toward others like a river! That's the day your relationships are going to be transformed. It's really a revolving circle. How we treat others is a direct reflection of our view and treatment of ourselves. Jesus said that one of the greatest commandments of all was to *Love your neighbor as yourself*.

> A best friend loves you no matter what. They accept what you look like. They understand your limitations, but love you anyway. A best friend never talks badly about you. They only want the best for you! Sometimes that best friend has to be you.

And so it is that **we must find a way to start loving ourselves the way *God* loves us, armed with the knowledge that we're fearfully and wonderfully made in His image.** And *His* is the only image we need to "bow down" to.

I can promise you that when you clear your head and accept that you *are* His, you will forever stop feeling inferior. You will stop hating yourself. Why? It's because you will have discovered your God-given value. Remember that God told Israel that they were His special treasure (Exodus 19:5)—and it's this knowledge that allows you to stop doubting yourself.

Instead, you will *rise* to the level of the image *He* has in His mind of you. And it won't matter how much you weigh, what clothes you wear, where you live, or what you own.

You're going to truly love yourself from the inside out.
So let's destroy self-hatred and forever stop the cycle of self-condemnation.

THE ROAD TO ACCEPTANCE

So how can we begin to love *ourselves*—and others?

1. *Put God First in Your Life—and Honor Him.* By giving this respect to the Creator of the universe, and knowing His love, you will begin to feel an overflow of dignity and respect for yourself and others. Putting Him first in all areas of your life will create a healthy and positive sense of respect, which is what really makes the world go round. When you do this, it restores order to your world. God first— then you. As it says in the Bible, "God will honor those who honor Him." When you honor God by putting Him first, you will feel a sense of dignity, a greater respect for yourself, and a greater love.

2. *Silence the Inner Critic.* In order to love yourself, you must eliminate self-derision. So once and for all, let's put an end to the "Charlie Brown syndrome." Charlie was a loveable loser with a permanent case of bad luck. He was always down on himself and taken advantage of. No more negative words about yourself, period. No more:

- "I'm so stupid."
- "What a klutz I am."
- "Why do I always blow it?"
- "I shouldn't have said that."
- "I'll never get out of this mess!"

continued

Doesn't it sometimes seem as if there's a demon sitting on your shoulder, judging you, giving you advice, telling you what's wrong with you, how you failed again, what you'll never be, what you'll never do? This is the demon of limitation, the negative voice that's always whispering into our ear, chattering away. Such demons feed on the negative emotions that we all have inside us.

These can be eliminated and silenced once and for all when we take in the love that God has for us. Speak to yourself respectfully. Praise yourself for what you do *right*! Silence forever that inner critic. Instead, listen to God's voice of acceptance.

3. *Remind Yourself You're Priceless.* As it says in Psalm 139:14, you are "fearfully and wonderfully made." Tell yourself that. Remember that you are tenderly loved by God, that you are the crown of His creation, made in His image. You may not feel it right now, but talk it and think it, and it will change you. We sometimes forget that we're more precious than anything in the *material* world, that we are a valuable commodity. Have you ever gone into an art gallery and looked at an abstract painting? I recently saw one appraised at $20 million, but, honestly, it looked like a child had splattered paint all over the canvas! It was pretty ugly and worthless in my eyes. So where did it get its *value*?

The value of a thing is not determined by how much money or time it took to make it. It's determined by how much someone is willing to pay to have it.

The Bible says God valued us so much that He was willing to sacrifice His own Son's life so that we might live and prosper. That's how valuable *you* are—as precious as the thing with which you were purchased, which in this case was Jesus Himself. God values you as much as He does Him.

Start telling yourself: *I'm a child of God. I'm special. God paid a great price for me. He values me therefore I value myself.*

4. *Abandon Perfectionism.* Surrender the idea of ever having angel wings and a halo—and realize that you're human. Doing your best is a worthy goal, but you can't do it all (and you can't do it all perfectly). Perfectionism is actually the *lowest possible standard*, because it always sets you up for failure and disappointment. We may desire a "perfect" body or a stratospheric bank balance, but realize that our happiness (and worthiness for love) does not depend upon it. If you're stressing out because you don't feel you will ever be good enough—GIVE THAT UP!

Are you always criticizing your performance? Do you disregard compliments and praise, because you feel you could have done better? Do you seem to have trouble finishing something, because you're always adding or changing one more thing? If so, it's time to *let go and let God.* Do your best at life, and trust God with the rest! Sow the best seeds you can in life, and go to bed trusting that God knows how to take it from there.

5. *Avoid the Comparison Trap.* When you attempt to be *like* somebody else or compare yourself to that person, you drag yourself down. Doing this saddens your heart and prohibits your unique talents and qualities from ever being discovered, enhanced, and appreciated. They remain hidden. And so you must embrace the individuality that God has placed in you, nurture it, and let it shine. You weren't made to be like anyone else but you. Remember: Comparing your "insides" to someone else's "outsides" is always a mistake. Yet it seems we're always comparing ourselves at our worst to other people at their best.

Isn't it funny how we always compare ourselves at our worst to other people at their best? *If I only had his job or her looks—then I'd be happy.* As I said earlier, we have to remind ourselves that we are fearfully and wonderfully made in God's image. So be the best

continued

you can be. You are not only enough—you are more than enough. Otherwise, trying to be like *them*, you'll always wind up number two, because their first slot is already taken. So stop looking sideways at others and start being "up" on yourself, not "down," and your unique gifts and qualities will show up in your life!

6. *Surround Yourself with the Right People.* As it says in 1 Corinthians 15:33, "'bad company corrupts good character.'" So who you hang around with matters, as it will directly impact on your feeling about yourself. I have seen many people held back from their potential because of the wrong associations. Ask yourself: *Where does this person place value? Do they desire popularity? Do they talk about the "in crowd" and what's "cool" in the eyes of others? Do they always talk about themselves? Do they criticize others? Do they long for compliments and despise criticism?*

We have to stop hanging around these kinds of people. Find some friends who have a happy and healthy view of themselves and others. As the Bible says, "Pursue righteousness, faith and love with those who call upon the Lord out of a pure heart" (1 Tim. 6:11). This verse not only shows us what to go after in this life, but "who" to go after it with!

Let's receive God's love and accept His grace, which allows us to love, appreciate, and accept ourselves (and others) just the way we are. Know that you are beautiful in every sense of the word, that you are a divine creation and deserve to feel proud of yourself and cherish the uniqueness of you.

Remember to knock that demon of self-hatred off your shoulder. And give up those feelings of unworthiness and low self-worth. Stop comparing yourself and seeking perfection. And, instead, find satisfaction in who God made you to be.

Secret #8

Forgive Yourself

PRONOUNCE YOURSELF: "NOT GUILTY!"

He who is devoid of the power to forgive is devoid of the power to love.
— MARTIN LUTHER KING JR.

Suzanne, the eldest of three, was a high-strung, sensitive girl. Her mom, Arlene, was a nervous woman who lost her temper easily. Sound familiar?

And the combination of their two temperaments created nothing but conflict.

As Suzanne grew into her teens, Arlene was always making "helpful" suggestions about her daughter's appearance, while laying down the law about her curfew, dating boys, and choosing friends. Her dad was mostly absent at work.

Although Arlene was, in truth, only trying to help, Suzanne felt smothered, perceiving her mother's restrictions and nagging as criticism. The two would wind up in screaming matches with Suzanne slamming the door to her bedroom, barricading herself inside. The situation became pretty intolerable.

By the time Suzanne had gone off to college, she had completely demonized her mom. At age twenty-one, her bitterness and resentment finally boiled over. She wrote her entire family a letter, telling them she never wanted contact with any of them again! She even legally changed her name and moved as far away as she could, from the East Coast to Hawaii.

Arlene was devastated and tried to communicate with her daughter, apologizing many times for the past—but Suzanne would not back down.

Why? Because she was *unforgiving*.

And Arlene, racked with guilt and grief over the loss of her daughter, was likewise unforgiving—of *herself*.

THE ABILITY TO FORGIVE AND FORGET

How many of us, like Suzanne, have ever held a grudge against a family member or a close friend? We've all been there, right?

Every one of us has been hurt by the actions or words of another. It's impossible to escape this. Your mother-in-law criticizes your parenting skills; a close friend gossips about you; your boss undermines you; your teacher criticizes you. A careless word here, a selfish action there—and we're off and running.

When any of these things happen, we often lose our cool and get incredibly upset—and wind up saying or doing something we later regret.

No matter how large or small the offense, underneath our anger is *hurt*. You may feel crushed, confused, sad, or resentful. These feelings might start out small, but if you don't deal with them quickly, they can get bigger and more powerful.

Resentments that start off as *scratches* can become *wounds* that leave you feeling bitter, cynical, and even vengeful. Why? Because we let our grievances build up in our minds until they explode. People can even become animalistic—territorial and retaliatory—without really understanding why.

Equally destructive is turning our anger *inward*, when we mercilessly blame and berate ourselves, feeling intense guilt and shame for our shortcomings, mistakes, and imperfections.

All of us have someone in our lives that we either *need* to forgive or receive forgiveness *from*. And "moving to Hawaii" doesn't solve the problem. Sure, we can run away to another place (or permanently cut off relationships), but it just never works—because that unresolved conflict is robbing us of the invincible spirit and satisfied life that God promises.

Well, *no more*!

In this chapter we're taking control of unforgiveness toward others and, most important, toward ourselves.

Isn't it true that when it comes to reflecting on our own mistakes, we condemn and punish ourselves; while the mistakes of others turn us into *blame* specialists—resulting in anger and broken relationships. Both sides of the coin require the forgiving balm that only God can give.

When it comes to forgiving others, have you ever thought, *I'll forgive them as soon as they* apologize—*or as soon as they* change!" So we hold on to our grudge *until* the other person has done something to get back into our good graces. In the meantime we remain imprisoned in the pain of *unforgiveness*. Why? It's because we mistakenly think that forgiveness must be earned, deserved, or worked for.

And when it comes to pardoning *ourselves*, we're no more forgiving. We beat ourselves up about everything we've done wrong. We tell ourselves that we don't do enough for our kids, our parents, our jobs, or our spouses. Or we feel immense guilt over something from the past that we just can't seem to shake.

No matter what the offense, we pronounce ourselves guilty—deserving of blame and punishment.

Who doesn't need forgiveness? Who hasn't fallen short, or blown it, or done something that they would give anything to *undo*? We all have!

Yet, we feel we can forgive ourselves *only* when we have beaten ourselves up enough to *deserve* it. Well, let me make this announcement, my friends: **Whether it's forgiving others or ourselves, the idea of *deserving* it is not the point.** That's why the middle syllable of the word "for-*give*-ness" is "give," not "earn."

In just a moment we'll talk about *how* to experience the power of forgiveness, but first we need to better understand the true meaning of this indispensable tool to a satisfied life.

The components of this word can give us powerful insight into its meaning and how it works in our lives. Let's take the word apart:

1. **For**
2. **Give**
3. **Ness**

For starters, the first part of the word simply means we offer forgiveness "be-**FOR**" it's even deserved. After all, it's not "*after*-giveness." By forgiving in *advance* of any apology, it *frees* us just as it frees them. This is the ultimate act of *giving* with no condition attached; i.e., forgiving be-*for* they deserve it just because we choose to, and be-*for* you necessarily "feel" it. The middle part of the word, as we said, is "give." Forgiveness is simply that — a gift.

The final part of the word, "*ness*" adds a continual action to its meaning; as with any word ending in "ness" (i.e., kindness, faithfulness, dizziness, etc.), it is a constant state of being. It tells us that the art of forgive*ness* must become a habit that we can practice throughout our lives — a *continual* action, *not* a onetime event.

So, in its essence, forgiveness means to continually give mercy and pardon to people, including ourselves, without demanding or expecting anything in return — or requiring anything in advance of our gift. This allows us to step into a totally new way of living delivering us from the bondage of guilt and regret. I call this the GUILT-FREE life!

> **WHAT IS FORGIVENESS REALLY?** It's the decision to give up and to let go of punishment toward ourselves and resentments and thoughts of retaliation toward others. It's a full pardon, absolving yourself and others from blame and restoring faith in ourselves and in life itself.

I'm sure you've heard of the "guilt-free" diet. That's the eating plan that allows you to eat from a wide variety of food groups (including desserts!)

without ever feeling guilty — *and* still lose weight at the same time. (Yeah, right!)

But when it comes to the "forgiveness" diet, we really *can* arrive at the destination of guilt-free living, the place where we're no longer imprisoned by our past or our sins.

THE GUILT-FREE LIFE

Imagine for a moment a life completely free from guilt! How would it be different?

For starters, you would be *free* of all anger, resentment, blame, and obsession on the past — all of which come from feelings of guilt. That five-hundred-pound bag of rocks would be off your back for good. You're so much lighter on your feet.

You would be able to quickly recover from your mistakes, **separating a mistaken action from *being* a mistake yourself!** You would be able to accept your shortcomings and weaknesses without crumbling and feeling bad about yourself.

You would also give up those defense mechanisms — making excuses and blaming *others* for things you feel guilty about. Instead, you would take responsibility for what you do and how you do it. "Innocence" actions will be a by-product of "innocence" thinking.

You would avoid saying and doing things that are *guilt builders* — things you're later going to regret. No longer is that guilty shadow trailing you! Satan is no longer the accuser on your tail, and you're no longer living by his verdict.

Armed with this freedom from guilt, you would no longer succumb to the manipulation of others. No longer would they have the power to cast a GUILT TRIP on you. When people say: "If you really loved me, you'd do this," you'd answer: "I really *do* love you — and I'm so sorry, but I can't do that." Why? It's because guilt is no longer your master.

Living the guilt-free life, *you're* in charge of what you say and do. This means you set *practical limits* on your time and energy, without expecting more of yourself than you can reasonably handle. When you do this, your feelings and mood will improve making it easier to treat those around you with more respect, love, and patience.

At last, we're liberated from the *blame game*. We're free. We can reclaim our innocence and purity of heart.

That, folks, is what life is like when you are totally free from guilt!

This is true freedom. No longer will you need other people's *approval* when you have God's. He swallows up all the accusations and says: "You are forgiven." And when you live like this, your life becomes like a peaceful river. It flows naturally. You're not fighting the current. You're flowing *with* it. You have a clear, peaceful conscience.

THE BLESSING OF A CLEAR CONSCIENCE

So think about it. How come we're *not* experiencing this dreamy existence? What's keeping us from the guilt-free life?

Maybe you're still bothered by the time when you cheated on a test at school, or stole something from a store, or exaggerated or lied to someone you loved, betrayed a confidence, or made a cruel remark. Maybe you've gone so far as committing adultery or something even worse.

I'm sure you felt terrible about what you did because you realized you'd fallen short of God's standard. But the fact that your *conscience* was bothering you also was a *good* thing. It shows you have a moral compass—a clear understanding that there *is* a right and a wrong way to live.

> "While conscience is our friend, all is at peace; however once it is offended, farewell to a tranquil mind."
> —LADY MARY WORTLEY MONTAGU

Our conscience is that inner voice that, when respected and honored, will tell us the right thing to do.

The problem begins when the conscience becomes a nagging, punishing voice inside our heads, making us (or others) *pay* for the mistake. It's like the guy who wrote the IRS the following letter:

> *Dear Gentlemen:*
>
> *Enclosed you will find a money order for $250. I cheated on my income tax return last year and have not been able to sleep ever since. If I still have trouble sleeping, I will send you the rest.*
>
> *Sincerely,*
> *A Taxpayer*

Friends, that voice of conscience must be answered—if not like the taxpayer above, then how?

We can do it—first and foremost—by being open to receiving *God's* forgiveness. That's why it's called "grace." It's a free gift—undeserved and unearned. God gives it freely because He loves you and doesn't want you to live a life of guilt.

Children often understand this better than adults. There was a poll taken among kids, ages five through nine, on the meaning of *conscience*, and here's what a few of them said:

- "A conscience is the spot inside that burns if you're not good."
- "Something to do with feeling bad when you kick girls or little dogs."
- "It's a voice that says 'No' when you do something like beating up your little brother. My conscience has saved me lots of times!"

I've found that most children have the innate capacity to make a mistake, wipe the slate clean, and move on free of nagging guilt and remorse. But as adults, as I noted a moment ago, our conscience often becomes *punishing*.

I can tell you that **nothing robs us of the satisfied life more than feeling guilty.** We know, too well, the gnawing agony of it, right?! We feel we don't measure up. We're not skinny enough, smart enough, kind enough, or patient enough. In fact, that guilt is always hitting us over the head, talking right to us: "You don't pray enough, give enough, or earn enough. If you really cared about your children, you'd buy them the latest and greatest games they want and prepare them better for Ivy League colleges. You'd take them to piano and dance classes, gymnastics, spelling bees, talent contests," on and on.

And when we succumb to temptation, we later try to wash away our guilt, or attempt to bury it, hoping it will just go away, when, of course, it never does. Or we end up hardening our hearts, searing our conscience with all sorts of rationalizations, reasons, and excuses. We blame *others* for whatever's wrong in our lives, never accepting responsibility for it, because it would be too crushing for us to admit our own fault. Or, of course, we beat ourselves up, realizing less than our full potentials in life, feeling unworthy of all that God and life offer us.

Once we're snared in this guilt trap, we then plot ways to escape it, right? We may try to pray enough to get rid of it, exercise enough, diet enough, work enough, or compensate to the people we failed — or *supposedly* failed.

How often has a critical relative manipulated us into feeling guilty? (They're really good at it, too, aren't they?)

And sometimes, to relieve our guilt, we'll do the right thing for the wrong reason. We may give to a charity to cover up the guilt of our sin or mistake, believing that God will forgive us if *only* we show ourselves to be generous-hearted.

It reminds me of the time a thirteen-year-old Girl Scout was asked how she was able to sell 11,200 boxes of cookies. She explained, "Well, it's simple. You have to look them in the eye and make them feel guilty!"

Now, there's a young lady who has tapped into the motivating power of guilt!

And while it may seem harmless in the Girl Scouts, it's anything but harmless in real life. **Guilt is an evil taskmaster, relentlessly trying to manipulate and control our lives.**

As we've seen, we're continuously filled with remorse about what we've done, or failed to do right. It's almost like we use guilt as a weapon against ourselves — a form of penance, allowing it to punch away at us until we feel finally *worthy* of receiving forgiveness. We're weighed down and broken down as we convict, punish, and berate ourselves, replaying the memory of what we've done over and over again.

Folks, in the words of a brilliant, old McDonald's ad, *YOU DESERVE A BREAK TODAY!* Why? It's because all this self-condemnation is exhausting. It's not only painful and useless, but also very bad for your health.

HEALTHY HEART, HEALTHY START

Remember: our choices should protect our health, not our hurts, for the Scripture shows us that a guilty heart does much to harm us.

In the Bible, before David admitted his adultery and murder, he experienced the physical, emotional, and spiritual anguish of searing guilt. In Psalm 32:3–4, describing how his guilt affected him, he wrote, "When I kept silent, my bones grew old through my groaning all the day long [emotional]. For day and night Your hand was heavy upon me [spiritual]; my vitality was turned into the drought of summer [physical]."

Consider this: guilt and unforgiveness usually turns into anger, which when directed inward can lead to depression and numerous stress-related illnesses, including headaches, stomach problems, body pain, exhaustion, and, most notably, heart disease. Yes, your heart is designed to weather problems, but not to endure stress continually, the stress of which can lead to premature death.

In fact, a recent CNN report stated that heart disease is the number one cause of death among both men and women in the United States today. One out of every three women in the United States dies of heart disease! And while proper diet and exercise are vital in preventing this, the emotional stresses of hurt and unforgiveness are often the triggers for this staggering statistic.

The Benefits of Forgiveness

- Lower blood pressure,
- Stress reduction,
- Less hostility,
- Better anger management skills,
- Lower heart rate,
- Lower risk of alcohol or substance abuse,
- Fewer depression symptoms,
- Fewer anxiety symptoms,
- Reduction in chronic pain,
- More friendships,
- Healthier relationships,
- Greater, spiritual, emotional, and psychological well-being.

Not surprisingly, forgiving ourselves and others can save our lives.

Indeed, forgiveness offers numerous benefits. A 2001 study revealed the correlation between *replaying hurtful memories* and the human stress response. When those tested were encouraged to think *forgiving* thoughts, their heart rates and blood pressure were significantly decreased. Forgiveness fostered better anger management skills, lower risk of alcohol or substance abuse, fewer depression and anxiety symptoms, reduction of chronic physical pain, healthier friendships, and, of course, greater spiritual well-being.

Wow! Is all *that* worth the simple act of forgiveness? You be the judge and jury and decide.

HOW TO FORGIVE YOURSELF

As we learned in the previous chapter, in order to love our neighbor, we have to first love *ourselves* (in a wholesome, godly way).

Likewise, using that same simple truth, we must learn to *forgive* ourselves first, so that we will have something to give to others when we need to extend forgiveness to them.

I can tell you that the most *unforgiving* people in the world, more often than not, hate *themselves* for the mistakes they've made. They're the ultimate perfectionists, who punish and deride themselves, never giving themselves a break. And they end up extending that same attitude toward others. THERE IS A BETTER WAY!

One of the most famous, riveting trials of all time was, of course, the O. J. Simpson murder case, which had an amazing impact on our culture. No matter what evidence was presented, or what most people concluded, and no matter whether he did it or not—O. J. was found: "not guilty."

I like to sometimes tease my very multiethnic church members by joking that both black and white cultures have a little idiosyncrasy. Black folks think O. J. didn't do it, and white folks think Elvis is still alive!

Notice, though, that although O. J. was found "not guilty," he wasn't found "innocent." There's a big difference, right? It's the same in our lives.

We are clearly *not innocent*. Why? It's because we're human. We have all failed, sinned, and fallen short. We've all lost our temper, hurt others, committed sins, and thought unspeakable evils. So we're *not* "innocent."

However, in God's great love, even after looking at all the obvious evidence, and hearing all the accusing testimony against us, and even after having caught us red-handed in our wrong ways, He cleanses and declares us NOT guilty.

His grace gives us the secret to releasing our guilt:

1. *Accept God's Merciful Verdict over Us.* Most of us have heard the Bible story about the woman caught in adultery. Several "religious" leaders brought her to Jesus and told Him that she should be stoned for her sin. She remained silent while they went on and on about her guilt. In the midst of this, Jesus stooped down to the ground and began writing in the dirt, though no one knows what was written. Perhaps it was a list of the accusers' sins!

But the beauty of this imagery is that *Jesus would not listen to their accusations and judgments* against this woman. As He proclaimed: "Let the one who is without sin among you cast the first stone at her." Then He told her: "I don't condemn you. Go and sin no more."

This teaches us that when we judge and criticize others, God has no part in it. He doesn't accuse or condemn. This realization alone is liberating. It tells us that **if we stop trying to defend ourselves, God will defend us**. This leads us to our next step in forgiving ourselves.

2. *Honestly Admit the Wrong We Have Done.* Notice that the adulterous woman in question above did not fight back, argue, or pretend she was innocent. She knew she had sinned and that she was wrong. She was willing to accept whatever God said about her, but refused to defend herself against her accusers. We need to stop pretending that we didn't do anything wrong. Too often, our pride gets in the way, and we don't want to recognize our sins, shortcomings, and failures. God already knows what we've done. But he's waiting for us to come clean. We need to get a clue and give up our denials. This becomes much easier to fully embrace after step one—accepting God's merciful verdict of us: NOT GUILTY!

3. *Give Up the Self-Punishment.* Without much conscious effort, we often say to ourselves, *I'll punish myself to pay for what I've done.* As a result, our self-recrimination and blame can turn into depression, which becomes the "self-inflicted" penalty for doing wrong. But since nothing can pay for our sins except God's mercy, we find ourselves remaining stuck in depression. Why? It's because we feel our debt is never fully paid. We learn all this, of course, as kids. How often do parents tell their child, "Go into your room and don't come out until you feel bad enough for what you've done!" Like this works, right? Do we actually think that our kids feeling bad will prevent them from misbehaving again? A lot of good that did me growing up! I kept doing wrong, but I was much more careful about being caught. Friends, punishing ourselves may be how we *grew* up, but we'll never "grow up"—out of guilt and shame—until we stop doing this to ourselves. Remember: God is in the business of forgiving sin. But His forgiveness does us no good, until we stop punishing ourselves and receive His mercy deep into our hearts. When this happens, guilt disappears. Depression flees. And the vitality and joy of life is restored.

4. *Put First Things First.* What do I mean? *First* God forgives us; then we are released from the power of the guilt that keeps us enslaved to doing it again and again.

Most people have it backward. They think that if they stop sinning, *then* God will forgive them. But it's the exact opposite. When we realize and accept His forgiveness FIRST, the by-product of that mercy is that we will desire to stop living that way. When we receive mercy, it changes us, because in our utter honesty, we realize that we really don't deserve it.

The mother of a young man accused of treason came before Napoleon, just before her son was to be hanged for his crimes. "I implore you, Great Emperor," she said, "that you would have mercy on my son."

"Mercy?" Napoleon responded in disbelief. "Do you have any idea how great these crimes are that your son has committed against our country? He doesn't deserve mercy!"

With innocent hope, she responded, "Sir, you are right. If he deserved it, it wouldn't be mercy." At that, the emperor freed the man.

So it is in our lives. It's when we realize we don't deserve it, that we become candidates for mercy and guilt-free living.

As we've seen, all our lives, we fight against guilt, or yield to it, by justifying our wrongs and defending ourselves. But when we make ourselves vulnerable by letting down our guards and standing naked before Heaven, God clothes us with mercy and righteousness. That's when His forgiveness becomes real in our lives.

And, folks, if GOD can forgive us—then we must certainly forgive ourselves.

HOW TO NEVER BE HURT AGAIN

The final process for attaining freedom from guilt and resentment is the art of forgiving *others*. Let me give you some motivation for mastering this key to the satisfied life. For starters, remember that unforgiving people are no fun to be around. They're typically overcritical, negative, judgmental, and mistrustful. Yikes! Moreover, they often make bad decisions—tainted by resentment and blame. In this way, by refusing to forgive others, our hearts are poisoned from *within*. It's like a snakebite. It isn't the bite that kills you—it's the venom. Likewise, when we hold a grudge, we allow the poison of bitterness, blame, hatred, or revenge to destroy us.

What are some signs that it's time to forgive? Here are just a few:

- Obsessing on the wrong done to you,
- Hearing from others that you're wallowing in self-pity,
- Being avoided by family and friends because you're a drag,
- Erupting in angry outbursts at the smallest perceived slights,
- Feeling misunderstood,
- Drinking excessively, smoking, or using drugs to try to cope with your pain,
- Having symptoms of depression or anxiety,
- Feeling consumed by a desire for revenge or punishment,
- Automatically thinking the worst about people or situations,
- Regretting the loss of a valued relationship,
- Feeling like your life lacks meaning or purpose,
- Feeling distant from God.

That's why I believe God has put a longing into every human heart to forgive and be forgiven. As we saw in the story at the start of this chapter, the mother desperately wanted her daughter to forgive her and be restored to her family. And in so many of our lives, all we want is the forgiveness from our family or our friend. Here's how to do it:

1. *Believe that God Can Turn Any Situation Around.* After being sold into slavery by his brothers, Joseph ascended politically in Egypt. He saved the world from starvation, and rescued his brothers when they came begging for food. While they thought he would avenge their sins against him, he took the high road and responded by saying: "You meant evil against me; but God meant it for good."

Joseph's example is the epitome of forgiveness, proof that even if someone tries to harm us, nothing can ultimately prevail against what God has destined. And therefore, there's no need to hold a grudge against those who are bitter and hurtful. They don't have the power to stop you from living the life God intended. Why? Because God is powerful enough to convert even the most sinister plots of those who hurt us for the good of those who forgive.

2. *Let Go.* Who are we to hold something against someone when God Himself doesn't hold it against them? We must see that withholding forgiveness only hurts us. Turn it over to God. Then, trust that He will get involved to work it out.

Sometimes we mistake "holding a grudge" for "sticking to principle." But let's not be deceived. Principles are, of course, good rules to live by. But "holding a grudge" is not one of them! One of the things that has helped me "let go" of some of the "wrongs" that I've experienced is realizing that unforgiveness is spiritual POISON. If we don't get rid of it, it will eventually kill us (as in the heart disease statistics we saw earlier). It's like the game Hot Potato. The object is to get rid of the hot veggie before you get stuck with it and it burns you!

To put this idea another way, we need to live by the Golden Rule—doing unto others as we would want them to do unto us. But so many times, we do the opposite—doing unto others what they have *done* unto us. Or we do unto them even WORSE than they've done unto us. Perhaps you've heard of the unforgiving servant in Scripture, who owed millions of dollars to his master. When he could not pay, he begged for forgiveness and received it. When he found one of his lesser servants who owed him merely hundreds of dollars, he refused to forgive the lesser debt. Had he forgotten so quickly the grace that was extended to him?

We must never forget the enormous debt that we have been forgiven by God. This will keep our heart soft and able to forgive others—not because they deserve it, but because it is the overflow of what we ourselves have freely received.

But remember that **genuine forgiveness does not depend on the *other* person apologizing or changing.** Don't expect anything in return from them. Love them and release them.

3. *Declare Your Forgiveness Out Loud (to God and Yourself)!* Remember the hurt as a whisper, but declare forgiveness with a shout! We need to verbalize forgiveness for our own sake. Say something like this, out loud, to yourself: *"I choose this day to forgive "_____" for what he did to me. I release him from the judgment of it. And I let it go. My decision today is greater than my hurt feelings and I deliberately close the chapter on that offense. As an act of my will, I release him and bless him. I refuse to hold on to the bitterness or resentment that has been in my life from this person's failure or abuse of me. I am free!"*

This doesn't have to be a deeply emotional experience. It might be, but don't be guided by the presence or absence of feelings. Forgiveness is a quality *decision*. The trauma and deep emotions have already been experienced...the hurt has already taken place. Now you FORGIVE BY FAITH. So whether you feel anything or not, you declare aloud before God, *"I forgive that person for hurting me, neglecting me, abusing me,"* etc.

Also, when you forgive someone, declare out loud to *yourself*: *"They owe me nothing—not an apology, not even an explanation."* This kind of affirmation frees you from the inaccurate expectation that your freedom depends on something that the other person must do.

4. *Stop Talking About It.* A little boy was so proud of the scab underneath his bandage, that whenever he saw one of his friends or

continued

relatives, he would rip off the bandage to retell his exploit and reveal his badge of manhood! There was just one problem: the wound wasn't able to heal because every time the boy pulled off the bandage, it reopened the wound. It's the same thing in our lives: when we *rehearse* our hurt, we inevitably wind up reopening the wound, hurting ourselves and others. Sure, we want to talk about how much we were hurt, so we continually reopen up the wound. But this only delays the process of healing. Some people *never* recover from hurt and unforgiveness because they refuse to stop talking about it. They wear their wound as a badge of honor, when, in fact, it brings them nothing but *dishonor*. So stop discussing the wound and give it a chance to heal completely.

5. *Stop Making Excuses for How Sensitive You Are.* We must give up justifying why we are so prone to being hurt. Having thicker skin is going to be an asset in shaking off resentments. Don't take things so personally! What people say and do is more a reflection of themselves than a judgment on you. Also, sometimes we're overly sensitive, using our race, gender, background, or limitations as justification for being so sensitive. In fact, it's funny how most people are sensitive and *insensitive* all at the same time. They are sensitive to how they are treated, but insensitive to how they treat others. We are all sensitive by nature. But allow your sensitivity to be directed *toward others with understanding and compassion* rather than being so caught up in what's been done to you.

6. *Believe That It Is Done and Don't Look Back.* Move forward *through* thankfulness. Thank God for your freedom from unforgiveness. Surely, this is cause for celebration! Sing, dance, and rejoice. At last you've been liberated from a damaged past *and* an imprisoned, limited future. Remember, forgiveness is a quality decision, regardless of second thoughts or lingering feelings. You may be tempted to

think, *I'm still angry—so maybe I didn't really forgive!* WRONG. You made the decision. Mark the date, and don't turn back. Sure, feelings of bitterness or resentment may return. But you need to just resist them by thanking God that you are free and healed. As you continue to practice forgiveness, you will feel less and less of the pain until it vanishes forever, freeing your heart to experience the satisfied life you deserve!

A NEW FUTURE

Forgiveness may not change the past, but it opens up an incredible future, one that is unhindered by your past hurt and pain, grudges, or regrets.

No longer will you bring residual anger from the past into new relationships. No longer will you *act out* your hurt—by being withdrawn, moody, or even nasty.

Even better, when you forgive, you automatically cut off one of the main inroads to addiction. You no longer need to numb the pain with smoking, drinking, drugs, prescription medicines, food, gambling—you name it. You're free of all that—and can now tap into the energy and optimism that surface when you're willing to GIVE UP the right to strike back and punish yourself or others.

This kind of all-encompassing forgiveness is life-changing. It's much more than just letting *go* of the past. It's moving *beyond* it—to the future life we truly want, the one we thought was impossible—free of guilt and pain.

As we said at the start, people will inevitably hurt you—but they don't hold the power *over* you unless you allow it. So go ahead and make a quality decision. **Give that pardon. Let it go. Move on. Believe in God's forgiveness.** I promise you that when you forgive, you're well on your way to the satisfied, guilt-free life, the one of your dreams, the one that God intends for you.

In closing, let me tell you about a father and son in Spain who had a falling-out, and had not been on speaking terms for years. The son ran away, and the father set off to find him. He searched for months, to no avail. Finally, in a last, desperate effort to find him, the father placed an ad in a Madrid newspaper. It read: "Dear Paco, meet me in front of this newspaper office at noon on Saturday. All is forgiven. I love you. Your father."

On Saturday, eight hundred Pacos showed up, looking for forgiveness and love from their fathers.

Are there any Pacos listening here? Get to that newspaper office today!

Secret #9

Fall Out of Love with Your Feelings

MASTERING YOUR EMOTIONS

Let us not forget that the little emotions are the great captains of our lives and we obey them without realizing it.

—Vincent Van Gogh

A young boy once asked his father, "Dad, how do wars begin?"

"Well," said his father, "take the First World War. One of the ways that it got started was when Germany invaded Belgium."

Immediately his wife interrupted him: "Tell the boy the truth. It began because Belgium provoked Germany."

The husband drew himself up with an air of superiority and snapped back, "Are you answering the question, or am I?"

Turning her back upon him in a huff, the wife walked out of the room and slammed the door as hard as she could.

When the dishes stopped rattling in the cupboard, an uneasy silence followed, broken only by the son when he said, "Never mind, Dad, you don't have to tell me any more; *now* I know!"

Any of this sound familiar? I'm sure we've all experienced family arguments and times of tension when we blow up and lose our tempers, allowing our feelings to skid out of control.

What if I told you that this husband and wife were actually very much in love? Would you believe it? Well, it's true!

The problem, though, is that they weren't in love with each *other*.

Instead, they were, like so many of us, in love with their ... *feelings*.

It's so easy to become addicted to, or fall "in love" with emotions like anger, fear, anxiety, depression, frustration, and impatience—all roadblocks to living the satisfied life. It's these feelings that so often run our lives.

Negative emotions do nothing to bring us closer to God—or to the people we really care about.

Yet these emotions often seem to go everywhere we go, and do what we do. They want to be with us *all the time*! They are, in fact, the prime culprits of our distress.

According to recent statistics, one out of every four Americans is "crazy," suffering from some form of mental illness. Think of your three best friends. If they're okay, then it's gotta be *you*!

Seriously, though, these negative emotions, as we've seen, have us by the throats. They're very, very possessive. They influence our decisions. They tell us what to do and when to do it. They become routine *habits*— addictive, predictable patterns. Not only have we *fallen in love* with these negative feelings—we've married them, too!

Why would we do this? Well, believe it or not, we actually get a "high" from it. You know what it's like to vent anger—when we explode and blow off steam, right? We know it's wrong, but it sometimes feels *so* good! It's the same thing when we wallow in self-pity, feeling sorry for ourselves. That pity-party hurts *so* good! And then there's the high we get from feeling superior or dominant, prompting us to belittle someone else.

You may be thinking, *Everyone has emotional outbursts at times; that doesn't mean that people are* in love *with their feelings.*

But consider one of the definitions of love. As we saw in the "Be Loved" chapter, the Hebrew word for "love" is *"ahav."* It means "to be attached to" or "cling to." And that's just what happens. How often do we stay more attached to our negative feelings than to God or to the people in our lives? We cling to our anger and depression, not letting go no matter how much we may want to get rid of them.

So we get intolerant and lose our temper. We say and do things we regret. We're sarcastic or spiteful, unforgiving or retaliatory. We punish ourselves and others — and ultimately wind up feeling guilt and regret.

Why? It's in that moment we've lost control of ourselves. We act impulsively. We're literally driven by emotion and can't seem to put on the brakes.

The end result is that we hurt the people we love most and destroy the peace of mind that God wants for us.

Having emotions, of course, is only human; but, unfortunately, as we can see, they often have *us*. These powerful feelings are like tidal waves, sweeping over everything in their path, wreaking chaos and destruction, including damage to our physical health.

In a Johns Hopkins study, medical students were classified into three personality groups: Alphas were cautious, reserved, quiet, and undemanding; Betas were spontaneous, active, and outgoing; Gammas were moody, emotional, and demanding.

Thirty years later, scientists looked at the health records of these former students and they found that 77 percent of the Gamma group, which were the moody, emotional folks, suffered from major disorders, including cancer, high blood pressure, heart disease, and emotional disturbances. These problems were seen in only 25 percent of the other groups.

The lesson? **Falling out of love with your feelings will not only change your life — it can *save* your life!**

So make no mistake about it. Emotions are mighty things. In fact, they are the source of just about all the problems you'll ever deal with in your life.

Overeating, for example, is not merely a *physical* problem — it's an *emotional* one. Many people tend to eat when they're lonely, tense, bored, worried, or angry. And it's the same thing with many addictions and habits. In this way, for better or worse, emotions *move* us to action.

In fact, the root definition of emotion is *internal motion*. **Inside each of us, there are a great number of feelings "moving" us in certain directions, and leading us to make the decisions that shape our lives.**

Sometimes it almost seems as if we're puppets on a string, our emotions pulling us haphazardly up in one direction and down in another. We become *reactive* to whatever it is we're feeling.

Folks, we need to harness our emotions, get control of them, so that they move us in the direction that *we* want to go — not in the direction that *they* want to go.

I can tell you that if we don't control what is "in us," we end up trying to control those "around us." This leads to anger, manipulation, domineering attitudes, as well as depression, anxiety, and a host of other negative emotions, all arising from our sense of powerlessness.

When we feel we *have* no control — we *lose* control. The result is chaos — with people sabotaging their careers, ruining relationships, and splitting their families apart.

That's why I believe that the outcome of our lives **is not determined by the *chances* we get, but by the *choices*** we make. And we can't make them impulsively based only on what we're feeling at the time. As I always say, "Don't do what feels good; do what produces good."

THE MOMENTUM OF EMOTION

January comes along and we're feeling guilty about all those desserts we ate during the holiday. So what do we do? We order the "Hip & Thigh Sculptor" from TV. But when it's delivered four weeks later, we stick it in the garage. Why? Because by the time it arrives, the emotion that drove us to order it has subsided.

Next we *feel* inspired to eat better, so we buy a juicer from the Juice Man. We use it once, and put it away in the pantry. Why? Because it takes too long to prepare the recipes and it's too much work to clean the contraption!

Later on, we're watching TV again and *feeling* a little down or depressed; so *feeling* nostalgic, we order the oldies collection. It seems like a great escape from our current woe. But when it arrives, we're no longer in the same *mood* as when we ordered it, so we don't even listen to it!

These are just a few of the countless ways that emotions drive our decisions to spend money better used in other ways. It may all seem somewhat harmless, but let's continue.

You might be feeling lonely and try to escape that uncomfortable emotion by visiting Internet chat sites—so you end up with a bad habit.

Or feeling desperate, you might latch onto someone who is unhealthy for you, but who, at the time, fulfills an emotional need—so you wind up in a bad marriage or with a broken heart.

Or you might lust toward a coworker and start flirting with them, only to find yourself accused of sexual harassment and losing your job.

And let's not forget this one: You feel frustrated with your toddler. You've repeated yourself five times, counted to ten, and instead of calming down, you're like a missile. You LIFT OFF and explode, doing untold damage to your child's little soul, not to mention the potential abuse that can follow.

Friends, no matter what the situation, *the damage is done*. **Your emotions have gotten the best of you—and brought out the worst in you**.

They have controlled your life, by controlling your thoughts, and your decisions. They've hurt you, and what's worse, they've hurt the people you care most about. We've all been there.

Life is made up of a series of choices. And no matter how smart or strong we are, our choices, so often, are based upon how we *feel*. Why? Again, it's because emotions run our lives—and too often, run them into the ground.

But all that is going to change beginning today. That's why I've coined a phrase that I believe will change your life forever: "Falling Out of Love with Your Feelings."

THE SECRET TO EFFECTIVE LIVING

Everyone knows what it's like to "fall *in* love," right? You feel the *euphoria* of infatuation and intense passion. You're on a high. You think about that person all the time. You want to go where *they* go, and do what *they* do. You might even become possessive or, unfortunately, obsessive. Remember *Fatal Attraction*? (Yikes, let's keep away from that bunny in a boiling pot!)

And when we're in love with someone, we'll do *anything* to avoid being separated from that person. While there is much more to be said about the subject of love, I only use this analogy to draw a picture of our relationship to our *emotions*.

As we've seen, too many people are not only overly "attached" to negative feelings, but they're stuck to them like glue. We can't be split apart from them. Although people sometimes convince themselves that *others* are to blame for their own behavior, we know it's never true. I can tell you that making other people responsible for what *we* choose to do puts *the power to change today* in somebody *else's* hands. And throughout this book we've seen that the revolution of change is in our own hands—not in somebody else's.

Yet, so often, as I said, people are impulsive in the way they behave. Why? It's because we've fallen in love with the wrong thing: our feelings.

How did we get like this? It all started in the Garden of Eden. Didn't everything? In Genesis 3, when God created Adam and Eve, He created them to be *in love* with one another. But after their historic and tragic choice to disobey God, they fell *out of love* with each other; and they each began a new love affair.

They fell in love with their feelings—becoming attached to their own desires, their fears, their worries, their shame, and their need to control one another. And so began the downward spiral of mankind.

Now, please don't misunderstand. I'm not saying we should ignore our true feelings or not take them seriously. I'm saying we must not allow our decisions to be *determined* by them.

In Genesis 4:7, when Cain was on the verge of falling in love with his feelings of jealousy and rage toward his brother, God told him: "Sin is crouching at the door, but you must master it." Cain obviously did not master his emotions and wound up murdering his brother.

In our lives, though not as extreme, sin is often crouching at our door, lurking and waiting for us to give in to our emotions. These feelings don't heal us, bless us, or make us prosper—though we still bow our knee to them so often. In this way **your negative feelings want to master you, but God is saying, "You must master *them*."**

We've been attached to our feelings for way too long! We've fallen head over heels in love with the wrong thing—indulging those negative feelings and expressing them for quick relief of our moods. We're been too *attached* to the *wrong* thing to do the *right* thing. We don't just need a *separation* from our negative feelings; we need a *divorce*.

We need to *detach* from the negative and *attach* to the positive— mentalities of *success* that can lead us to falling back IN love with the things we were created to love: our God, our family, and ourselves.

THE ANATOMY OF NEGATIVE FEELINGS

Changing the old way of expressing out-of-control emotions isn't as hard as you may think. **But we're going to need some good reasons to do it.** Since we so often justify a pity party or an angry rant, and believe it's normal or even therapeutic, why *should* we make the conscious decision to *fall out of love with our feelings*?

First, realize that our feelings are *schizophrenic*, a word taken from the Greek root meaning "to split." Our emotions are not only unpredictable, but often contradictory. It's almost like we have *multiple* personalities. Remember the movie *Sybil*? She had at least sixteen personalities and would constantly shift from one to the next.

No, I'm not comparing you to Sybil, but our feelings are equally volatile at times. One moment we're happy; the next we're sad. Tuesday, we're kind; Wednesday, we're mean as a hornet's nest. Today you forgive your husband; tomorrow you're plotting his demise. It seems our feelings can't make up their minds!

But when you can recognize that your feelings are always fluctuating, you learn not to take them so seriously, and not to act on the ones that don't serve you.

The **second** reason we need to fall out of love with our feelings is because they're *unfaithful* to us. They're oh-so seductive, luring us in, enticing us with their promise. But as soon as you commit to them, they cheat on you. They don't ever stay true and so often tempt you into taking actions you later regret.

The **third** reason we need to fall out of love with our feelings is because they never consider the *consequences* of their behavior. They're like undisciplined little kids — OUT OF CONTROL. They *will* express themselves, and don't care whom they hurt in the process. To them, there are no consequences.

But in our adult lives, there *always* are. Maybe one night you're feeling lonely, really desperate for a connection, so you wind up with someone who's no good for you. What really happened? Your feelings *deceived* you into taking actions that hurt you because they didn't care about the consequences.

Let me give you an example that we've all experienced at one time or another. You become angry at a friend or relative and immediately pick up the phone to "tell them off." You've said things that were cruel and hurtful. The next day you come to find out that the person you told off wasn't even the one who did it — or worse, they had just received news of a loved one's death or a terrible doctor's report. Now filled with regret, you despise what you just did. You feel like an idiot, because you listened to your impulsive feelings. The problem was: your feelings didn't listen to *you*, and they didn't consider the consequences of their behavior.

> Remember, emotions are internal motions trying to move you in whatever direction they feel. They don't care about the consequences of their behavior. Whatever you do don't let them control you.

The **fourth** reason we need to fall out of love with our feelings (as we saw earlier in the chapter) is because they can cause you to make *bad decisions*. And it's our decisions that produce the quality of our life. A bad life is the result of bad decisions — nothing less, nothing more. **Life is a series of choices, not a series of chances.**

So *how* long would you stay married to somebody who was schizophrenic, unfaithful, inconsiderate of the consequences of their behaviors, and always leading you to bad decisions?

Not very long. Out they go. Call your lawyer.

That being the case, how do you fall *out* of love with someone like that?

You would stop paying attention to them. You would stop taking their calls. You would stop letting them influence your decisions. You would stop spending time with them. And most important, you would stop respecting what they had to say.

Experts have gone so far as to say, if you are in love with someone you shouldn't be — like someone else's wife — start focusing on the flaws and shortcomings of that person. Start criticizing and second-guessing them. Question all their motives. Notice every wrong thing that they do. It won't be long before you fall out of love with that person.

Isn't that how so many marriages turn sour anyway? So treat your emotions that same way, and you'll find the surest recipe to "falling out of love with your feelings."

And even on days when those negative feelings are incredibly strong and you're tempted to give in to them, you *won't*.

To summarize, let me walk you through some simple steps to disarming the bomb of negative emotions.

1. *Realize That All Emotion Begins with a Thought.* If you're depressed, the thought goes something like this: *I'm never going to make it. Life isn't worth living.* And as you keep mulling this thought over, it becomes an emotion, which rises up in you until you make a bad decision based on that emotion.

continued

Folks, as we've seen, you change your life by changing your thinking. This means that as you fill your mind up with "right thoughts," they will produce right emotions, which will, in turn, lead to right decisions.

The Bible says in Philippians 4:8, "Whatever is pure, whatever is lovely, whatever is honorable, whatever is of good report, whatever is excellent, whatever is worthy of praise, *think on these things*." Instead of harping on the negative, which makes our emotions unstable, **we have to permit God's thoughts to be our thoughts**—which will bring our emotions under control.

Remember: **Emotions don't know reality; they only react to what we think**. A few years ago, my wife and I were in a restaurant, and after I'd paid the bill, my wallet disappeared. After looking everywhere for it, I was convinced that someone at the restaurant had stolen it. I was so angry—until an hour later when I took my coat off and realized my wallet was in a pocket I didn't ordinarily use. The reality was that the wallet was never lost, but I had all the *emotions* that accompanied thinking that it had been stolen. You see, my emotions were blind to reality. So what we have to do is fill our mind with the Word of God and our emotions will react to those new thoughts.

2. *Talk to Your Emotions Rather Than Letting Them Talk to You.*
Whether it's facing down anger, fear, revenge, or depression, you need to fight back.

For example, tell your anger: You ruin my day, you give me an ulcer, you raise my blood pressure, and you make my face contort! You're inconsiderate, rude, and selfish. You only think of yourself and never about what's best for me. And worst of all, you hurt people all the time. I'm better off without you!

Then finish that thought with: I can control my emotions. I react with kindness and love—not anger. I have patience, understanding—and a cool spirit.

You see, as simple as it sounds, you can overcome the habit of falling *into* these negative emotions by a deliberate choice to speak to them in a manner that will defuse them.

3. *Pray.* I'm reminded of Mark 14:32–33, where Jesus went with His disciples to a place called Gethsemane. As He prayerfully considered the sacrifice He would soon be making, He said to His disciples, "Sit down here while I pray." He took Peter, James, and John with Him, and though He was struck with sadness, terror, and fearful emotions—He never sinned.

Maybe, like Jesus was, you're in your own Gethsemane right now. What do you do about it? Let's look at what He did to resist the temptation of His feelings.

It says in Verse 35, *"And he went forward...a little."* When you're struck with frustration and sadness, those emotions are trying to move you *backward,* maybe into depression, maybe into making a bad decision. But perhaps you can move forward *just a little bit.* Even though you might feel that you can barely move, maybe you could make that phone call, or offer that apology, or turn that frown into a smile, a bad moment into a joke, and see the good in things rather than the bad.

The Bible says that Jesus then fell to the ground and *prayed.* So can you! As we learned in the "Be Healed" chapter, prayer changes things, which is why Jesus said: "Pray that you may not enter into temptation." By doing so He went forward into God's purpose for His life.

4. *Have Faith.* Believing, as we discovered in the second chapter, gives us the power to see the impossible become possible. When you have **CONFIDENCE** in God's promises, negative emotions are greatly lessened. You feel bold and brave. Nothing is going to defeat

continued

you. As Jesus says in John 14:1, *"**Let** not your heart be troubled; you believe in God, believe also in Me."* Yes, we do have control over whether we allow our heart to be troubled. And it comes from what we believe. Believing in God and His promises calms our emotions, our fears, our uncertainty. This power of faith is what brings rest to the troubled heart.

And so it is that not allowing our hearts to be troubled, and not allowing our emotions to control our lives, are the twin secrets to turning emotional bondage into emotional freedom.

5. *Walk in Love.* Remember that **the most formidable opponent to any negative emotion is love.** It is the most powerful force in the universe. 1 John 4:18 says, "Perfect love casts out fear." Since fear is the root of all negative emotion, then love is the answer. When we know we are loved by God, and express His love toward others, our fears, our anxieties, and the forces of negativity melt away. Resentments turn into forgiveness; jealousy melts into admiration; competition changes into respect. We are not threatened. We are touched by God's love and express this in our relationships.

Using the tools we've talked about, you're no longer going to be susceptible to the dark emotions that emerge when a sense of powerlessness takes over your heart and mind. In fact, you'll be amazed at what you can accomplish *when you fall out of love with your feelings and begin to master your emotions.*

Like a city whose walls are broken down is a man who lacks self-control. —Prov. 25:28

As it says in Proverbs 16:32: **"Better is a man who can rule his inner self, than one who can capture an entire city."** Indeed, one trait of the *victorious* life is *self-control.* Yes, we do have the ability to rise above our feelings when, at times, they're ready to explode or consume us.

Indeed, these feelings create pressure on us based upon outside circumstances. Maybe we feel financial pressure, physical pressure, marital pressure, or job pressure. We need to turn the valve of that pressure off instead of throwing open the switch and letting it rip. HOW? Get to the root. Some thought is flooding your mind, filling your emotions with energy and momentum. Change gears. Replace those root thoughts with thoughts of peace. As it says in Philippians 4:8, "...whatsoever things are pure, whatsoever things are lovely, whatsoever things are of good report; if there be any virtue, and if there be any praise, THINK ON THESE THINGS."

> Though trouble will come against me, it will not come into me.

You'll be amazed at how quick your emotions will improve.

Remember, as I mentioned earlier, all negative emotions come from a sense of *powerlessness.* Isn't it true that one of the reasons we get so upset with our spouse, friend, family member, or coworker is because they won't do what we *want* them to do? When we feel powerless to change them or get our way, we resort to anger or manipulation. We may try to intimidate or control them—all because we feel powerless to change them.

Persuasion of intimidation may work, at times, but it will damage your soul and theirs. Instead, ask God to bless them and leave the results to Him. That's real power.

God made you to be superior, to be a champion, to be a conqueror—not over *others*, but over *yourself*, over your emotions, the forces trying to control you.

So free yourself. Fall *out* of love with the feelings that no longer serve you—and prepare to live the satisfied life that you deserve.

Secret #10

Discover the Greatness in You

THE TREASURE INSIDE

> *Never underestimate the power of dreams and the influence of the human spirit. We are all the same in this notion: the potential for greatness lives within each of us.*
>
> —WILMA RUDOLPH

The little boy born with a rare form of muscular dystrophy was not only unable to walk, but unable to breathe without a respirator.

Although there was much in life that Mattie Stepanek could not do, he surprised his mother when he began writing *poetry* at age three—brilliant verses that belied his age.

He poured out his feelings in order to cope with the death of his older brother, who had died of the same disease, as had two other siblings. Mattie wasn't expected to live very long, either.

"Doctors told my mom I would die by the time I was three," he remembered years after he had defied those predictions. "My mom, who also has the disease, said: 'No! I'm going to train his spirit.' So I *lived* to three. At age four, [*sic*] they told her that was it. Then I lived to be five. Then they said ten."

Over the next few years, rather than surrendering to grief or wallowing in self-pity for what he could *not* do, Mattie, who lived near Washington, D.C., became a best-selling author and public speaker, captivating fans like Jimmy Carter, Oprah Winfrey, and Larry King—all of whom celebrated the boy's series of five books, *Heartsongs*.

How had he come up with the title? **"A heartsong,"** Mattie explained, **"is your inner beauty. It's the song in your heart that wants to be heard — that makes you become a better person, and helps others to do the same. It's the gift you have inside. *Everybody* has one."**

Mattie shared his rare gift right up until the end. He died in 2004 at age thirteen. "A champion," he wrote in one of his last poems, "is a winner, a hero, someone who never gives up, even when the going gets rough."

My friends, this remarkably optimistic boy, who suffered so much, who was denied the longevity many are given, was still able to discover the greatness within him and share it with the world.

I believe that each of us has a *heartsong*, a rare gift inside, a treasure just waiting to be tapped into. It's your God-given talent, your potential for greatness, the most unique part of you. This gift will unfold, like the petals of a flower — but only if we shine light on it.

You'll often hear people say: "I'm nothing special"; "I'm just average."

But I disagree. There is a *gold mine* in every one of us and you don't have to wait for a crisis or tragedy to discover it. Of course, as we saw in the "Be Expectant" chapter, people sometimes settle for mediocrity — but that's a choice, not a destiny.

God doesn't make junk. And he doesn't create failure. You are not designed to be average — or mediocre. As it says in Deuteronomy 28:13, "The Lord will make you the head, not the tail...you will always be above, and not beneath."

God has planted talent, power, wealth, and purpose inside each of us. This is the "Garden of Eden" that will flourish if only we plant the right seeds and *cultivate* them, which we'll talk more about in the later chapter, "Plant a Seed."

The story is told about a father who, as he lay dying, gathered his two sons close to him and whispered: "The back lot, the back lot."

For years the sons believed that their father had hidden a fortune of gold somewhere on the family property. So as soon as the funeral was over, the sons rushed home and began turning over every inch of soil on their ten-acre back lot, finding nothing but dirt.

Sorely disappointed, they became bitter, regretting that they had worked so hard for no reward, and believed that their father had misled them. Why would he do that? What lesson was he trying to teach them?

Suddenly it dawned on the older brother "since we've readied the field anyway, let's plant some corn." Four months later they *found* "gold" in the back lot—in the form of a very plentiful corn harvest!

You have a "back lot" inside you, too. When you dig it up, and clean it up, you'll find gold in it. It's right there, hidden in your soul.

God is waiting for you to discover the treasure—the greatness in you. Yet many mistakenly believe that there aren't any new treasures to be had. The truth is, there is so much untapped treasure in this world. And this chapter is devoted to discovering the greatest treasure of all—the one IN YOU!

MINING FOR GOLD

As we've seen from Mattie's example, it doesn't matter if you're ten, thirty, forty, fifty, or beyond. You have unique abilities. There is a musician, a poet, an artist, a teacher, a community leader, or a business owner (or countless other possibilities) *inside* of you that must come *out*.

Sometimes, of course, we hope to save ourselves the labor of discovering our greatest gift, hoping that others will bring it *out* of us—or find it *for* us, which only makes us dependent upon them. Other times we attempt to take a *shortcut*. Instead of planting our own harvest, we're like 'California prospectors mining for "gold" in the obvious places, where we expect to find it. We may believe that the treasure of our lives is going to be found in *someone* or *something* else—winning the right job, falling in love, buying a house or car, getting a degree, having a better body, or earning more money and prestige. The "treasure," we mistakenly believe, is something *external*, bestowed from outside of us, onto us.

We need to value *ourselves*, and mine out the best that is within us.

Andrew Carnegie, who became one of the wealthiest men in America, had the distinction of having forty-three millionaires who worked for him at the company that would become U.S. Steel.

A reporter once asked him how he had assembled such a team of established millionaires. Carnegie responded that those men had not been wealthy at all when they were hired, but they had *become* millionaires as a result of the men's hard work and the faith they had in themselves, supported by the faith Carnegie placed in them.

"But how did you train these men to become so valuable that you would pay them so much money?"

Carnegie replied that **men are developed the same way gold is mined**. Several tons of "dirt" must be moved to mine an ounce of gold out of the ground.

It's the same thing in our lives. We have to push aside the "dirt" of our low expectations, fears, and procrastination. We have to forget the odds against us and set aside the skepticism of others. We have to believe in ourselves.

And even if we have to struggle, we can't lose faith or interrupt God's plan.

STRENGTH COMES FROM THE STRUGGLE

I'm reminded of the man who came across the cocoon of an Emperor moth, which would one day become a beautiful creature with its wings marked with red and orange. Anxious to see the moth emerge from its cocoon, the man took it home. For several hours he watched as the moth struggled to break out of the cocoon, but it seemed to him as if it had gotten stuck. So he took a knife and cut off the remaining bit of the shell, allowing the moth to go free.

The problem was that the wings were shriveled and undeveloped — and the little moth, never able to thrive, soon died.

What the man in his kindness and haste had failed to understand was that this moth was created to emerge from its cocoon only when — *through its struggle* — it developed enough *strength* to survive, a process timed perfectly by God. Freedom and flight would only come from that struggle.

By robbing the moth of the time needed, he deprived the moth of his destiny — not just to fly, but to produce one of the treasured riches on earth, the finest quality of silk.

Even if you're struggling today, there is a treasure within, waiting to emerge—*if* you'll endure the effort required to discover it. *Strength comes from the struggle!* We need to fight through the obstacles, through the temptation to quit, to doubt, or to question God's love, or to give up on His Word.

Know that there is "silk" ready to be spun from your wings—to enrich the lives of everyone around you.

So instead of waiting for someone to *point the way,* or finding that treasure of gold "out there," *it's time to search within.*

Remember: Gold nuggets are not found on the surface of the ground. You have to dig in the "back lot" to discover them. And this takes persistence, discipline, hard work, and faith.

IMAGINE IT

It all begins with imagination. The greatest artists of Western civilization prove it: Where did the music of Bach, Beethoven, and Mozart come from? This was music that came from the soul, as a gift from God. How were the towering bridges and monuments of the world built? They were constructed through the imagination of architects who could see the invisible. How were the greatest novels or paintings created? Again, from within the heart of imagination.

But many of us, as we've seen, have stopped dreaming. We've become *practical*—focused only on the responsibility or task at hand. We're on automatic pilot, going through the paces of the day, but using little of our true potential.

In fact, scientists have discovered that most of us use a mere fraction—10 to 20 percent—of our brain's capacity at any given time. Imagine what we could accomplish if we were able to tap into more of this treasure? Similarly, we settle for less than we deserve, never bringing more than a fraction of our true potential to fruition.

How much more productive, inventive, giving, and loving could we be if we used more of our God-given abilities?

Kids instinctively do it all the time. Their imaginations are on fire! Just watch them. Their minds and skill sets are advancing at a dizzying pace. Spontaneity flows. Their imaginations are fertile and, often, very amusing.

But as we grow older, all this creativity seems to slow down. Life becomes repetitive and dull. Our big plans and dreams get delayed or forgotten because we "don't have the time" or are "too stressed out."

Our jobs, children, families (and worries), all take precedence over striking out in new directions. We feel stuck. We're bored by the predictable and consumed by our routines.

If you're anything like most people, you tend to be a creature of *habit*. Most days you *say, do,* and *feel* the same things, over and over again. You get up in the morning and have your coffee, take a shower, walk the dog, make breakfast, take the kids to school, go to work, drive home, have dinner, watch TV, play with the kids, walk the dog again, and go to sleep, right?

Our routines are predictable and so are the results we're getting in life. Our "jobs" become our lives.

In fact, the number one enemy of the imagination is **BOREDOM**. In a 2006 "drudgery report," a survey of **workplace boredom** by a British teacher-training agency demonstrated that millions find themselves in "mind-numbing" jobs, doing the same thing over and over again.

It reminds me of the woman at a job interview who was asked to list some of her accomplishments: "Let's see." She smiled. "I won a Sudoku championship and several crossword puzzle contests."

"That's great," the interviewer said, "but I meant your accomplishments at work."

"That *was* at work!" she answered.

What we need is *variety* and *growth*—and what we're getting is *monotony* and *stagnation*. Why does this happen? Sometimes we're just afraid. Sure, we want to do stand-up comedy, enroll in the culinary institute, or learn how to sculpt, but we're fearful of even attempting it. We figure it won't work out anyway. It's too risky, so it's crazy to even try.

We might imagine it, but fear stops us.

Instead, we get into our COMFORT ZONES—safe, protected, and bored. Rather than mining the treasure within, we become cautious and guarded, anything but bold. We avoid risk. We stop dreaming. We crave security and certainty.

But the comfort that protects us from the pain of growth also imprisons us in a life of mediocrity and emptiness. You feel stale and unhappy because you're not *expanding*. And as we saw in the "Be Healed" chapter, we lose our ability to have fun and see the world with wonder.

Rather than evolving—we're dissolving.

I believe it breaks God's heart to see so many people fail to live up to their potentials and instead live defeated lives. Discarding our true potential wipes out our creativity and the fulfillment of our true destiny.

I'm not telling you we don't need to earn a living or have a structured life. But there are twenty-four hours in a day, so let's devote at least a fraction of that time into developing the true treasure that lies within. We don't have to go on *American Idol, Dancing with the Stars,* or *The Biggest Loser* to mine our vocal talent, learn how to dance, or lose weight. Let's start by going within and searching our hearts and imaginations, recovering the hidden talents buried deep within us.

YOUR TREASURE HUNT…DISCOVER, DEVELOP, DISTRIBUTE

DISCOVER Your Treasure

If we want to discover the treasure within, we need to know *where* it's buried and *how* we can find it. In other words, we can't derive value or share our gift if we can't *identify* it. So we need to start excavating. And remember: We all have *multiple* gifts and talents, so don't get stuck trying to find the perfect one—the so-called *magic bullet*. Your gun is loaded. You have lots of ammunition in it. In fact, as we said in the introduction to this book, your "cupboard" is filled. So ask yourself: *What do I love to do? What am I good at? What do other people say I'm good at?* The answers to all these questions will lead you to discover your passions. So, to begin, what would discovering our treasure specifically require us to do?

> ∽ *Surrender the past.* Failure is a memory that must be forgotten.

1. *Surrender the Past.* Failure is a memory that must be forgotten. So stop going back over your failures and beating yourself up about them. We've all had disappointments and negative experiences, but we can't use them to *rationalize* why we can't do what we need to do to prosper and develop our great potentials. I can tell you that lugging around the past—all the stories we tell about what happened and how difficult or painful it was—will only hold us back. Don't get me wrong. It's okay to sometimes page through the scrapbooks of our lives. In fact, allow yourself to reflect on serious challenges you've faced and what you learned from them, for any of life's experiences can be the catalyst for discovering your greatest gift. In this way, *even bad news can be good news.* Why? Because when a bone is broken, it heals back even stronger than it was before. So if you're in a near-miss accident, or get fired from a job (or from a relationship!), or lose something precious to you, or get diagnosed with an illness—any *and all of it* can be a wake-up call. What did you learn from it all? How did it shape your *priorities* or change your *perspective?* But after this self-reflection, let's turn to a *new* page. Rather than looking *backward,* move *forward* and attack it with a plan.

2. *Let Go of Your Preconceptions About What You Can and Can't Do.* So often, we *limit* ourselves. We argue that based upon our family history, education, physical appearance, or experience—we simply can't change. We all have weaknesses and handicaps. But the

continued

greatest handicap of all is blaming others or outside circumstances for what we choose NOT to do. We've got to get over our *stereotypes* about ourselves—releasing procrastination and fear and launching out in bold new directions.

3. *Be Open to Growing and Changing.* Growth is our God-given capacity to stretch and evolve, reaching beyond where we *are* to become more of what we *can* be—stronger, smarter, kinder, funnier—perhaps more adventurous, openhearted, or patient. God has given each of us a sound mind—and all it needs is some *stretching*. Yes, like muscles that have gotten tight and tired, our mental muscles are cramped up and stiff, which means we can't move very quickly. With God's help, though, we can expand the borders of our minds and our expectations.

For starters, find ways to improve your home and environment. Why? Because clutter can leave you depressed, overwhelmed, almost unable to breathe. Sometimes our desks, bedrooms, and living rooms reflect the actual state of our lives, right? Are they a little disheveled or dusty, the same old things sitting there in the same old way? *Change things around.* Go out and get something to brighten your environment, to alter what you see and shift your perspective. You'd be amazed at how changing your physical surroundings can give you a lift. And when you're "lifted" you tend to see things differently, which leads to doing something new.

4. *Start with What You Love.* People often try to "figure out" a career, an expedient route to earning a living, forgetting that the source of our greatest treasure lies in what we feel *passionate* about. You can turn something you love *into* a profession. For example, even as a five-year-old, Debbi Fields loved making cookies. By the time she was twenty, bored as a young housewife, she daringly opened her first cookie store. From those humble beginnings she turned her Mrs. Fields franchise into a multinational business. And it all began in her kitchen. You don't have to become a mogul, but identifying what you truly love to do is the first step to discovering the treasure within.

DEVELOP Your Treasure

Clearing away the past, stretching yourself in a new direction, and knowing what you love to do won't necessarily be enough to bring your dream to life. You're going to need to do some *research* and take some *action*. Why? Because your ultimate success is not about how talented, fortunate, or lucky you are. In fact, a brilliant idea or innate talent is worthless unless you *develop* and *follow through* on it. In this way, talent is like a spectacular waterfall: it's beautiful but has no commercial value unless its power is harnessed to produce energy. You *are* that waterfall, innately powerful, but you are not going to fully develop your gift until you harness your talent and cultivate it.

> Begin with what you LOVE to do. But begin!

1. *Gear Up and Get Ready.* This is the getting prepared stage. It's often helpful to *change your perspective* by reading, listening, or witnessing things that capture your attention. A magazine article, a TV news report, or something you see or hear may directly inspire you to pursue a new path. You might be deeply moved by an act of kindness you observed. If you need ideas, go into a bookstore and just wander. We all have more than one "calling" that's calling out to us — if only we listen for the voice of it.

To gain perspective, you might also consider scheduling a vacation or a visit to a new place that fascinates you or spending some time

continued

out in nature. Sometimes, folks, we just need to get away. Going to a new place gives us perspective. This can help clear your mind and prepare for a new beginning. And even if you don't have time or money for a vacation, get into the park, onto the beach, into the woods. Being out in nature reminds of us of God's power and helps us get more perspective on what's important—and what's not.

2. *Create a Treasure Chest.* Compile a collection of written ideas and goals that can be your guide to greatness. It includes a list of resources, options, skills, hobbies, career ideas, solutions—everything and anything that will help tap into your God-given potential. Above all, start thinking *outside the box.* If something seems *impractical* or even *impossible,* don't let that stop you. As the saying goes: If you think you CAN or you think you CAN'T—you're *right!* Just a small step forward can be the beginning of a new life. Remember that the Spirit of God lives in *you. You* can do what *He* can do in you. As it says in 1 John 4:17. "Because as He is, so are we in this world."

3. *Take Action.* Prosperity begins in your dreams—but works itself out through your hands. As it says in Daniel 11:32: "That the people who know their God, shall be strong, *take actions* and do exploits!" This means that your spiritual knowledge and relationship with God need to turn into *action*—steps that will lead you to the greatness within. Metaphorically, you have to stoke the fire, get the flames fired up, and fuel that flame with wood. Whether it's sitting down to write that novel, learning French, volunteering at a hospital, weight lifting, mentoring a child, learning to cook, or starting a business— *any and everything* has the potential to stimulate us and mine the greatness within, but we must take the first steps.

Of course, you need to approach new endeavors with wisdom. Ellen DeGeneres once quipped: "My grandmother started walking ten miles a day when she turned sixty-five. Today she's ninety, and we have no idea where she is!"

But seriously, taking action is critical—though sometimes we don't do it until we're forced to. The best-selling mystery writer Mary Higgins Clark started off as a thirty-six-year-old widow with five children to raise. Writing was just a sideline at the beginning, though she was quite self-disciplined about it. Each morning, at five a.m., she always got up to write at the kitchen table, doggedly pursuing her "hobby," penning short stories. But after her husband's sudden death from a heart attack, with little money, she turned that hobby into a profession. To date, she's sold over *80 million* books and is the highest-paid female mystery writer in the world. How did she do it? It was because she took action to draw out the treasure in her.

What could *you* do at the kitchen table *today*? **Research** your passion on the Internet. **Network** with friends and colleagues. **Make a phone call. Sign up** for a class. **Choose a mentor**—someone who is *already* successfully doing what you want to do. Model yourself on their success. **Ask for guidance**. And remind yourself: *I have a special gift and treasure that God has given me. There is a portion and a place in God's kingdom reserved for me.* When you know this, developing that gift is a foregone conclusion.

4. *Discover the Boss Within.* As it says in 2 Timothy 1:7: "For God did not give us a spirit of timidity, but a spirit of power, of love and of self-discipline." So if you're thinking you don't have the time or self-discipline to take that first action, that's only because you've yet to tap into the boss within. This is the resourceful, daring, disciplined manager within you—the one you need to get to know. This boss is going to be your chief of staff, your captain—giving you self-discipline and self-control. This is the boss who is going to get you the interview, raise the money, master the musical instrument,

continued

and motivate others. When one of those familiar refrains comes to mind—*I'm too tired. I can't do it. This will never work.*—your inner boss is going to help push past your procrastination and your old habits. But much better than any boss you've ever known, he (or she) is only concerned about what's best for *you*! (That's a new one, right?!) This new boss is placing only *one* demand *on* and *in* you—to stoke the fire of your true potential. I like the story of the older woman who observed a teenage girl playing the piano beautifully. The sounds were soothing, almost healing to her. "My, you are gifted," she told the girl. "Not particularly," she answered. "I just kept at it—and *kept* at it." So can you.

5. *Stay on Your Own Course.* No matter what you choose to do, stay on your *own* course. Become *blind* to what others do and *deaf* to their critical opinions. We must eliminate doubters, cynics, and naysayers from our circle of influence. They only bring us down—and we're going up. The only thing we're competing against is our own inertia, that thing inside us that keeps us lazy, sometimes even immobile. Nobody can motivate us better than that boss within.

DISTRIBUTE Your Treasure

Once you're up and rolling and you've *discovered* and begun to *develop* your gift—**SHARE IT** with others. Turn your new vocation or perspective into something that can help others—in your neighborhood, at church, in school, at work, wherever you might be. Perhaps you can tutor a child, or help a friend in need, or call up your local animal shelter, retirement home, hospital, library, or college and offer to contribute what you can. If you've mastered the use of a computer or software or started a successful business, volunteer to teach a course at an adult education center;

if you've learned to cook, volunteer at church preparing and delivering meals to the homebound.

Remember: **Your treasure has no real value if it doesn't add value to others,** a subject we'll look at more closely in our chapter "Be on the Giving Side."

1. *Expand Your Social Circle.* Having a treasure to distribute allows you to broaden your horizons, going beyond your usual peer group. Once you're ready to share your gift—you'll be amazed at how rapidly you're going to meet new friends and associates. You'll find that your treasure is a passport to enlarging your world and creating more energy in it.

2. *Revitalize Your Spiritual Life.* As your confidence grows and your creativity expands, you're going to further expand your connection to God. He has the answers. He is the potter and we are the clay. God is working on you, to make you what He wants you to be. So trust the artist to make a masterpiece. See yourself as a great work in progress. And remember: faith is a tangible force. When you exercise faith, all fear and doubt pass away and you will be thoroughly convinced of God's promise in your life. So meditate on the love of God. Think: *My hopes are up! And I'm keeping them up. I expect God's promises to come to pass in my life today.* Making quiet time for prayer is essential for the process of distributing that treasure within.

3. *Don't Rest on Your Laurels.* Even once you're on a roll and distributing your treasure, keep challenging yourself to improve, challenging the status quo. Let's not settle for what we've *already* accomplished. No one is going to crown you, but you. So we must

continued

be devoted to our development and endure the struggle sometimes required. And in the process of trying out new things, remember that **nothing is beneath you**. Sometimes you have to start at the bottom to get to the top. Don't wait to be told what to do — do it! Don't think the hill is too steep. Climb it!

BECOME *IRRESISTIBLE*

We've heard of irresistible chocolates and babies (and certainly irresistible temptations), but now *we need* **to become irresistible people.** When we do, our dreams won't turn us down, and neither will the job we need or the people God is directing toward us.

So how do we become irresistible?

Be unafraid. Be passionate about everything you do. Create an atmosphere of victory wherever you go. Listen more than you talk. Increase your level of eye contact. Adopt a "What can I do for you?" mind-set. Make other people feel good about themselves. And above all, be loving—for love never fails.

Just like with a business, do an inventory of what's inside you. **Make sure you're stocked up on positive thoughts and attitudes about yourself *and* others.** Stock up on dreams. Stock up on a happy spirit. And remember that a person says more with a smile than with words.

In fact, a winning formula for getting a job or succeeding in business always begins with a smile. When a successful hotel chain was looking to fill five hundred positions for a new facility, they interviewed *five thousand* candidates—and instantly eliminated any of them who smiled less than four times during the interview! **Success is attracted to truly happy people.** Indeed, success comes from your relationship with God.

Remember Joseph. After enraging his brothers by sharing his dream with them, they threw him in a pit, then sold him into slavery to the Egyptians. Without a friend in the world, and seemingly without hope, Joseph was left to die.

As it says in Genesis 39:2, "The LORD was with Joseph, so he became a successful man." Notice, even though he was abandoned by his brothers, he was not abandoned by God. Though surrounded by defeat, he emerged victorious and prosperous. Why? Because God was with him, even as He is with you!

Joseph knew there was something inside of him — a gift, a calling, and a destiny. What did he do with it? He served Potiphar and helped make him successful; he served other prisoners, interpreting their dreams and helping them find their futures; he served Pharaoh and was exalted, helping rescue the world from the great famine.

No matter where Joseph found himself in life, his greatness was discovered in serving others, which ultimately led to the fulfillment of his own dreams.

Wherever you find yourself in life right now — serve the people around you. Help someone else figure out their dream. Serve others, pushing them up to their God-given potential. Even if you don't yet know the true nature of your treasure, set your purpose to helping others fulfill their dreams, and I believe it won't be long before you find yourself fulfilling a dream or two of your own!

> *If you want to lift yourself up, lift up someone else.*
> —BOOKER T. WASHINGTON

I promise that you will discover your own great treasure and gift, one that you can share with the world. Remember: **God wants you to succeed. In fact, it is impossible for you to fail when He is with you.** He wants you to be happy. And as His creation, He wants you to fulfill your God-given destiny.

Part III

FRAME YOUR WORLD AS YOU WANT IT TO BE

Secret #11

Plant a Seed

REAPING THE HARVEST YOU WANT

Anyone can count the seeds in an apple, but only
God can count the number of apples in a seed.

—ROBERT H. SCHULLER

Everyone remembers the words of the Cowardly Lion from *The Wizard of Oz*. When asked by Dorothy, "Your Majesty, if you were a king, you wouldn't be afraid of anything?" He answers: "Nothin', nobody! Nothin', no how!"

Then, joining in, the Tin Man and the Scarecrow also continue the questioning.

"Not even a rhinocerous?"

"Imposserous!"

"How 'bout a hippopotamus?"

"Why, I'd trash him from top to bottomous!"

"Supposin' you met an elephant?"

"I'd wrap him up in cellophant!"

"What if it were a brontosaurus?"

"I'd show him who was king of the forest!"

"How?"

"Courage," the lion answers, puffing out his chest. "What makes a king out of a slave?" he continues. "Courage. What makes the flag on the mast to wave? Courage. What makes the elephant charge his tusk, in the misty mist or the dusky dusk? What makes the muskrat guard his musk? Courage. What makes the Sphinx the Seventh Wonder? Courage. What makes the dawn come up like thunder? Courage. What makes the Hottentot so hot? What puts the 'ape' in ape-ricot? Whatta they got that I ain't got?" The trio's answer: "Courage!"

As grammatically challenged as this wizardly poetry may be, our Cowardly Lion playfully illustrates for us the simple yet profound truth—that there is cause and effect to everything in life. Indeed, if the Wonderful Wizard of Oz would only give him that one thing—if the seed of courage could have been *planted* in his heart—well, he just knew he would reap the harvest of bold action, fearless adventure, and mighty deeds!

Friends, this great truth—that *there is cause and effect to everything in life*—is not just limited to the movies. We, too, can be fearless and bold, turning our dreams into realities. But how?

We've all heard people say, "Everything happens for a *reason*." But have you ever wondered what that reason was? The answer is found in another well-known saying, "You reap what you sow." Indeed, there can be no harvest without a seed—and no reaping where there is no sowing.

Remember, after the floods subsided and Noah got off the ark, all that was living had died. Hopelessness must have set into Noah's heart when he looked over all the devastation and ruin—until he heard these words from God in Genesis 8:22—"As long as the earth remains, seedtime and harvest shall not cease."

In other words, whatever is devastated and ruined in your life can be overcome and *rebuilt* when you put this amazing principle to work. The fears and anxieties that often fill our minds will become a thing of the past once we learn the secret of *planting a seed*.

EVERYTHING IN LIFE BEGINS WITH A SEED

It is a fundamental truth that everything in life begins with a seed. Babies are conceived from seeds. Fruits and vegetables come from them, as do flowers and all that God has given us.

Even our *imaginations* are seeds. Why? Because everything tangible in our modern world—from the television and telephone to spaceships and the Internet—was created from the seed of a thought or inspired idea. Even the greatest works of art, inventions, and monuments have all sprung from the fertile soil of human imagination as well.

And in our everyday lives, we're inundated with seeds being planted in us all the time. For example, *advertisements* are seeds. Have you ever gotten a song from a TV commercial planted in your head? ["You deserve a break today!"] Those are some powerful seeds! Marketing firms strategize long and hard to plant their campaigns in our minds through billboards, flyers, TV commercials, jingles, and Internet pop-up ads—all in calculated expectation of their harvest of sales.

In fact, when a company is getting started, the initial investment made in the business is called "seed capital." And it's that initial seed, when planted correctly, that can turn a business into the fruitful enterprise the owners envisioned. Their success is not a coincidence; it's cause and effect, seedtime and harvest.

Every thought, every word, every decision we make, is a seed— that shapes the outcome of our lives. If we're helpful and kind, we generate the same response in others; and if we're impatient or angry, we know what to expect. It's the law of reciprocity. *What we put out is what we get back*. Every action has a reaction.

God wants us to see how simple life can be, that there are no complicated formulas for attaining the life of our dreams and no mystery to having an invincible spirit. If you want to experience the power to change anything—simply PLANT A SEED.

This universal law is totally predictable and works both positively and negatively. If we plant love, we reap it. If we work hard, productivity multiplies. If we take good care of our bodies, our health gets better.

> *If we don't plant flowers, we will forever be pulling out weeds.*
> —DR. JOHN F. DEMARTINI

Conversely, if we spend more than we earn, we wind up in debt. If we exceed the speed limit, we get a ticket. If we take drugs, sooner or later, those consequences are going to show up, too. We either reap the reward or pay the price for virtually everything we do.

Once you start observing the universal law of cause and effect, you quickly see that *there is no such thing as an action without a reaction.* What goes around comes around.

Whether it's a sixteen-year-old who sows good study habits *consequently* reaping entry into the college of her choice, or a president or governor who lies to a nation and *consequently* gets impeached—**all actions and decisions cause a *chain reaction* or *domino effect*—which ultimately determines our realities.**

Sometimes seeds brew and fester and show up in one big bang! In marriages, for example, how many husbands have ever planted the seed of thoughtlessness, reflected in an innocent remark that caused their wives to suddenly blow up?

I must admit that early in our marriage, I told my wife how her hair looked better the way it was *before*—and I reaped a very swift and decisive harvest in the form of a can of beans flying by my head. Good thing I like beans! My comment about her hair was just the final straw, but the true cause of her response, as in so many conflicts, was the insensitivity I had expressed time and time before. I'd planted the wrong seeds—and though they didn't come up right away, when they did, it was quite a harvest!

So like a stone thrown into a lake causing a rippling effect across the water, each thought, word, or decision we make—large or small, good or bad—always leads to a similar effect.

Nothing just happens—for *everything* begins with a seed.

YOUR LIFE IS A GARDEN

Think about it—when God created Adam and Eve, He didn't put them in a house, in an igloo, or in a cave. He put them in a garden! And what do you do in a garden? You plant seeds. The first thing God told them to do: *Be fruitful and multiply.* But you can't have fruit without seeds. It was

God's original intention for mankind to govern their lives and harvest their dreams by the seeds they sowed.

And although we are no longer "in" the Garden of Eden, the Garden of Eden is "in" us. You see, the Bible says that our hearts and minds are the soil of our lives. We can grow whatever we plant. Proverbs 4:23 says that we must watch over our hearts with diligence, for out of our heart flows the harvest of our life.

So even though the wisdom of Scripture has always given us the secret to the satisfied life, religion

> The Kingdom of Heaven is like a single mustard seed, which a man planted in his field. Even though it is the smallest of seeds, it grows into one of the largest plants. And when it is grown, it is the size of a tree, and birds come to live in its branches.
> —MATTHEW 13:31–32

has become, in so many circles, a system of rules and regulations. One mantra goes: "Don't drink, don't chew—don't run around with those who do!"

But God hasn't designed us to be governed externally by rules, but rather by a system of sowing and reaping that empowers us to produce the life we want from the inside out. When governed by this principle, YOU DECIDE the kind of life you will enjoy or suffer, by the seeds you sow. Since life on earth is governed by this principle, your destiny is entirely in your hands!

So remember: **Your life is a garden.** And you determine how your garden grows by the seeds you sow. If you want it to be lush and beautiful rather than parched and withered, you have to water it, work in it, cultivate it, and harvest it properly, a simple process

> He which soweth sparingly shall reap also sparingly; and he which soweth bountifully shall reap also bountifully.   —2 COR. 9:6

we'll see in a moment. But it's not going to happen by magic or by accident.

How many people think (or have believed that) the *grass is greener* on the other side of the fence? The person next door (or in the next office) seems to *have* it all. In fact, their grass is not only greener, but it's taller and thicker, too! But have you ever thought that perhaps it's that way because they've been watering and fertilizing it—and planting the right seeds?

So rather than being envious or jealous, we're going to learn how to take control of the seeds we sow. I can promise you that if you focus on *your* grass, you can grow a lush garden and achieve the satisfied life you envision while also becoming an inspiration to others.

As we know, many people blame the condition of their "grass" on what someone did to them, or on the "bad luck" they had, or the side of the tracks they were born on, or the breaks they weren't given. This victim mentality has to be eliminated from our thinking.

And so it is that **seeds are powerful things that have the ability to create something out of almost nothing.** In Scripture we see the parable of the mustard seed, the smallest of all seeds. Yet it produces the largest tree!

If you ever doubt the power of a seed, just start smiling at people. I promise you that nine out of ten times you'll get a warm smile back. Your friendliness is contagious.

So plant a seed.

And have you ever noticed that even when seeds are *accidentally* scattered in between cement, a flower can bust right through the cracks anyway!

It's like that in our lives as well. Even when we're born with the toughest of challenges, when the odds are against us and victory seems unlikely, **planting the right seeds can break through any ceiling, limitation, or boundary that life has set over us.**

Anything is possible, folks. Give and you shall receive. Plant and you shall harvest. As it says in Galatians 6:7, "For whatsoever a man soweth, that shall he also reap."

Manny, a popular neighborhood pharmacist in Manhattan, who works near 9/11's Ground Zero, has a bedside manner better than most physicians. Soft-spoken and calm, he fills 120 prescriptions daily, offering his customers more than just medicine. "I view my job as much more than just counting pills," he explains. "I set out to do one good deed for the day—to plant a seed—something that's going to grow and make somebody else happy. I ask God to give me strength and humility, patience and a little wisdom, and the ability to love people." It's planting this seed of kindness that produces purpose and meaning in his life. "If a customer leaves smiling or laughing, and feeling reassured," Manny continues, "I know I've succeeded."

Why? Because Manny understands the secret to the satisfied life—planting the right seed.

THERE ARE NO ACCIDENTS

Let's face it, when we see a pregnant woman in the mall or grocery store, no one says, "I wonder how that happened?" And you don't look at an orchard full of apple trees and say: "Wow, somebody really got lucky here, didn't they?" No. That apple orchard got there because seeds were planted and cultivated. Where there is a seed, there is a harvest.

Nothing just happens.

Even when you look at what people refer to as "accidents," there's usually a cause and effect.

You go to an event or gathering, engaging and friendly, and you end up meeting someone who becomes the love of your life. Was that an accident? You probably didn't sit in the corner eating peanuts, with your knees crossed and your head down, playing Sudoku all night by yourself! You planted "relationship" seeds of conversation, warmth, kindness, and humor. That was no accident.

Or you generously offer a helping hand to a business associate who, in turn, refers the most lucrative account you've ever had. Was this dumb luck? I don't think so. So while we sometimes claim things are mere accidents—they rarely are.

I don't know about you, but my kids' rooms never got cleaned by accident. They (or often their mother) had to plant the seed of diligence.

And if you've ever cut your hand in the kitchen, as I have, you could call it an accident, but the fact remains that we probably **planted the seed** of haste and carelessness. Nothing just happens!

Even a car wreck is rarely an "accident." It's usually because one of the drivers planted the seed of speeding, or texting while driving, or hurrying through the red light, or drinking alcohol.

Now, I'm not saying that every bad thing that happens in your life is because of a seed *you* sowed. Sometimes it's the seed that *others* sowed in us—a teacher who said you were stupid, a parent who abused you or was always negative and critical. Why did that happen? Was it your fault? No, it's just the way those people happened to be. It had nothing to do with you. However, your *response* to those adversities has everything to do with you. *Their seed*

> Sometimes people think they've inherited a bad seed, that they're cursed because members of their family always had the "same problem." Stop asking yourself: *Why do bad things keep happening to me?* My response is nothing just happens. If you don't like the harvest you're reaping—change the seed you're sowing.

may have been planted, but *your seed* is what will determine your harvest in life.

So whether it's a thought, word, attitude, or action, *anything* we put our energy into returns to us like a boomerang. What you think and what you do always leads to a reciprocal result. In this way, our actions are *seeds* planted—investments in our future—that either grow and bear fruit, or wither on the vine.

But the quality of the fruit depends on the *quality* of the seed.

I'VE GOT THE POWER!

The principle of planting seeds and harvesting them seems obvious, like following the directions for assembling a toy or baking a cake. You do one thing; you get the other.

We certainly respect this truth when it comes to the laws of gravity or electricity, right? You would never step off the roof of a twenty-story building or touch a wire charged with ten thousand volts—because you know what the results of those actions would be. Cause and effect would kill you.

Yet, we'll take other kinds of risks, defying the law of sowing and reaping. We sometimes believe we can make bad choices and "get away" with them. We tell ourselves it's okay to tell a little white lie, cut corners at work, say one thing and do another, ignore our responsibilities, neglect our kids, or lose our tempers. It's not that God won't forgive us or that He loves us less, but He has set up a system of reaping and sowing that governs the world. This universal law plays no favorites and makes few exceptions.

> ⁓ *Every choice carries a consequence. For better or worse, each choice is the unavoidable consequence of its predecessor. There are not exceptions. If you can accept that a bad choice carries the seed of its own punishment, why not accept the fact that a good choice yields desirable fruit?*
> —GARY RYAN BLAIR

So we can't blame God for the consequences of our own lives, though we are often tempted to. In fact, many people think God is in control of everything, and whatever happens is up to Him or *because* of Him. He gets all the credit or the blame. This isn't true. **God has given us the power and responsibility to manage our own lives, to take responsibility for our own decisions, and to determine our futures by the seeds we sow.**

The story is told of a man who bought a run-down old farm. Thorns filled the land, and the decrepit house was crumbling. Over the next year the man toiled furiously, rebuilding the house and replanting the farm. When he was all finished, a neighbor came by and said, "My, how you and God really turned this farm around."

"Well," the man replied, "if you had seen the farm twelve months ago, then you know what it looked like when God had it all to Himself!"

You see, God wants the best for us, but He has given us the power to create the satisfied life for ourselves. And if we don't, it's simply not going to get done. It's not because God doesn't care, but because He has set up this world to operate on the system of seedtime and harvest.

SEEDS MEET NEEDS

As we've seen, God created us to be in control of our lives, giving us the power to plant the seeds of our own futures rather than living in fear of them.

Have you ever wondered why God made us out of the dust of the earth—out of dirt?

He could have chosen to make us out of something else—gold, silver, or emeralds. But no, He chose the soil of the earth.

Why? Because *soil is capable of growing and developing life,* a God-given resource for bearing fruit. It's the place where seeds are cultivated and brought to harvest.

This means that God designed us to be cultivators—producers and creativity centers—empowering us to yield a rich harvest from the seeds we sow.

Unfortunately, some people are *passive* about creating a new future, even fatalistic or pessimistic, just waiting for something to happen, even expecting the worst to happen.

In our own lives, how often have we sung the song—*"Que sera sera? Whatever will be, will be. The future's not ours to see."* That is a lie! The truth is: *"Whatever you sow—will be."* And *"Whatever you plant—will be."*

Remember, we saw earlier in the book that **powerlessness is the root cause of all negative emotions**—resentment, depression, anger, and worry, among many others we know all too well.

So when we feel powerless to change our futures—unable to take control and have mastery over our lives—we become depressed, angry, or fearful.

In truth, friends, YOU'VE GOT UNLIMITED POWER! If you don't

like the life you have right now, you can change the seeds you're sowing. You can plant something else and bring in a brand-new harvest.

That's the beauty of a seed! It contains the POWER to create the life you want.

That's why I always say: **seeds meet needs**.

Small though they may be, they flourish when we water them and give them the right climate to live in so that they will eventually come to bloom.

Yet many people have said to me, "I just don't have a lot of friends" or "I'm not good with relationships." Yet they hope or may pray that things will change. I can tell you that no farmer prays for a harvest without first planting a seed.

The solution to any challenge you're having? **Plant a new seed**. As it says in Proverbs 18:24: "If you want to have friends, show yourself friendly."

Likewise, *If you want love, be loving. If you want attention and respect, give it to others. If you need a friend, be a friend. If you need favor, show favor. If you need forgiveness, give some.* It's really the essence of the Golden Rule—do unto others, as you would have them do unto you. This is a universal law that is undeniable.

And finally, in assessing the state of your harvest, deal with **the cause— not the symptom.**

What's *really* causing the stress, weight gain, or fighting at home? We have to start dealing with the causes (the seeds we're planting)—not the symptoms (the harvest we're reaping). When we pinpoint the source, we can uproot it from our lives.

When we are sick, often all the doctor has to offer is a prescription or treatment that can help the symptom but doesn't necessarily deal with the root of the problem. It's often the same with formalized religion. So much, of it is centered on fixing the *outside* of our lives, striving to do right and avoid wrong; when, in fact, **if we don't change the root, we won't change the fruit**.

In Mark 4:37, we find Jesus and His disciples "crossing the sea when a fierce gale of wind arose, the waves breaking over the boat, causing it to fill up."

What does this have to do with our lives? Well, we may not be in the middle of a literal storm, but we all face the emotional, medical, or financial storms of life. This story gives us insight into how to deal with them from the root.

While the disciples were bailing water out of their boat, we're told that Jesus got right to the true root of the problem. He arose and rebuked the *wind*.

Why? Because the cause of the crisis wasn't the water filling the boat or the waves crashing against it. Those were only the symptoms of the real problem, which was the wind. In fact, those disciples could have bailed water out of the boat all night, but it would have never solved the problem, until Jesus stopped the wind.

So, too, in our lives we medicate the symptoms of our physical pain, for example, or we desperately borrow to cover up our bad financial decisions. But the root of the problem remains, and the situation never improves.

But when we tackle the *root* (i.e., the cause) the *fruit* will take care of itself.

START PLANTING

Whatever you're lacking in life is within your reach. But as we've seen, it won't come along by accident, or just because you're hoping for good fortune. Nor is it a magic potion. Prayer alone won't do it, either!

In fact, many people don't understand that the Bible is not a *book of rules*, but a *bag of seeds*! All the answers and seeds of greatness lie within it. The words of the Bible are described as the seeds that, when planted, will surely produce the satisfied life. *You can truly be happy and confident, for your abundant future lies within your hands.* Here are some simple steps to get you started:

1. *Choose Your Harvest.* Decide what kind of "harvest," i.e., what kind of life, you truly want. If you want to have tomatoes in your backyard, you don't plant carrot seeds. Likewise, if you want to have friends, you can't sit home alone (every night) watching TV. Even if you're a *Star Trek* fan, you still have to put on your pointy ears and costume to go hang out at the convention center with the other Trekkies.

You must start with the end in mind, then work your way backward! This resolve will guide you in the seeds you sow. Most people are not living "by cause," but rather just "because." So many just go through life, trying to make the best of it—doing things just *because* they feel like it; *because* that's how they grew up; *because* others are doing it. Instead, we need to *live by cause.* Knowing that there is a cause and effect in everything will motivate us to determine in advance the kind of harvest we want, avoiding the seeds that would yield us something contrary. Envision your dream, write it down. Observe others who have reaped the harvest you desire; and identify which seeds will make that dream a reality.

2. *Plant the Seed.* The winter is over, the soil is rich, and we're ready to roll. This step is all about *taking action*—no longer *planning* but *doing.* You've mapped out your strategy, your goals are clearly defined, and you're putting your plan into action. Once you have determined the kind of harvest you want, you have to plant the seeds that will produce it. It's not that hard. Do you want your children to turn out right? Plant the seeds of love, respect, encouragement, sacrifice, and godliness in them. Do you want that promotion at work? Plant the seeds of diligence, excellence, commitment, and loyalty—and you will reap a harvest of success and victory. Our words, our choices, and our actions are all seeds.

3. *Protect Your Field.* Your heart is the "soil" of your life. So what goes into your ears, your eyes, and your mind goes directly into your heart.

continued

But your heart can't *decide* on its own which seeds are good and which ones aren't. Your heart is set on automatic pilot—vulnerable to accepting whatever you put into it. In my backyard the soil will produce whatever seeds I plant in it. For example, if I plant marijuana seeds in it, the soil doesn't yell back at me and say, "Are you crazy? Do you want to get arrested?" No, it has no bias, no opinion. **It will grow what I sow.**

Our hearts are like that, too. They will accept whatever we plant into it. So, if we fill it with pornography, we will reap corrupt thoughts, promiscuous lifestyles, hardened hearts, perverted views of men and women, devastated relationships, and so much more. Again, the Scripture says, "Watch over your heart with all diligence. For from it, flow the issues of life" (Prov. 4:23). So clear out the things that will kill the harvest you desire. Eliminate the contaminants to your heart—criticism, unforgiveness, bitterness, resentments. These choke out the good harvests you desire.

4. *Rest.* Once the seeds are planted, expect nature to take its course. Now it's time to trust in God—and rest! After all, you're a "farmer"; so trust the power of the seed to bring itself to pass. Trust that the sun will shine, that the rain will fall, and that God will make it happen. In the meantime, the seeds you planted today know what to do once they're in the soil. As it says in Mark 4:26–27: "The farmer goes to bed at night and gets up by day and the seed sprouts and grows. He himself does not know how." Yet, so many times we stay up worrying about the future, afraid of what *might* happen. Folks, I'm not going to tell you what *might* happen. I'm going to tell you what *will* happen: you're going to reap the harvest of the seeds you sow. So relax. The seed knows what to do next. Just as the farmer cultivates his land, plants his seed, and goes to bed—so can you!

5. *Don't Give Up.* So many times we get discouraged by the process and give up just before our harvest comes. Galatians 6:9 says, "Don't

grow weary in doing good, for in due season you shall reap, if you do not faint." So many people dig up their seed prematurely after planting it, fearful that maybe it won't grow. You may say something kind or express affection to your spouse with no reciprocal gesture returned, and so you take your compliment back or become sarcastic or offended. Be faithful. Be patient. **Keep sowing that seed of kindness.** It may take some time, true. But we need to have faith in the process. There's no luck or mystery involved here. We will reap—*if* we don't give up. I can tell you that the greatest harvests often take the longest to grow. You may think it's not working, but underground it's building a root system, to sustain its future growth.

The Chinese bamboo tree when planted and watered doesn't grow at all the first year or the second or third. By the fourth year, you might feel like giving up for sure, but keep watering it anyway. Still nothing happens! But, friends, in the fifth year, suddenly the tree grows and grows up to three feet per *day*! Within six weeks, it grows to an amazing ninety feet.

Life is a lot like that bamboo tree. We do the right things in our job, family, or heart. We prepare the ground, plant the seed, faithfully fertilize and cultivate; yet nothing happens. And with seemingly no results, we get discouraged, losing faith, and often abandoning the effort. But we must remember that during the long seasons where there was no evident growth, we are, in fact, developing a mature, long-reaching root system that will sustain and nurture the explosive growth we will soon experience—if we DON'T GIVE UP!

6. *Harvest It.* The crop is *finally* ready and it's time to reap the reward of your effort. Having toiled so hard, you see that your life is now completely different. Those mentalities of failure have been replaced by mentalities of success. The new seeds you planted have

continued

yielded a much sweeter fruit for your life. You're happier, calmer, and less reactive to what other people say and do. Enjoy the new harvests of your life, like the vineyard owner, who celebrates a great crop with his new wine.

By enjoying the harvest, you can appreciate the process that got you there, and expect it to work again and again. The consistent application of this simple principle will secure for you a future beyond your wildest expectations. Become as patient and faithful as the farmer who plants the Chinese bamboo tree. You can start right now. See *everything* you say and do as a seed that has within itself the DNA to bring itself to pass over time.

So, friends, when you look at life through the eyes of a farmer, a sower, you will make the right decisions, maximize each moment, and live with purpose. The result will be the satisfied life—not just a dream for the rich, the famous, or the lucky. It will be your own abundant crop—an everyday experience—thanks to choosing wisely which seeds to sow.

Remember: you hold in your hands the power to live the life you desire by choosing the seeds you plant. No one can stop your harvest, but neither can anyone plant the seeds for you! So begin cultivating the right seeds today, and enjoy the harvest that you so richly deserve, the destiny that God has in store for you.

Secret #12

Find Your Calling in Your Conquering

TURNING ADVERSITY INTO OPPORTUNITY

He who is not every day conquering some fear has not learned the secret of life.

—Ralph Waldo Emerson

There I was, in eighth grade, frozen in my seat, when my civics teacher, Mr. Sutherland, announced that the next day he'd be picking ten students from our class for a debate about slavery in early America.

I was deathly afraid of being picked. It was as if my whole world would have crumbled if I had to speak in public. Compounding my already exaggerated sense of self-consciousness (feeling observed, but not approved) was an overwhelming fear of speaking to thirty 14-year-olds!

That could intimidate anyone! In me, it created pure terror.

So as Sutherland continued talking about the great debate about to happen, everything in my world stopped. With all the determination in me, I decided to find a way *not* to get picked.

There was only one sure solution: I'd skip school until well after the selections were made. My plan was that I'd hide behind the couch in our family room until my parents left for work, and then I'd stay home and watch television all day.

And that's exactly what I did for three days in a row, just to make sure I wasn't around for that dreaded debate. Of course, I had only delayed the inevitable confrontation that would, one day, have to occur.

I can see now that I would have to *conquer* this fear and insecurity if I were ever to find my true calling in life. But back then, I was relieved just to *find* a place to hide!

INVITATION TO GREATNESS

So, how did I get from scaredy cat to pastor, international speaker, and television host? (Someone who, at the very least, is no longer hiding behind the couch.)

Well, the secret to that transformation is what we're going to answer in this chapter, demonstrating how to turn a painful weakness into a mighty strength—no matter what your challenge. Following some simple steps to get you there, we're going to discover how to overcome the obstacles that are keeping you from reaching your true purpose.

Overcoming our greatest fear—the thing we're most sensitive about—is often the pathway to our destiny, our true calling. Our *vulnerability* becomes our *opportunity*—a direct channel to greatness. So what seems like a liability actually becomes an asset—which leads to what you were *meant* to do in life.

Everyone has a calling, a purpose for which they were born—an overarching reason to live. And people desperately search for this calling. In fact, in survey after survey, the most crucial questions people ask are always the same ones: *"Why am I here?" "What is my purpose?" "What am I meant to do?"*

I can tell you that the number one question people ask me is *"How can I find the will of God for my life?"*

And my answer is always the same: **Your calling is found in your conquering.**

What do I mean? Usually, during the first half of our lives, each of us faces any number of physical, emotional, and spiritual challenges, things that trouble us deeply. These adversities are actually the *starting* place for discovering what you're meant to do.

As I told you earlier, I grew up with incredibly low self-esteem, feeling inferior and rejected. I was the last one picked for recess, and the last one chosen for a date. If someone asked what position I played in football, I'd answer: "Tailback." Why? Because every time I got off the bench to try to get into the game, the coach yelled out, "Hey, Dickow, get your 'tail back' here!"

At home, things weren't much better. With so little affection I felt unloved and insecure. And nobody I knew could help me overcome the inner demons that waged war in my soul. So I just withdrew, got connected to the wrong crowd, and wound up using and selling drugs.

But when I discovered God's love for me, I found worth, significance, and purpose. I overcame my deep-seated emotional pain — *and* my terror of public speaking. The very thing I most dreaded became the exact thing I needed to do. And therein I found my *calling*. Had I not — by God's grace — overcome these challenges, I would not have been capable of leading others to conquer their own demons. That's the beauty of a calling — it allows you to help people.

So, yes, that obstacle, trauma, bad childhood, painful divorce, betrayal, loss of a job, or health crisis are all *opportunities* — invitations to our destiny.

Our trials, mistakes, and liabilities are actually stepping-stones rather than stumbling stones. Why? Because enfolded in our human frailty is a gift, a lesson, and a rare opportunity. Folks, **each of your trials is a message calling out to you that can lead to the PURPOSE for your life — the mission that you were meant to accomplish.**

I am convinced of this truth: we will never be truly satisfied in life until we *do* what we were *born* to do. And it's ironic that the answer to this search, so often, is found in the very thing we needed to conquer in life.

I can tell you that even after my miraculous conversion to Christianity, deep-seated insecurities still plagued me, causing a huge tug-of-war inside. In my junior year of college, every class I was enrolled in required a public speech at the end of the semester. What was

> Who wouldn't like to be able to say with confidence: "This is what I was born to do." By the time we're done with this book, that's exactly what you will be able to say!

my response? I dropped my major and decided to find one where I could hide "behind the couch" again. It was crazy the way I was so driven by fear. It was like I had this demon on one shoulder, making me shy away from speaking publicly, and an angel on the other shoulder, pushing me to press through the fear.

In certain situations I would boldly share my faith; while at other times, some sort of social anxiety would overtake me. *Who* would ultimately be the winner of this battle? And how could I rid myself of this fear? I knew my destiny hinged upon it.

I found a verse in Psalms 34 that says: "I sought the Lord and he delivered me from all my fears." I read it a thousand times and started praying that God would free me from these fears and insecurities.

The next day, as I sat in my dorm room, looking through the college course listings, wondering what I was going to switch my major to, I heard a voice tell me: "I want you to major in public relations."

Huh?! Talk about jumping out of the frying pan and into the fire. This was the ultimate absurdity. Yet, I now see that it was the first necessary step to finding my calling, the voice of God urging me to conquer my fear.

So, is there a fear or weakness in your life that is limiting you? I believe your assignment in life is to conquer it, as mine was.

We see people doing this all the time. The emotionally battered child becomes a psychologist; the class clown becomes a comedian; the converted and rehabilitated in prison becomes a counselor, helping inmates turn their lives around.

Fourteen years ago, a man joined my church just as it was getting started. He had just been released from a five-year prison term. While in prison, his life was transformed by the power of God. Today he heads up our prison outreach ministry, reaching thousands of inmates with the love of God. It's amazing how discovering your calling is truly life-changing, both for you and for others.

There are countless such examples proving that we can and often do find our greatest calling in what we conquer.

Helen Keller, deaf and blind, became a prolific author, lecturer, and role model for countless children and adults alike. Eleanor Roosevelt, once painfully shy and awkward, became an international diplomat, eloquent and confident, helping to shape the world!

These were among the most powerful souls of this world. And so are you!

THE MONUMENT WAITING
TO BE SCULPTED

During the early, most painful years of my life that I've described, I knew that the "real me" was somewhere buried inside. In fact, I can see now that God had embedded into me a purpose—to change people's lives with a message of love, power, and grace.

But, first, all the damage on the outside had to be chiseled away—the fears, the insecurities, the hurt, the rebellion, and the pain all had to be conquered. These were the stumbling stones that were preventing me from finding my calling. Yet they were also the inspiration to move me beyond my suffering.

So whatever stumbling blocks you're facing, don't see them as deal breakers, but as assignments to conquer on your journey to destiny!

Let's take a look at Michelangelo, one of the supreme artists of all time. His sculpture *David,* which soars seventeen feet into the air, is considered one of the greatest works of art ever created. But what raw material did he start with? It wasn't great at all. The marble used was actually damaged, neglected for twenty-five years

> *If you listen to your fears, you will die never knowing what a great person you might have been.*
> —ROBERT H. SCHULLER

and exposed to the elements, a block of stone riddled with imperfections. His contemporaries had sneered at the slab, declaring it "a thing of no value."

But within that stone, Michelangelo saw his *David.* And so it was, that after chiseling away at the marble for three years, *David* was finally unveiled in 1504, declared a masterpiece, just as God sees a masterpiece inside you.

We have to carve out our futures, smoothing down the rough edges, sanding away the resentments and fears, chipping away at the bitterness and procrastination, seeing the *potential* in that block of stone that is *us*. When we do, the masterpiece will be revealed.

So often, of course, the "DNA" of our past will try to mark us, corner us into a predictable, boring, and uneventful existence. We take the path of least resistance, or make a truce with our vices, weaknesses, and infirmities. Because of this programming, we're conditioned to stay small, limited, and insecure.

That's what happened to me. My weaknesses, idiosyncrasies, and fears had to be conquered or they would fence me in the rest of my life. There was a *David* inside me, just as there is in you, but I had a lot of damaged stone that needed to be cut away.

So, yes, everyone has obstacles that keep their destinies locked inside. Life has damaged everyone in a devilish attempt to undermine our calling and get us focused on simply *repairing* the damage. We often run around, putting out fires—scratching around and just surviving. We find "a job," rather than a calling. We settle for mediocrity, rather than greatness. We expect little—and that's what we get.

But Michelangelo wasn't interested in just *repairing* that damaged block of stone; he was determined to *transform* it into legend. Likewise, God wants us to transform ourselves so that we can experience the satisfied life.

Ready to begin? Let's find out how...

The Future Begins

STEP #1: CONQUER YOUR *PAST*

The first key to finding your calling begins with conquering your past—and letting go. This is not as hard as some may think. Many times we dwell on an issue for too long, becoming attached to it and allowing it to define or disable us.

To conquer our past, we first have to *acknowledge* it. I'm not saying we need to crawl up into a ball on a therapist's couch and get all fetal! But we can't hide from it, either, or cover it up. Yes, it happened, and after acknowledging and understanding exactly what occurred in our past, we must make peace with it and decide we're no longer going to be a hostage to it.

We need to *disengage* from the endless stream of old memories that keep looping back around our minds, like a tape recording that never stops. Stop talking about it, trying to explain it, or using it as a rationalization for not moving forward.

Next we need to *disengage* from preconceived ideas of how we're *supposed* to be. You have to make a deliberate break from the patterns you grew up with, low expectations, or unrealistic ones—which we'll take a closer look at, later in the book. You have to burn your own trail, and carve your own path.

Sure, it takes courage to do this. A friend of mine who was intensely shy as a child was driven by self-hatred. In fact, he was incredibly fearful of rejection, avoiding social situations like the plague, just as I did. How did he overcome the past and heal the scars of his early years? He went into a profession that demanded him to be front and center, becoming a TV interviewer—a highly social profession that defied his past shyness. It was by pushing through his pain and nervousness that he was able to conquer it and become the very thing he thought he could not be.

How can any of us do this?

First, accept that we were all "messed up." Indeed, acceptance is crucial to healing the past. But how, you might ask, does one find acceptance amidst humiliation, shame, despair, grief, and all those other emotional ghosts? Can we just wave a wand over them and create order from chaos?

No, of course not. **We can't change the past. But we need to see it differently.** Rarely can we skip over our painful feelings and create change in short order. Often we want difficult life situations to be rewritten some other way. But the key is to *accept* that although it has been that way, it will not *stay* that way.

Give up trying to figure it all out; and trust, as it says in Romans 8:28, that "God can cause all things to work together for good to those who love Him and are called according to His purpose."

Believe that God can take every life experience and turn it around—making it work *for us* rather than *against us*.

If you've ever seen great chefs, they don't throw away the butts and ends of celery or carrots or onions, or even some remnants of fat. They put them in a pot and turn them into delicious broths, soups, and stews.

God's that way, too. He takes our leftovers and left outs, he takes what others reject—our shortcomings and our old "butts"—and makes soup out of them!

As we accept life's challenges and difficulties as opportunities, God turns them into sweet and savory victories.

Ask Him to turn your situation around. Go to Him with arms open wide, and accept the second chance He offers. As it says in 2 Corinthians 5:17, "If any man is in Christ, he becomes a new creation—a new species of being." Realize that a new birth is the beginning of a truly satisfied life.

And to support you in your new path, surround yourself with people who are already *in* the future you desire. That doesn't mean getting rid of everyone from your past, or condescending to them. But distance yourself from the people in your life who are stuck and don't want to get out of their past — *or* yours.

STEP #2: CONQUER YOUR *PAIN*

Pain is universal and inevitable, but it can be healed. We learned that the only escape from mental and emotional pain is replacing *mentalities of failure* with *mentalities of success.* We also learned that prayer, joy, and laughter can do much to heal our bodies and spirits. We also learned to shift our *focus,* knowing that we're going to feel whatever we direct our attention to. We saw the value of *taking care of ourselves* and having fun, reclaiming our spontaneity and childlike energy. All this contributes toward healing the pain.

Sometimes, of course, rather than trying to relieve it, we actually flame the fires of it. I once had a vision of a man I knew who had a knife in his side. It was stuck there, and he *wouldn't* pull it out. The knife represented the pain that others had inflicted upon him. Yet, inside him were buried a number of great talents — the potential for positively influencing people all around him. But these gifts could not emerge. Why? Because the knife was blocking the way.

> The wounds that others cause create the opening through which our new life can flow.

What was the meaning of my vision? First, if we don't pull the knife out and stop nursing our pain, no good can come forth from our life. We will blame our failure to reach our potential on what others have done to us when, in fact, *we're doing it to ourselves.*

Second, remember that **the wounds that others cause create the opening through which new life can flow.** Consider Jesus, who was lanced in His side, on the cross, where water and blood flowed. The blood cleanses, while the water washes away old mind-sets, which have kept us limited and defeated. So the wound caused by an ignorant and mis-guided Roman soldier opened the way for blood to flow and new life to be born.

View the wound you've endured as an opening from which new life and love and purpose can flow. But you have to get to the root of the pain — you have to pull out the knife.

Chances are, you've heard the story about the guy who went to the doctor and said, "Doc, it really hurts when I lift up my arm like *this*." The doctor performs a thorough exam, hands the patient a bill for $500, then looks him straight in the eye and says, "Don't lift your arm like that anymore!" This is often the way we deal with our pain. We just try not to move that part anymore, rather than getting to the root and fixing the cause. There is a cause and effect to everything — get to the root!

And one of the best ways of doing this, as we saw earlier in the "Forgive Yourself" chapter, is to *release* those who contributed to this pain. Let go of anger, resentment, and bitterness. Forgiveness is not a feeling, but a *decision*. If you wait until you "feel like" forgiving, you may be waiting a long time. Make the choice, and whether you feel it or not, stick to the decision like glue.

Also, *consider past pain to be present gain*! **We have to realize that our pain, once conquered, produces sensitivity to others who have suf-fered too**. And it makes us stronger, able to withstand future challenges with faith that we can get through anything.

And, of course, *employ the power of positive words*. As it says in Prov-erbs 12:18, the tongue of the wise is healing. Words heal. Words restore. Words build. So talk to yourself in a positive, encouraging way. Include not just your family and friends in your prayers — but yourself as well. Speak God's language — and you'll experience His success.

Make it a point to set the course of your life each morning with words that build you up. Start out your day and prayerfully declare: *This is the day the Lord has made. This is my day. This is my week. This is my moment. I am somebody, because God made me special. I am more than a conqueror. I'm not going down, I'm going up. I'm the head, and not the tail, above only and not underneath. I'm blessed coming in and blessed going out. Something good is going to happen in my life today!*

The Bible says that the tongue is like the rudder of the ship. Whichever direction you turn it, is the direction your whole life will eventually go.

STEP #3: CONQUER *YOURSELF*

The true cause of the defeated and unsatisfied life is the *unconquered* self. As Plato said: "For a man to conquer himself is the first and noblest of all victories."

Indeed, friends, **success or failure in life is almost always determined by the degree to which we're able to conquer our self**.

So how do we do this? We begin by dealing with our *thought life*.

> *Better is a man who can rule his own self, than one who can conquer a city.*
> —Prov. 16:32

Have you heard the story of the lady who was robbed? Though many things were stolen, her insurance covered everything and all of it was replaced. But within weeks she was robbed again! This time the police told her a repeat robbery was quite common, for once a thief discovers an access point left uncorrected (or unconquered), he often comes in the same way again.

Friends, our unconquered thoughts are the access point by which our enemy gets in and tries to rob us of the satisfied life.

The access point for defeat and destruction in our lives is how we think. As we saw in the "Be Healed" chapter, such mind-sets as these must be conquered: *I can't. There's never enough. I'm overwhelmed. My life is not as good as yours. I'm not that important. That's just the way I am. I'll always be this way. I wish I were you!*

Never wish you were somebody else. It reminds me of the man who was sick and tired of going to work every day, while his wife stayed at home. He wanted her to see what *he* went through at work, so he said this prayer: *Dear Lord: I go to work every day and put in eight hours, while my wife merely stays at home. So please allow her body to switch with mine for a day. Amen.*

God, in His infinite wisdom, granted the man's wish. The next morning, sure enough, the man awoke as a woman! He arose, cooked breakfast for his mate, woke up the kids, set out their school clothes, fed them breakfast, packed their lunches, drove them to school, came home and picked up the dry cleaning, took it to the cleaners and stopped at the bank to make a deposit, went grocery shopping, then drove home to put away the groceries, paid the bills, and balanced the checkbook. He cleaned the cat's litter box and bathed the dog.

Then he hurried to make the beds, do the laundry, vacuum, dust, and sweep and mop the kitchen floor. He next ran to the school to pick up the kids, set out milk and cookies, and got them organized to do their homework, then did the ironing. At four-thirty, he began peeling potatoes and washing vegetables for salad, breaded the pork chops, and snapped fresh beans for supper. After supper he cleaned the kitchen, ran the dishwasher, folded laundry, bathed the kids, and put them to bed. At nine P.M., he was exhausted, and though his daily chores weren't even finished, he went to bed, where he was expected to have sex, which he managed to get through, also without complaint.

The next morning he awoke and immediately knelt by the bed and prayed: *Lord, I don't know what I was thinking. I was so wrong to envy my wife's being able to stay home all day. Please, oh please, let us trade back.*

The Lord, in His infinite wisdom, replied: *"My son, I feel you have learned your lesson, and I will be happy to change things back to the way they were. You'll just have to wait nine months, though, because last night—you got pregnant."* So much for trading places!

Our negative mind-sets must be conquered by systematically replacing wrong thinking with right thinking.

That's why, as I mentioned in an earlier chapter, I launched a concept called: "From the Inside Out—a Fast from Wrong Thinking." Instead of fasting from food, I took people on a forty-day journey of "fasting" from wrong thoughts.

The results were amazing. People reported losing weight without even trying. Others said that they had been freed from smoking, from depression, from suicidal thoughts, you name it.

Folks, **all these changes were the result of people conquering wrong thinking.**

⁓

Another way of conquering yourself is *taking responsibility* for your life, eliminating the *victim mentality*.

It is so easy in our culture to find other things and other people to blame for why our lives turn out the way they do. We tell ourselves, *It's not my fault. It's my parents. It's the government. I was mistreated. No one gives me the same breaks as others.*

Sure, other people and circumstances had something to do with how you got into your situation, but only *you* can decide whether or not you're going to stay in that situation. The victim mentality is looking for someone else to take the blame—and the responsibility.

But when you eliminate all vestiges of a victim mentality, you are empowered to take full CREDIT for your life. You see the truth is **no one can keep you from the destiny that God has for you, but you**.

Don't wait for someone else to give you a break. **Make your own break**. I started a church, a radio talk show, a TV program. What do you want to start?

Take control. Don't give away your power to anyone else. You are the voice. You have the power to choose, to forgive, to recover, and to conquer *anything*.

So conquer yourself and take your power back, shedding other people's judgments, expectations, and rules—and create the life you want.

STEP #4: CONQUER WHAT IS RIGHT IN FRONT OF YOU

So far, we discussed the need to conquer your *past,* your *pain,* and your *self.* But what I'm about to say might be the simplest and most powerful thing I could tell you about finding your true calling.

Everyone knows the story in 1 Samuel 17, where young David faced a giant that taunted both him and the armies of God. This giant Philistine threatened the very existence of the nation of Israel. What did David do? With five smooth stones and a sling, he conquered the giant.

But did you know that defeating the giant was not where David's destiny was born? As a young boy, when he was entrusted with his father's sheep, a lion threatened the flock. **David conquered the lion!** A bear later came for the little lambs. **David conquered the bear. By the time the giant came, he was ready.** His faithfulness in the previous smaller battles had made him ready for the one that would catapult him to legendary status!

He had found his calling in his conquering. How? He conquered whatever was *right in front* of him.

Frequently we try to look all the way down the road to the finish line. People go after a giant that they are not yet prepared for. We want to get to our calling and purpose right *now.* Living in a quick-fix culture, we're impatient, so we expect instant results.

But transforming our lives is not like ordering Chinese food or a new blender on the Internet. Sure, we want to conquer our greatest weakness and achieve our highest dream as quickly as possible. But we don't get there that way.

Start with the seemingly "insignificant" sheep. Defend them from the lion—and the bear. And one day you will be catapulted into your ultimate life calling.

How do you get to Carnegie Hall? *Practice, practice, practice!* You don't jump from musical knucklehead to superstar. First you learn how to read music, and begin perfecting your hand position, practicing scales, presenting recitals for the neighbors, until eventually you get to the bigger audiences.

Likewise, don't attempt to achieve all your life goals today. When Jesus walked this earth, He didn't start out healing the sick and preaching to the multitudes. He didn't start out dying for the sins of mankind.

First He simply conquered the temptations that the devil brought Him in the wilderness. Conquering what was *right in front* of Him was the passageway to His purpose, as it is yours.

Remember, we are not "entitled" to all of God's power and blessing just because we're born. **We need to pass some tests**. When we're faithful in the little things, God will put us in charge of so much more.

So **conquer what is right in front of you!** Rule your desk—and maybe one day you'll run the entire company. Start by feeding one child in Africa before taking on the world's starvation. Lose a few pounds, gain a new friend, take that class that you've been avoiding—and before you know it, you may find yourself right in the middle of God's perfect will for your life—a complete and satisfied life.

So, before you turn the page, what's right in front of you right now? **What obstacle or challenge seems to be** *standing* **in your way—rather than** *leading* **the way?** Release the idea that fate or circumstance is against you, and remember that God is always *for* you. You're not the victim, you're the victor. And even if you're confronting a crisis, trust that facing it head on will bring you into your true calling.

Tell yourself: *This* setback *is a* setup *for my* comeback*!* It might have taken its best shot at you, but you're still standing. It might have had you down for the nine count, but you're getting back up. It can't stop you. You are more than a conqueror. You can do all things through Christ.

Whew! Doesn't that make you feel like dancing? Or jumping? Or climbing the legendary Philadelphia Museum steps in your gray sweatshirt, black winter cap, with your hands held high, and your smile tilted to one side, yelling: "Yo, Adrian, I did it!"

Think of Jared Fogle, known to most people as "the Subway Guy," who by his junior year in high school weighed 425 pounds! Yet, by his early twenties, he was exchanging his ten-thousand-calories-a-day diet for turkey sub sandwiches made by the Subway restaurant chain. By the end of the diet (plus an exercise program that he religiously adhered to), he had lost *240 pounds,* able to finally retire his old pair of pants with a sixty-two-inch waist.

Jared conquered the weight that was right in front of him and has been paid handsomely for it. His conquering allowed him, as it will allow you, to contribute positively to the lives of others.

In short, you, too, can turn your liability into your greatest asset.

So go ahead, my friends, and conquer what is right in front of you and get ready for the greatest days of your life ahead.

Secret #13

Be on the Giving Side

AND LET YOUR BLESSINGS TRANSFORM
THE WORLD

> *It is every man's obligation to put back into the world at*
> *least the equivalent of what he takes out of it.*
>
> —ALBERT EINSTEIN

Just after the Korean War ended, a native woman had a brief affair
with an American soldier, becoming pregnant, though the relationship ended quickly and the soldier returned to the United States, never to
see her again.

The baby girl was cruelly ostracized by her community because of her
light-colored skin and curly hair, for this was a time when the Korean culture frowned heavily upon children of mixed races.

In fact, it was known that some women would even kill their children
because they didn't want them to face such rejection, though this girl's
mother decided to raise her child as best she could.

But after seven years of relentless insults and abuse, the mother did
something that few of us could even imagine: she abandoned her little girl
to the streets!

There, the child was ruthlessly taunted, called the ugliest word in the
Korean language, *"tooki,"* which means "alien devil." And after two years
of wandering the streets, the desperately ill girl was finally placed in an
orphanage.

Despite her great suffering, this girl was, at heart, a *giver*—loving and
compassionate. Indeed, when it was learned that a couple from America
was coming to the orphanage intending to adopt a *boy,* she spent the entire

day giving baths to all the little boys and combing their hair—hoping that one of them would be adopted by the American couple.

The next day the couple came, and, years later, this is what the little girl recalled: "I saw this man with his huge loving hands lift up each and every boy. I saw tears running down his face and knew he adored every one of them as if they were his own. And I knew that if he could, he would have taken the whole lot home with him.

"At the very end of his visit, he saw me out of the corner of his eye. I was nine years old at the time, but only weighed thirty pounds—a scrawny little thing. I had worms, lice in my hair, boils all over me, and was full of scars—not a pretty sight!

"But the man came over to me and gently laid his hand on my face. I could hardly believe the words that came out of his mouth: 'I want this child. This is the child for me.' And that was the day my life was saved."

BE A GIVER, NOT A TAKER

In that moment, *giving* rescued that child who had, herself, been willing to give away her chance of adoption for the sake of another. And in the instant when the man chose the little girl, *his* giving changed her life.

In a society where we want the perfect life and the perfect child—one with no weakness, sickness, or inconvenient condition—this man demonstrated the definition of true love: giving to someone who cannot give back.

This is a demonstration of God's love in action and a reminder of what He has done for each of us—giving life itself to us. He gave us His son and a second chance even after we were *tooki*—aliens or strangers, rejected and used.

In this way, God says about you, "I want this child. This is the child for me." And when you discover this, you are forever struck by unselfish love. Suddenly you see others as objects of your love and generosity, rather than opportunities for your own personal gain.

That, my friends, is the beauty of real giving, knowing that we're created by God, each of us blessed with the unique ability to *help* one another. Indeed, **the capacity to see a need and fill it is one of the most powerful secrets to the satisfied, invincible life.** Real giving has nothing to do with self-interest, gaining a profit, getting something in return, or a secret motive.

Instead, **being on the giving side is our capacity to reach out and *contribute* whatever we can, whether large or small, to the people around us.** It's an unselfish act that creates an intimate bond between giver and receiver.

This is true love—and true living—which is why I say: *to live is to give.*

In fact, the thing I love most about the previous story is that the little girl discovered the greatest blessing *after* she demonstrated giving and unselfish love. She was the one hoping the little boys would be adopted. She was the one who gave them baths and got them ready. She gave pure love and *then* she was the one to receive it.

With a little more of that kind of generosity of spirit, we could all make a true difference in the world. And you don't have to go halfway around the world to do it. Instead, consider your mission field your own circle of family and friends, the world in closest proximity to you. If you just look around you, you'll easily discover people who could be forever impacted by your act of kindness and generosity.

Teach and inspire a child in Sunday school. Offer to pick someone up when you find out their car is in the shop. Buy someone lunch for no reason. Give a small gift to someone when it's not their birthday. Send some flowers, hold an elevator, anything at all. Aren't these the kind of things we do for someone when we fall in love with them? Well, why wait for that? Let's *live to give*—and live in love—rather than waiting to fall in love before we give freely.

Make people the most important thing in your life, for an existence of self-importance and self-absorption is a miserable life.

Indeed, sometimes we're so selfishly focused on our own needs, desires, and survival that we forget about the reward in giving to others, not realizing that new answers (and real joy) come when we give. And when we only *take,* we ultimately hurt ourselves.

Perhaps you've heard the story about the smartest man in the world, who was flying to the West Coast on a small plane. The two other passengers were a retired priest and a Boy Scout. Suddenly the door from the cockpit swung open and the pilot rushed out, wearing a parachute.

"The engines have failed," he said, "and the plane is going to crash. I'm sorry to report that there are only two parachutes left. Good-bye." Then he swung open the side door and jumped off the plane.

The plane began to shudder violently and the three passengers looked at one another.

The smartest man in the world jumped up and spoke first. "As the smartest man in the world, the contribution I can make to the future of civilization cannot be calculated," he said. "You're an old man, and you're just a kid. It's my duty to mankind to save myself." He grabbed one of the packs, went over to the door, and jumped out of the plane.

The retired priest turned to the Boy Scout. "He's right," he said. "I am an old man, and I've lived a long and wonderful life. You should save yourself."

"Don't worry about it, Father," the boy replied. "The smartest man in the world just jumped off the plane with my backpack."

I promise that you're always happier when you're on the *giving* side!

A fascinating study was compiled by the Institute for Child Behavior with regard to the principle of the Golden Rule. The institute found that "the happiest people are those who help others." Each person was asked to list the ten people he knew best and to label them as happy or unhappy. Then they were to go through the list again and label each one as selfish or unselfish (using the following definition of selfishness: *a tendency to devote one's time and resources to one's own interests and welfare — an unwillingness to inconvenience one's self for others*).

The results showed that all of the **people labeled happy were also labeled unselfish.** The researcher wrote that those "whose activities are devoted to bringing themselves happiness . . . are far less likely to be happy than those whose efforts are devoted to making others happy."

And there are legions doing exactly that—whether it's Mom leading a Bible study, kids raising money for abused children, a volunteer at a nursing home, a community banding together to rebuild a house, missionaries feeding the hungry, or teachers mentoring children.

These influencers contribute *unconditionally* from the heart, giving their time, energy, knowledge, skills, resources, and talents with *no strings attached.* They are the generation that will make a difference in society. They will help restore this nation to the benevolent and selfless people that made it great years ago.

And believe me, it's not someone's profession that determines the giver mentality, but rather the character of the person doing the job. We might believe that a stockbroker, for example, is someone only interested in making money, but he or she can be as great a giver as a nurse or a teacher. It just depends on their *perspective* on life and their ability to give in *any* situation, no matter what the setting. That's why living on the giving side is not just about being charitable, generous, or handing over your time, money, or possessions.

Giving is not just what you do; it's *who you are.*

Friends, you don't have to be an organ donor, a saint, or a missionary to give. And you don't have to wait to be a millionaire before you do it, either. You can make a difference *today.*

Giving is an attitude. It's seeing people through the eyes of God. It's realizing that you are blessed and can, in turn, be a blessing.

I was recently walking down the street in downtown Chicago on one of those freezing winter days when I wished I were in Hawaii! And I came upon a homeless man holding up a sign, FEED ME, begging for spare change. We all know how uncomfortable it is to be approached by someone possibly *posing* as homeless, but this man looked pretty ill, obviously not "faking it." Yet, two well-dressed people walked by, one of them expressing disdain for him. "That's disgusting," she told her friend. "*I never give*. It only encourages them."

Hmmm. She *never gives*. That's quite a statement.

If any of *us* were homeless, wouldn't it be comforting to know that *someone* would reach out to help? Although this may be an extreme example of someone lacking empathy, it underlined my belief that there are two kinds of people in this world — *givers* and *takers*.

THE TAKER MENTALITY

Takers are essentially selfish, excessively focused only on themselves — on their own advantage, pleasure, or well-being (like a ball of twine, all wrapped up in itself). The taker's life is geared toward *self-fulfillment* rather than interest in the welfare of others. Their life revolves around thoughts like *How do I feel? How do I look? What do I need? Where am I going? What do I want?*

And never before have we seen such a selfish time in America. I often ask myself: whatever happened to the values that Tom Brokaw wrote about in his book *The Greatest Generation* — the generation of the 1940s that understood sacrifice, commitment, love, and duty? The freedom won for us by these heroes was trampled on by the spoiled "me" generation of the '60s and '70s, which now seems to have grown into a culture caught up in materialism, greed, and self-absorption.

> *He who lives only to benefit himself confers on the world a benefit when he dies.* —TERTULLIAN

Indeed, the "taker" feeds on a *consumer* approach to life — the goal being to acquire as many products, services, and achievements as possible. An extreme example of this selfish spirit is the person who embodies what I call the "hitchhiker mentality," a taker who wants someone else to not only drive the car but also to pay for the gas! This is the guy who eats out of your refrigerator, listens to your CDs, and excuses himself when the bill comes at the restaurant. He takes anything he can — and too many of us allow him to take us for a ride.

This cultural selfishness shows up in our country's casual approach to commitment in relationships, too. We have become accustomed to self-serving relationships that turn out to be temporary and disposable. We selfishly blame our partner for the dissolution of our sacred union — "that relationship just wasn't good for me" — and move on to the next one. (Of course, there are cases where divorce is necessary and appropriate, but that's not my point here.)

Selfishness also shows up in our lack of appreciation for the people we're closest to — our parents, siblings, friends, colleagues, and pastors — those who have always been there for us. We find subtle ways of manipulating or blaming them for our own lack of responsibility, dragging them into our problems.

And, of course, selfishness shows up in our detached attitude and even coldheartedness toward the suffering of others, like the example of the homeless man. We give little of our empathy, time, or resources — because we're not directly affected.

But as we'll see in a few moments, while our giving greatly benefits the receiver, it also gives back to *us* in profound ways. We get instant results: a smile, a moment of

> *You're always going to be lonely and depressed if you think only about how you're feeling, how you look, how to color your hair. That's because the self is a deadend, ultimately boring. If you concentrate on that, God help you.*
> —KATHARINE HEPBURN

connection, the pleasure of seeing someone else blessed, and an exchange of heartfelt thanks. And afterward, we feel a thousand times better, *satisfied* as God intends us to be.

As the saying goes, "Look around and you'll be *distressed*. Look within and you'll be *depressed*. But if you look to God, you'll be at *rest*."

Why? It's because we were created by God to look up, to look out, and to give. As Jesus said, if you want to live the satisfied life, you have to deny selfishness and put your eyes on God and *others* (Matt. 10:37–39). And undoubtedly, giving is the greatest antidote for selfishness.

Selfishness is rooted in fear — the fear of losing what we have, the fear of not having enough, the fear of running out. If we want to overcome selfishness, we have to break out of the fear of losing what we have.

And the way to break out of that fear is to believe the promise that as we give, it will be given back to us.

If we truly believe this promise, this universal law of giving, we will never run out. We will never lose what we have. There will always be enough because of the miracle of giving.

So to live the invincible life that God intends for us, always remember these four words: ADD VALUE TO OTHERS. I can tell you that when you gauge what you can *contribute* to a situation, how you can add value, you will always be blessed and satisfied, with your happiness ever expanding.

> *Make it a rule...never to lie down at night without being able to say, "I have made one human being at least a little wiser, a little happier, or a little better this day.*
> —CHARLES KINGSLEY

Take the heroic example of Sandie Anderson, a Starbucks worker in Tacoma, Washington, who, last year, donated a kidney to a longtime customer, Annamarie Ausness. Why would she potentially jeopardize her own life to do this? "It just tugged at my heart," said Sandie, whose blood type matched the woman. "I told myself, *'If I can do something for her, I'm going to do it.'*"

How could Annamarie ever thank Sandie? "There are no words of thank you that would have been enough," said the grateful woman. "She gave me the gift of life."

TO GIVE IS TO RECEIVE

Everyone is familiar with the Scripture: "It is better to give than receive." But let's take a closer look at *why* it's better.

We've all experienced the pleasure that comes from making somebody *else* happy. That's it in a nutshell! You can see the look of joy, surprise, or appreciation in another person's eyes. And I'm not only talking about giving something *material*. It can be a compliment or a prayer. It can be concern, time, affection, humor, or insight—all gifts that "cost" you nothing.

I promise that when you live to give, you will experience the liberating awareness of true *abundance,* rather than scarcity. In fact, giving sets off a *chain reaction* inspiring others to give, too, which creates *a circle of giving.* What goes around comes back around a thousandfold. In this way, generosity is contagious, one kind act inspiring another.

I can also tell you that giving increases faith and trust in God. As His blessings unfold before you, you become more aware that God is at work in every area of your life.

It's the universal law: the more you give, the more you receive. As Jesus said in Luke 6:38, "Give, and it will be given to you. They will pour into your lap a good measure—pressed down, shaken together, and running over."

As we get older (and hopefully smarter), our favorite part of Christmas becomes the giving, not the receiving. Like so many others, it's the giving that gives me the most pleasure. Sadly, though, some people regard giving as an obligation rather than a pleasure. **True giving is an overflow of love.** The best-known verse in the Bible says it all: "For God so loved the world that he gave his one and only Son" (John 3:16).

Let's think about that. God gave. He demonstrated His love by giving.

If there were no giving, there would be no love. True love gives. It doesn't take. That's why I tell young people that premarital sex is really shallow. I tell ladies that "if that guy really loves you, he won't 'take' from you. He'll demonstrate his love by giving his life to you." Once a marital commitment is made, sex becomes a gift within that relationship, which is valuable, honorable, and truly satisfying.

> *If you wish to travel far and fast, travel light. Take off all your envies, jealousies, unforgiveness, selfishness and fears.*
> —CESARE PAVESE

Whether it's a material thing or an *act* of kindness, giving away *whatever* your gift is, is always an expression of love. In fact, **we must make giving a lifelong habit, one that can be cultivated.**

As a young boy, John D. Rockefeller (who would later become America's first billionaire) had always been taught by his mother to *tithe*— contributing a tenth of whatever he had to his church.

As he once said: "I had to begin work as a small boy to help support my mother. My first wages amounted to $1.50 per week. When I took this home to her, she told me that she would be happy if I would give a tenth of it to the Lord. I did, and from that week until this day, I have tithed every dollar God has entrusted to me. And I want to say, if I had not tithed the first dollar I made, I would not have tithed the first million dollars I made. Train up a child to tithe, and they will grow up to be faithful stewards of the Lord."

You might be saying, "Well, if I was a Rockefeller, I could *afford* to give!" But he did it when he had almost nothing. Ponder this: A recent Gallup Poll about highly affluent people considered a variety of theories about why such people had become so successful. Was it their education, family background, lucky breaks, or what? One fact that they all had in common was that 90 percent of these superachievers gave regularly and significantly to charity.

Those who have read the Bible are not surprised. God always multiplies what is given. The little boy who gave five loaves and two fish was part of the miracle that fed five thousand. After that miracle the little boy got twelve baskets full of bread in return for his gift.

When we talk about "tithing," I want to make it clear that it means much more than just giving money: It includes money, but at its core, it's *about honor.* By giving 10 percent to God, you're really saying: *God, you come first in my life. You were the first one to love me, to forgive me, to believe in me; therefore, you should be the first one to receive my money, my giving, and my heart.* That's what I mean by "honor." When you do this, giving has amazing power.

As it says in Malachi 3:10, when we honor God with our tithe, He will open the windows of Heaven and pour out a blessing—which could include joy, wisdom, ideas and so much more!

> Live to give, and have the nerve to serve, and you will never lack any good thing all the days of your life.

This blessing is God's gift that He wants each of us to experience. The word "blessing" itself is profoundly important and it appears in the Bible more than five hundred times. **God wants you to be blessed—which means *happy, fortunate, and empowered to succeed.*** And I can tell you that the number one way to *become blessed* is to give.

I like to refer to the great patriarch Abraham, who experienced the satisfaction of a life of giving. In Genesis 12:2, God told him, "I will bless you so that you will *be* a blessing." When Abraham discovered this secret to living the satisfied life, he became one of the most successful men in history. He was later described as a man whom the Lord had blessed "in every way" (Gen. 24:1).

There was a purpose for God's blessing in Abraham's life—so that he would be a blessing to others. And so it is in our lives. When we understand the purpose of God's blessing we will end up far better off. So **being on the "giving side" really translates as: be a blessing.** This becomes easy when you realize how precious people are to God.

I think we have all experienced the incredible feeling that comes from being a blessing. Giving really does make you happy.

In fact, a 2008 Harvard University study proved that "regardless of income level, people who spent money on others reported greater happiness, while those who spent more on themselves did not."

This only proves what the Scripture says: When you give, it shall be given to you again. God multiplies it back to you in more ways than one.

Scientists have even proven that being on the giving side creates a positive emotional punch, which, in turn, has a beneficial effect on physical health. Positive emotions enhance the immune system by increasing the body's number of T cells that resist disease; they release endorphins—the body's natural tranquilizers and painkillers—and they stimulate dilation of the blood vessels, which leads to a relaxed heart.

> *Giving is a very good criterion of a person's mental health. Generous people are rarely mentally ill people.*
> —DR. KARL A. MENNINGER

In fact, **when we perform an act of kindness or generosity, we get a**

"helper's high," a kind of euphoria, a warm glow in the chest and a sense of vitality that come from being simultaneously energized and calm.

A recent study proved that volunteering not only increases physical energy but can even lengthen our life span. University of Michigan researchers who studied 2,700 people for almost ten years found that men who regularly did volunteer work had death rates 2½ times lower than men of the same age who didn't.

And so it is that giving has amazing power, leading to an invincible spirit and a satisfied, healthy life.

BECOMING A GIVER

There were several men in the locker room of a private club, taking showers and getting dressed after an afternoon of exercise. Suddenly a cell phone, which was on one of the benches, rings. A man picks it up and the following conversation ensues:

"Hello?"

"Honey, it's me."

"Sugar!"

"Are you at the club?"

"Yes."

"Great! I am at the mall two blocks from where you are. I saw a beautiful mink coat...it is absolutely gorgeous! Can I buy it?"

"What's the price?"

"Only five thousand."

"Well, okay, go ahead and get it, if you like it that much..."

"Uh, and I also stopped by the Mercedes dealership and saw the latest models. I saw one I really liked. I spoke with the salesman and he gave me a really good price...and since we need to exchange the BMW that we bought last year—"

"What price did he quote you?"

"Only ninety thousand..."

"Okay, but for that price I want it with all the options."

"Okay, sweetie...thanks! I'll see you later! I love you!"

The man ends the call and raises his hand up, holding the phone in the air, asking to all those present: "Does anyone know who this phone belongs to?"

It's amazing how generous we can be with someone *else's* stuff, right? Well, this is the real key to stepping over into the giving side. We need to realize that the good we have in life is all a *gift* from God. It's not our own. It came from Him. We are not the owners; rather we are the stewards of these "things." And we are measured by what we *do* with what God has given us stewardship over.

We free ourselves from selfishness when we recognize *it's not our stuff*! Everything we have belongs to the true Creator and Maker of all things— God. When we realize this, we are no longer so attached to what we own or so self-centered, which makes the act of giving a whole lot easier.

Then, giving becomes a *responsibility*—a "response" to His "ability."

So develop a conscious desire to help and love others unconditionally. Start with your family, your church, and your friends. Then move beyond your inner circle, extending yourself to help your community or a stranger. It's so easy to do. See an opportunity and seize it. Give your time. Give understanding. Give love. Give appreciation. Give a listening ear. Give encouragement or hope. Give a smile.

You won't believe how good you're going to feel, knowing you're making a difference. There are so many ways you can benefit others. Why wait until later?

Start giving now without expectation of return from the one you gave to! Certainly, you should expect to receive back from God; but don't wait for the person you gave to give back to you. When you do, it's really not a gift. It's a trade.

Perhaps you remember the film *Schindler's List,* which told the incredible story of Oskar Schindler, a wealthy German industrialist who saved the lives of nearly 1,200 Jews during the Holocaust by having them work in his ammunitions factories. He moved mountains with his charm and persuasiveness to protect them. Yet, at the story's end, Schindler (played by Liam Neeson) has an epiphany, realizing that he could have done even *more* to save the lives of others. He was a hero, and a true giver, and he realized that *the giving in life will always be infinitely more valuable than merely having possessions.*

Remember, give and it shall be given to you. So get on the "solution" rather than the "problem" side of life. Giving is contagious. It serves humanity. It demonstrates true love. It satisfies a deep need in our lives. And it honors God.

Give and it will be given back to you in amazing and miraculous ways. When you're on the giving side, you're on *God's* side—the winning side—where the satisfied life awaits you.

Part IV

SMILE AT
THE FUTURE

Secret #14

Don't Be Afraid of the Dark

STEPPING INTO THE LIGHT THAT
DISSOLVES ALL FEAR

> *The best remedy for those who are afraid, lonely or unhappy is to go*
> *outside, somewhere where they can be quiet, alone with the heavens,*
> *nature and God.*
>
> —ANNE FRANK

One night the little boy who had always been afraid of the dark was helping his mother around the house. Since they were living on a farm near the woods, there were always sounds of the forest nearby, which scared the five-year-old.

That evening, working industriously to get everything "spic and span," his mother told him to go out onto the back porch and bring her the broom. His eyes instantly got wider. He felt so afraid. So he breathlessly turned to her and said: "Mama, I don't want to go out there—it's dark."

She smiled reassuringly, went over to him, and gently stroked his forehead, then told him: "You don't have to be afraid of the dark, darling. Jesus is out there—and He'll look after you. *He* will protect you."

The hesitant boy looked at his mom with a serious expression: "Are you *sure* He's out there, Mama?"

And with absolute conviction she answered, "Yes, darling, I *am* sure. He is *everywhere* and He's always ready to help you in your time of need."

The boy mulled this over for about a minute, walked reluctantly to the back door, cracked it open just a little bit, and stuck only his hand outside, peering into the darkness.

Then he yelled out: "Jesus! If you're out there—would you hand me the broom?!"

IN THE SILENT DARKNESS OF NIGHT

Have you ever had a moment or a season of *uncertainty* and *discouragement* in your life, when it was "pitch black outside," when darkness surrounded you? Maybe it felt like you were never going to get out of the situation that you were in.

We all face frightening times when we don't know what to do or where to turn. There seems to be no light, no answer, and no peace. Dark moments may turn into dark months; and it may eventually feel as if we are surrounded by a black cloud from which we can never escape.

Maybe you felt like Joseph in the Bible, stripped of his multi-colored coat and thrown by his jealous brothers into a dark pit, where it seemed as if all hope was lost. The very people that he had counted on the most had turned their back on him and betrayed him. So there he was, at the bottom of that pit, in darkness.

Folks, **every one of us has had a Joseph moment**—a too-afraid-to-go-outside-to-get-the-broom moment. In such times we want somebody to turn the light on and rescue us from fear and uncertainty.

In my life I've sure had my share of dark moments. One, in particular, stands out. A trusted confidant turned on me, twisting everything I said and everything I had done for him around—using it against me. Sound familiar? We've probably all experienced that vulnerable moment when we share something in confidence with someone, knowing that only in that context can it be understood; in any other situation it could damage you or someone else. It's one thing to have an enemy say something against you; it's altogether another thing to have a friend do it.

Do I regret confiding in him? Actually no, because this betrayal gave birth to something special in my life and ministry. With darkness and discouragement all around, I heard God tell me, "Find someone hurting more than you, and heal *them*."

It was then that I traveled to Africa, to minister to thousands of orphans whose suffering made my own situation pale in comparison. My trip gave birth to one of the most important outreaches we have ever undertaken — The Food for Life World Outreach, a ministry that feeds thousands of children every day, bringing light to their dark world and showing them the love of a Heavenly Father, one who will never leave or forsake them.

NOTHING NEW TO GOD

When I speak of "darkness," I'm referring to times of uncertainty and discouragement, yes; but I'm also speaking about those moments when the warmth of God's presence and the answer we need seem miles away. There are seasons of our lives when darkness falls, when we're spiritually cold or we've lost our bearings.

The things we've trusted in can no longer be believed. The people that we looked up to for confidence and comfort either don't understand us or seem distant from us. We may feel vulnerable, lonely, confused, or even hopeless. All these feelings gang up on us, and they make us afraid.

Friends, as has often been said, **fear is crouching at the door in times of darkness — trying to steal from us the faith, hope, and love that will never fail.**

The letters of the word itself say it all: *F*(alse) *E*(xpectations) *A*(ppearing) *R*(eal.) We envision the worst, and expect it. This painful emotion kills pleasure and gratitude. It blocks love. And it negates our ability to give.

Fear makes us surrender. We settle for less than we deserve, and stay safely in the background of life, never living up to our true potentials. And as we saw in the "Be Healed" chapter, a fear is a mighty enemy — a *mentality of failure* that brings much pain.

We're afraid that we're *not* enough or that we won't *have* enough. We're afraid that we'll be rejected or unloved, that something bad will happen to our children, or that our health will fail, or that God won't come through for us. And we're afraid of death. You name it — people are afraid of it!

But the good news today is that darkness is nothing new to God.

As the Bible shows us, He's faced it *many* times and masters it *every* time. **In fact, God thrives in dark times.** In the beginning of creation, Genesis 1:2 says, "Darkness covered the face of the deep." This didn't stop God for calling for light. It didn't stop God from creating the world He dreamed of. And it's not going to stop you, either.

We all know the words of Psalm 23:4 and must remember them: "Though I walk through the valley of the shadow of death, I will fear no evil: for thou art with me; thy rod and thy staff, they comfort me."

Notice that the words don't say: "I'm not going to fear this dark hour because *it might not last too long*" or "*I'm getting out of it soon!*" We have to have faith that we can endure the midnight hour for as long as it takes, because **God is with us.**

Remember Daniel's friends in the Bible—Shadrach, Meshach, and Abednego who refused to bow down and worship the gold statue of the king? As punishment they're thrown into a fiery furnace; yet they emerge from it unscathed, without even a hair on their heads singed. When King Nebuchadnezzar looked into the pit, he saw not three men, but four, the fourth being the *Son of God*. They couldn't avoid the fire, but with God's presence in their midst, they could emerge from it *unharmed*.

Nor can *we* avoid fiery trials and adversity. But with God's help, we can be delivered from them. **He always shows up in troubling times.** So don't be afraid of the dark.

Not long ago, a dear friend of mine, Oral Roberts, founder and chancellor of Oral Roberts University, was experiencing one of life's darkest moments. His school, burdened by nearly $50 million in debt, was, he told me, just a few months away from closing its doors for good. Making matters worse, his organization had come under intense fire, enduring prolonged media scrutiny over financial matters. But Dr. Roberts, who never faced a problem without praying and planting good seeds, trusted God in this moment of great uncertainty. He told me he faced that dark cloud in the eye and said, "I've done what I can do. Now let's watch and see what God will do."

And during this trying time, when all hope seemed to be gone, his phone rang. A generous and concerned friend called and asked Dr. Roberts if he could use $70 million for the school! (Who couldn't use that?!) Not only did the gift pay off the debt, but an additional substantial gift went toward upgrading the school even beyond the excellent status it had known in the past, keeping the university on solid ground for decades to come.

What was most amazing about this? The donor would never have known about the need and made the call if the dark hour of adversity and media attention had not occurred.

So instead of avoiding or hiding from the "dark," or trying to desperately find the light switch, we need to *embrace* the midnight hour we face. This isn't a tacit acceptance or con-sent to ongoing darkness, but it's your ability to see it as the stage being set for God to present His most stunning performance in your life. This means that even in your moment of greatest uncertainty, fear, and confusion, God is going to do for you what you cannot do for yourself.

> God presents His most stunning performances in our darkest moments. Trust Him.

In my own life there have been many times when I would be sitting at my desk on a Saturday night, preparing for a sermon. The light in the room would be bright. And I would have my Bible and notes out, the computer turned on, the concordance by my side studying feverously—and guess what? I would sit there for hours and I wouldn't hear a thing. And I'd pray: *Lord, I want to share your word. What can I share that will truly help others?*

Guess what happened? Nothing! Getting no answer, oftentimes in frustration I'd tell myself: *Fine, I'm going to bed. If I don't have anything to say tomorrow, that's your problem, Lord.*

So I'd turn the light off, get into bed, put my head on the pillow, and as soon as silence enveloped me, as soon as all the books were closed, I sud-denly began to hear the voice of God. Although I would want to write it all down, I didn't dare turn the light on and ruin the moment. It's often in times of darkness that His faintest light can be discerned and appreciated.

So even in those moments of grave doubt, when it seems there's nothing to light the way, God's still, small voice will speak to us. **The light of His truth will awaken our hearts and illuminate our minds, because we're *embracing* the darkness, not running away from it.**

There's an incredible verse in Exodus 20:21. It says, "The people stood afar off, and Moses drew near unto the thick darkness where God was." Think about that. Moses drew near to the darkness *WHERE GOD WAS*. God's not afraid of the dark, and so neither should we. He is *omnipresent*, meaning He is everywhere all the time. He is in your darkest moment, ready to light the path.

What I'm saying is that no matter how dark it gets—whether it's a financial storm, a divorce, a bout with sickness—the dawn always comes. Psalm 30:5 says: "Weeping may last in the night, but joy comes in the morning."

So, **embracing the dark means we're willing to face our midnight hour with confidence that God will be there to show us the way**. We're believing even when we don't understand. We're following His voice in the night. And most of all, we're letting go, instead of trying to figure it all out—trusting that the light will come in our hour of need.

THE COMFORT OF DARKNESS

Don't be afraid of the dark, folks, because God is there in the midst of it, which is where He shines the brightest. In fact, we can often derive the most benefit from God's Word when it's darkest. After all, when the lights are all on or when the sun is shining bright, turning on yet *another* light isn't going to help. That's because the light that you turn on is being swallowed up by the light that already exists. But when it's dark, God's light will guide you every time.

So if you're feeling doubtful, fearful, unsure of what to do or where to go, reverse the old maxim "Don't just sit there, *do* something." I say: "Don't just do something, *sit* there!"

It's been said that it's darkest before the dawn. So if you're facing a dark moment, be encouraged. The light is coming!

Why? It's because sometimes the darkness is actually a gift. **In your weakest and most vulnerable moment, when you're feeling most uncertain and afraid, God is**

actually *hiding you, protecting you* **from the enemy or obstacle that could injure you.** He's wisely enveloped a cloud of darkness around you to make you stealth and invisible. And He will only remove that dark covering and put you back into the "light" once you're strong enough to reengage and fight the battle of life—to fight the fight of faith.

Maybe you're not yet ready to resolve a deep conflict or move on to the next step—letting go of something in your life that no longer serves you. Sure, you might feel depressed or forsaken, discouraged or rejected, but remember: *rejection may be God's protection.* Just as His hand will guide you through that challenging hour, He will guide you into the light. And you will emerge from it victorious, in all God's glory. As it says in Proverbs 4:18, "The path of the righteousness is like a light of dawn and it grows brighter and brighter until the full day."

Take comfort in uncertain times. Pause. Rest. Walk by faith—not by sight. Don't panic or freak out in times of doubt. And don't be consumed with having to turn on the light immediately. Isaiah 12 tells us what to do: "I will trust and not be afraid." Notice the progression of this verse. First he says, "I will trust." This is an act of the will, a choice to trust God even in the midst of darkness and uncertainty. Then he gives us the result: I will "not be afraid."

So don't fight for the light. Learn to trust that He is there. As it says in Hebrews 13:5, " '*I will never leave you nor forsake you.*' " He will not relax his hold on us. We take His hand by following His words: "Your word is a lamp to my feet and a light to my path."

As we've seen, both *fear* and *uncertainty* can be a way of *protecting* us and *challenging* us to grow. Yet so many of us have been programmed to believe that uncertainty is a bad thing. What we must remember is that, in our dark times, though we may not see Him, God is always present. Psalm 46:1 says, "He is *an ever-present* help in a time of need." What a comfort to know this. **When I feel Him—and even when I don't—He still IS. When I see His hand in my life and when I don't, His Hand is still on me!**

I always believe that God's hand is protecting my entire family. My children, for example, sleep in rooms not very far from mine. So whether the light is on or it's pitch dark, they know that their safety is assured. Why? It's because I am still "there," whether they actually see me or not.

Sometimes, though, even as adults we often forget that we are safe. I can remember hearing the voice of God one night when I was feeling especially afraid and uncertain, and beginning to believe that perhaps He had forsaken me.

Why did I feel that way? Well, Satan is clever at making us fear that our mistakes and shortcomings disqualify us from experiencing God's best for our lives. But in that moment, I heard these words: *"Son, I have not taken my hand off you, and I never will. You may feel as if you're lost, but I can assure you, I am with you and I will never let you go. We're going to walk through this together."*

So trust in God. And remember: uncertainty is the soil in which light can grow. We sometimes have to go through the discomfort of *not knowing* what to do next to get to that place of surrender to God.

THE KEYS TO FINDING LIGHT IN DARKNESS

How can we ultimately heal our deepest fears when darkness envelops us? What will give us the strength to turn fear and doubt into hope, courage, and optimism? Here are some keys to doing it.

1. *Walk by Faith, Not by Sight.* In times of doubt, first and foremost, we need to exercise faith. Remember: Fear comes when we demand that we see with our *physical* eyes something that can only be seen with our *spiritual* eyes. Faith sees what our natural eyes cannot see, allowing us a glimpse of a world of light—God's world. In this way, faith is

simply believing God's promises regardless of how it *looks*. Psalm 119 says, "The entrance of His Word brings light." So, as we allow God's Word to act as our eyes (much like a Seeing Eye dog), we will not only be safe, but we will arrive at the destination God intends.

I've been referring to times of darkness as times of uncertainty. That's why "faith" is the remedy, for Hebrews 11:1 says, "Faith is the assurance of things hoped for." One translation says, "Faith is being certain of what we cannot see." This kind of faith drives out fear no matter how dark the moment.

Where does such faith come from? The Bible says it comes from hearing the promises of God. Indeed, as you listen with the "ears" of your heart, you'll begin to see with the "eyes" of your soul, and the darkness will soon be swallowed up by the light of His Word.

2. *Find Your Anchor.* **Establish an anchor**—a dependable, stable, secure base that you can hold on to, one that keeps you firmly planted, no matter what winds or storms may come. It's amazing to think that the anchor of a naval ship weighs over forty thousand pounds! When that anchor drops, nothing else can move. With God as your anchor, you won't be blown out to sea or off course, no matter how troubling the storm is. And while the anchor of a ship reaches down to the bottom of the sea, the anchor of our soul reaches up into Heaven itself and gives us our bearings. David asks himself in Psalm 42:5, "Why are you downcast, O my soul?" Then he answers his own question: "Put your hope in God." In other words, we get downcast and depressed when our hope is placed in anything other than God Himself. Get anchored in His love, and watch Him work!

3. *Reach Out.* **One of the great remedies for dark and uncertain moments in life is helping someone *else* out of their dark hour.** No matter how bad it may be for you, there's always someone else

continued

out there who is struggling even more. Find a hurt and heal it. Find a need and meet it. You'll be amazed at the LIGHT that goes into your own soul when you bring comfort to "the least of these," as Jesus put it. I also like what Isaiah said in 58:10: "When you give to the hurting and share what you have with the suffering, then YOUR light will break forth like the dawn." So don't be so introspective and focused on yourself; reach out and help somebody else who is hurting and broken. Minister to them. Maximize every talent and ability at your command, using it in the service of others. You'll discover that you also illuminate your own soul.

4. *Talk* to *the Problem, Not* about *It:* As we've seen throughout the book, **what you say to yourself and *how* you say it has much to do with turning darkness to light.** Our words have power! As it says in Proverbs 18:21, "Death and life are in the power of the tongue." The words we say have power over us and influence every aspect of our emotional and physical lives.

Too many times we use a torrent of words, going on and on about our "problem." Obsessing on it can actually make it worse. The irony is, however much we talk about it, nothing ever seems to change. Still, we believe that *telling* someone else all about it will somehow help. Most people don't have the energy or time to help us anyway.

Mark 11:23 says: "You say *to* this mountain, be removed and cast into the sea. And it will obey you." Notice it says "you" and "to." *You* have to say it—and you have to talk *to* the problem, not *about* it.

Maybe your "mountain" is depression, worry, or your spouse. Talk to it and command it never to return!—except, of course, in the case of your spouse.

5. *Close the Door to the Enemy.* When under attack, a submarine dives underwater, battening down the hatches, protecting itself by

submerging into the deep, dark waters below. Likewise, when we're under "attack"—deeply doubting, confused, or afraid—this is the time we must protect ourselves, keeping at bay people, places, and things that are not our allies.

So your moment of uncertainty and fear is a calling to dive deeper with God. In Luke 5, when the disciples were fishing, they had caught nothing all night. When Jesus showed up in their boat, He said: "Launch out into the deep and let down your nets." That's where the fish were. So many people remain shallow in their journey with God, and never experience the depth of His love and care. Dive down into His promises. Dive down into praise and worship; set out into the deeper walk with God, where your enemy can't reach you!

Following these simple steps, God will turn your darkest hour into light. Midnight will become morning. Sadness will become gladness.

How? By trusting in Him to guide you through it all.

There are many definitions of trust in dark times, but I can't think of many better examples than the story of blind skiers before the 1988 Winter Olympics being trained for slalom skiing—impossible as that sounds. How did it work?

A legally blind skier was paired up with a sighted one, and together they created a series of vocal cues and signals that allowed them to race down the hill together. Skiing right beside the blind partner, the sighted skier would shout, "Right" and "Left" at various points. As the blind skiers responded to the command, they were able to handle the course and cross the finish line.

How did this work so effectively? The blind skier had to put his *total* trust entirely in the hands of his partner. He depended solely on the sighted skier's word, it was either complete trust or catastrophe.

In our world we are often "blind" about what course to take and what to do in our midnight hour. We must rely on the promises of the only ONE who is truly sighted — God Himself. His words give us the direction we need to finish the course.

He is our true anchor. He is our sight — and light — in the midst of darkness. So if you don't feel enough strength to carry yourself, know that you *will* be carried.

A man had a dream one night in which he saw two sets of footprints in the sand, both tracing the path of his life. One set was his; the other God's.

> *God is light; in him there is no darkness at all.* —1 JOHN 1:5

And as the dream progressed, he noticed that at the most difficult times of his life, when things were the worst, one set of footprints disappeared.

So he asked: "Lord, how could You have left me in times when I needed You most? Why did You forsake me?" And the Lord calmly replied, "My child, I have always been with you. When you saw just one set of footprints, it was then that I *carried* you."

And so, though you may face hard times and great adversity, *you're not alone,* for God is always there to support and carry you, even though you may not feel it.

He knows the dark hour that you might be having or may yet come up against — the disappointments, the temptations, the moments of trouble and vulnerability. And He is with you. According to His will, you are, and will forever be, safe and secure — a beloved child of light, not darkness.

Secret #15

Live in the Moment

THE SECRET OF THE CONTENTED LIFE

Yesterday is history. Tomorrow is a mystery. And today? Today is a gift.
That's why we call it the present.

—Babatunde Olatunji

This is the day the Lord has made, I will rejoice and be glad in it.

—Ps. 118:24

Freeze. Slow down. Stop everything.

Just for a second, put aside every stray thought, worry, or care.

Right now, in this moment, where are you? What do you see?
What are you feeling?

Are you relaxed or tense? Warm or cool?

And as you're reading these words, are you fully concentrated
and curious — or is your mind beginning to wander?

Perhaps you're anxious or worried about something coming up in
the future; or maybe you're focused on the past — filled with
regret.

Distracted by such thoughts, as we often are, how frequently do
we miss the blessing of the present moment?

On a recent trip to New York, while passing through Central Park on
a warm, sunny afternoon, I decided to sit down on a bench and relax for
a few minutes.

Caught up, I must confess, in people watching, I was struck by the sharp contrast between two people I saw.

One young man came by, looking relaxed and carefree. Smiling as he strolled down the winding path toward me, he was obviously enjoying the parade of joggers, mothers with babies, and horse-drawn carriages.

He stopped at a vendor's cart, bought a pretzel, then walked down to the pond, where he began sharing his lunch with the ducks. (Those ducks have it made, don't they? Free food, swimming all day long, able to fly — plus problems roll off them like water off their *own* backs!)

Close by, I also observed a young woman all dressed up who came rushing into the park, talking furiously into her cell phone, her head down. She was all business — tense and distracted — as she walked over to a shady spot and sat down on a bench. Then she pulled out a plastic container, and as she ate a salad quickly, she got back on the phone and started barking out orders to some poor soul on the other end. When a dog came by wagging his tail, she gave him a stare that made him run off with his tail between his legs! I doubt she even noticed that there was a newborn baby a few feet away, smiling up at her from the carriage. Finishing her salad, she made one more phone call and dashed out of the park. She was the picture of discontent.

TAKE CARE OF *TODAY*

While the man I saw was actually "*in*" the park, the woman, like so many of us, was merely "*at*" the park, *absent* in the moment and preoccupied by her thoughts. She missed the pond, the ducks, the baby, the scent of the trees, and the sun!

Like that woman, how many people find it almost impossible to relax and enjoy the moment? Instead, we get lost in our thoughts, either living in *anticipation* of the future (worrying about

> How can we be content in this moment when we're actually somewhere else?

what *might* happen) or living in *reflection* of the past (remembering what *did* happen).

We base our happiness on looking *forward* (to the future time when everything will finally be *right*) and our unhappiness on looking *backward* (to the time when things went *wrong*). Sure, our reflections of the past are sometimes happy, but often they're tinged or heavily overlaid with regret and sadness.

When we are tormented by the past and anxious about the future, the *present moment* is all but lost or ignored. **Using this comparison only in a symbolic sense, just as Jesus died on the cross between two thieves, we "crucify" ourselves between the two thieves of *yesterday* and *tomorrow*, robbing us of our today!**

So we wind up feeling burned-out and disillusioned—living on a skimpy diet of promises about the future made to those we care most about. We tell them that we'll have time *later on*—when conditions are just right. But they never are. There's always *something* that needs fixing at home, finishing at work, or replenishing at the bank. In fact, we're so absorbed in our worries, fears, hopes, and expectations—that we miss out on the only life we really have, the one happening right *here,* right *now.*

I'm no exception. In my own life I've found that every time I focus on something past or future, I'm robbed of the moment God wants me to enjoy.

Recently, while sitting around the kitchen chatting with my kids, I was beginning to feel overwhelmed by the flurry of events, meetings, and responsibilities I had to deal with over the next few days. I was looking at one of my sons in a daze, not hearing a thing he was saying, when I suddenly stopped myself, took a deep breath, and decided tomorrow is not going to rob me of the joy of my kids.

Isn't it true that we're often so consumed with trying to make our futures better that we don't appreciate what God is trying to do in our "now"?

We've got to stop waiting for the *perfect conditions* to be fully engaged in our lives. In just a few moments, I'm going to give you eight simple steps to living the contented life in the here and now—bringing God's blessings and true satisfaction into your life, so that you can live it as He intended it.

I tell people all the time that whether they're unhappy with their marriage, their career, or their financial condition that the key to overcoming it is living fully in the moment.

A recent survey—admittedly quite unscientific, since it was on the *Family Feud*—asked viewers, on a scale of one to ten, "how worried are you about the future?" The overwhelming majority answered ten (which was the most worried)! I wonder how true that is. So many of us lose ourselves in daydreams (or nightmares), feeling anxious or afraid. People get caught up in predictions of doom and gloom, their negative thoughts circling around and around in their heads.

What do we most commonly fear? It's that we'll lose what we *have* or not get what we *want.*

So worry lives in the background of our lives, like a radio channel that never stops playing. I can tell you that if you worry about what might be, and wonder what might have been, you will ignore what *is.* The result is discontentment, frustration, stress, and often hypertension. Sure, we intellectually know that the past is *gone,* and that the future isn't here. But that doesn't stop us from *living in* both!

How often do we waste countless hours anticipating that an event or experience is going to be *better* or *worse* than it actually turns out to be? Later on, we reflect on how disappointed we are that it *wasn't* what we hoped for. Why is it like this? It's because we don't know the secret to *inward contentment.*

> ꭈ Living in the now is the ability to enjoy the present moment, the one you're actually in—not the moments you were in, or the ones that you aren't in yet.

"In-the-moment" living is our ability to be completely present and undistracted, to take in, enjoy, and appreciate what's happening *right here, right now.* When we do this, our attachment to the past and future ends. And our worry and anxiety fade away.

In Matthew 6:27, Jesus said, "Who of you by worrying can add a single hour to his life?"

What was his remedy for the anxiety that grips all of us? He said, "Look at the birds of the air and the lilies of the field." What did he mean? I think he was saying: *"Go outside and look at what I made. Pause—and enjoy the beauty of creation. Get some fresh air and enjoy what God made."*

Living this way stops your mind from bombarding you with regret and worry. It's a *mind-set* that refuses to allow the past or future to contaminate it.

No words say it better than Matthew 6:34: **"Therefore do not worry about tomorrow, for tomorrow will worry about itself. Each day has enough trouble of its own."**

So let's take care of *today*—immerse ourselves in it—and tomorrow will take care of itself.

NO ORDINARY MOMENTS

Observe what happens when you're totally engrossed or consumed by *anything*. Let's say you're watching a gripping, suspenseful movie. Have you ever noticed that, for that space of two hours, all your problems disappear? Time flies. Worries and regrets vanish. Anger and resentments are forgotten. The tension of the day melts away. You experience total relief from it *all*.

How does this happen? It's not magic. It's because if you're completely *immersed* in the experience at hand, you're *focused* on something other than your pain. You're completely *"there"*—your mind is contented and at peace.

Have the actual circumstances of your life changed?

No, but you're so fully present in the moment that you can enjoy yourself and disengage from worries. You get to relax. Life becomes less of a struggle and more of a pleasure. Your body calms down. There's an ease and a flow. You're no longer paralyzed or imprisoned by thoughts of the past or future.

But afterward, when you leave that movie, you also leave that *peace* behind. You think, *Okay, back to the real world.* But the so-called real world is actually waiting for you to carry that peace right into it. *Don't leave it in the theater.* Capture that feeling and let it be an example of how to delight in the present moment. I can tell you that an enjoyed moment will turn into an enjoyed hour, day, week, and ultimately a LIFE fully appreciated and thoroughly savored.

God meant us to live this way. In fact, He is always described as *omnipresent*—not omni-*past* or omni-*future*. He is present. He is here now. He is with you. He lives in the now and He wants to bring you into it.

You can experience His blessing in virtually anything you do. It can be savoring a succulent orange on a hot summer morning; reading a good book out on the porch with a soft breeze against you; feeling invigorated shooting hoops—and sinking most of them!—seeing the pleasure in the eyes of your toddler or grandchild when he or she climbs onto

> I got the blues thinking of the future, so I left off and made some marmalade. It's amazing how it cheers one up to shred oranges and scrub the floor.
> —D. H. LAWRENCE

your lap to give you a big hug; feeling drawn to God's Word while praying in church and lifted up by the sounds of the choir; or simply lying on the beach, lulled to sleep by the sound of the tide. In each and every case, using all your senses, you're able to capture the richness of the world around you.

Friends, *there are no ordinary moments.* As a member of my church put it, sharing his experience of mowing the grass: "Instead of being wrapped up in my head—worrying about the future—I began enjoying the sun, the breeze, the time to myself, the smell of the grass, the feel of exercise, and my sense of accomplishment. This left me with a sense of peace, allowing me to actually enjoy an 'ordinary' moment I would otherwise have missed."

Such moments aren't *ordinary;* they're *extraordinary.* At least they can be. Each of them is precious, and you won't ever miss them if you're fully present and connected to God's world.

You may think, "Life is too challenging to be able to stop and smell the roses. That's too idyllic." O Contraire! It is, in fact, the capturing and maximizing of these moments that empower you with the

energy, creativity and hope you need—to face your everyday trials and responsibilities with the winning edge and conquering spirit!

Unfortunately for so many people, their life with God is consumed with what they *don't* have, what they haven't done right, or how they might *escape* their present trial, rather than just walking with God in the cool of the day as He originally intended (Genesis 3:8). That's the kind of relationship that Adam and Eve had in the Garden of Eden before they took their eyes off what they already had, and focused on what they didn't have.

BROKEN FOCUS

As we've seen in our grown-up lives, **our pleasure in the moment is often obliterated by the weight of our own thoughts**—the mentalities of failure we talked about in the fourth chapter. As we learned, all negative emotions come from a sense of *powerlessness*. When we feel powerless over our *past*, we feel guilt and regret; when we feel powerless over our *future*, we feel anxious and afraid; and when we feel powerless over our *present*, we feel sad and depressed.

In order to overcome the sense of powerlessness, we need to realize what we have right now. The Bible says in 2 Timothy 1:7 "God has not given us a spirit of fear, but of power, love and a sound mind." These things we have right now. And we need to enjoy them.

There's an amazing passage of Scripture in Philemon 1:6, "Our faith becomes effective as we acknowledge and appreciate what is already ours..."

Indeed, *this is the key to the satisfied life—recognizing what you already have and enjoying it in the moment God has given*. It's the ability to focus NOW on what God has already given you, which will propel you into the abundant life that He has created for you.

So what robs us of all this God-given power? It's becom-

> When one door closes, another door opens; but we often look so long and so regretfully upon the closed door, that we do not see the one which has opened for us.
>
> —ALEXANDER GRAHAM BELL

ing apathetic or sidetracked in the midst of relatively good and blessed lives. Indeed, it's amazing what someone will do when they *lose focus* and get out of the now.

For example, how many of us have ever been on a crowded airplane, traveling in coach? (I'm convinced those seats are made for stick figures, not real people!) Maybe you've been stuck between a crying baby and a two-hundred-pounder! We start thinking: *I wish I were in first class. This is just miserable.* So rather than the happy anticipation of our destination—we begin resenting what we don't have.

It's the same thing as the person you know who always resents the weather. On a warm summer day he complains about the heat. On a fall day it's too windy. In spring it's too rainy. In winter it's too cold. He's never satisfied.

Likewise, we frequently can never enjoy and treasure what we *do have* because we're so focused on the job or the spouse we don't have. I can tell you that the satisfied life will always elude the grasp of anyone who is looking *outward*. This broken focus is the antithesis of *inward contentment*.

The secret to turning a broken focus into 20/20 vision is being grateful for what you *do* have. It's right in front of you, if only you'll take the time to see it.

The great prophet Elisha and his servant were completely surrounded by an enemy army in 2 Kings 6. His servant was afraid and panicking: "What are we going to do, Elisha?" Notice what Elisha prayed for at that moment: "Lord, OPEN THE EYES of my servant, and **let him see** that there are more for us than those against us." At that moment the Lord opened his eyes, "and he saw and behold, the mountain was full of horses and CHARIOTS OF FIRE around Elisha!"

Notice, he didn't pray for more angels. He didn't pray for more help. He prayed for the man's eyes to be *opened* to what was already there!

This is such a powerful secret to the invincible and satisfied life.

> *The best thing about the future is that it comes only one day at a time.*
> —ABRAHAM LINCOLN

Although we're not likely to be surrounded by enemy armies in our lives today, we do find ourselves on a different kind of battlefield, don't we? We become alarmed by the "enemies" around us. Whether our challenge is financial, physical or emotional, we need to open our eyes to what is "for" us, right now. This is the secret to overcoming whatever is "against" us. Let's not forfeit the good in this moment for the potential good that we hope to feel or enjoy later in life, once our problems are solved. I used to always think, "If I can just get through this issue, life is going to be great." But as soon as I got through it, another "issue" arose. Sound familiar? Let's find the great in life, right now! For example, how many parents become impatient with their children, looking forward to the day they'll grow up and get on with their own lives, only to later regret their absence when they're gone? In fact, the number one regret most people have is that they didn't fully enjoy or appreciate the people and the goodness that filled their lives—at the moment it was happening!

EIGHT SIMPLE STEPS TO LIVING IN THE MOMENT

As we've seen, living in the moment (and being grateful for it) is the route to contentment and the satisfied life. But as we know, we tend to revert to replaying the past or feeling anxious about the future. In fact, we saw in the "Be Still" chapter that the present moment is frequently hijacked by a high level of distractibility in our lives.

As we said, our cell phones, e-mails, faxes, voice mails, pagers, and BlackBerries are continually *interrupting* the moment at hand. I'm sure you remember the story about the man who even looks at his BlackBerry while in bed with his wife!

Just turning off our machines isn't enough, though, to

> *Do not go where the path may lead; go instead where there is no path and leave a trail.*
> —Ralph Waldo Emerson

transport us into the present and keep us there. We need to use some of those tools I told you about at the start of the book, focusing our attention on redirecting our restless minds and hearts back into the present. Here's how:

1. *Live on Purpose.* We have to stop drifting in life, being continually *distracted* and living at *cross-purposes*. If we're playing with our kids, we feel the gnawing guilt that tells us we should be cleaning. Then we start cleaning and we feel we should be updating our résumé. While we're at the computer doing that, we're distracted by a TV show. We're constantly either disengaging or second-guessing ourselves, and the second guess is usually the wrong one. Pour yourself into whatever you're doing. And remember: **You can only be in one place at a time**. So be aware and alert to what's going on around you—and don't be like the guy who was out hunting in the woods when his buddy suddenly clutched his chest and fell to the ground. Immediately he calls 911 on his cell phone. "I think my friend is dead," he tells the operator. "It might be a heart attack."

"Try to stay calm," the operator says. "I'll notify the forest ranger and then I'll stay on the phone with you until help arrives."

"Thank you," the man said. "What should I do now?"

"Well, first, we need to make sure he's really dead," the operator said.

There's a long pause, and then a shot is heard.

The man gets back on the phone. "Okay, now what?"

You see the pressures of the moment often cloud our clear thinking and purpose.

Folks, live on purpose in everything you do—right at the moment you're doing it. There's power in such purpose. Don't allow outside distractions or being superbusy to pull you away from the moment. Multitasking isn't all it's cracked up to be. Although people sometimes admire us when we're insanely busy (physically doing one thing, mentally doing five others), it really isn't conducive for being *in the moment*. So turn off those machines. Slow down. Calm down. Do one thing at a time. Instead of living with a broken attention span, live with directed focus—and on purpose.

2. *Maximize Today.* It's *God's* job to make the day, but it's *our* job to make the most of it! In this sense, joy is a decision. You make the choice to rejoice! An Eskimo proverb wisely says, "Tomorrow is ashes, yesterday is wood. Only today does the fire burn brightly." So as you go through your day, take note of the *good* in it. And make it better. Sure, you might have obligations that weigh on you, but find the silver lining, something to laugh at or be happy about. Take pleasure in everything you do — and people will take pleasure in you.

Joy is like fuel. You have to *re*joice, just as you have to *re*fuel. Stop waiting for a feeling of happiness to arrive. You don't wait until you "feel" like getting gas, do you? You know that in order to get to your destination, you have to refuel. It's a decision. In the same way, to get to the destination of "the satisfied life," you have to rejoice. Fill your mind up with what you already have and fill your mouth up with the good things God has done, and joy will begin to crank up your engine!

3. *Don't Be Offended.* Nothing robs us of the present moment like being easily insulted, upset, or assuming the worst of intentions. Someone may either purposefully or inadvertently say or do something to tick you off. What happens? You feel disrespected and wounded, which leads to being resentful and angry. Some people get offended by almost *anything* that happens. I recently heard the story of someone who cut off an entire relationship with a longtime friend because they had not been included in a business lunch! Feeling discounted and insulted, they decided that was the end! And when we feel we're not included, that our opinion isn't appreciated, we take it personally. Let it slide right off your back like that duck we talked about earlier. Who cares? Remember, you have much to be grateful for NOW.

continued

4. *Stop Beating Yourself Up.* It seems that we're always berating ourselves about what we HAVE done and what we HAVEN'T done. The result is a life of regret and guilt, as we saw in the "Love Yourself" chapter. Now IMAGINE A GUILT-FREE LIFE! No more self-condemnation. You would be able to handle your mistakes without self-derision. You would be able to take correction without being defensive. You wouldn't continuously need or seek out people's approval. You would be free from manipulation. Best of all, you'd have *a clear conscience.* You wouldn't condemn yourself. Jesus came to not only forgive us, but to free us from the guilt that keeps us bound to our past sins and mistakes. If He can be that kind to you, extend the same kindness to yourself. So stop beating yourself up for all that you have done wrong, and start "building yourself up" for all that God has done right in your life!

5. *Trust.* Trust that God will provide and that you have the resources within to find contentment and peace. Remember, God cares for our every need when we *trust* Him. But trust is sometimes the hardest thing to do, though it's one key to living in the moment. So here's the secret to learning to trust: First, you can't trust someone who doesn't keep their word. The foundation for trusting someone is that they have a proven *track record* of integrity. How about this track record? There are over one thousand predictions or prophecies in the Bible—promises that God made before they happened. The chances of merely 17 of these coming to pass is one out of 450 billion x 1 billion x 1 trillion! Yet, *not one* of these one thousand promised have failed. In fact, to this day, 668 of them have already been fulfilled. What does that tell us? God has integrity. You can trust Him! Relax! He will never let you down.

6. *Stop Holding Your Breath!* Yes, this is a play on words, but it's true in both the figurative and literal sense of the expression. We

have to stop waiting to win the lottery before we enjoy the day! DON'T HOLD YOUR BREATH! At the same time we need to USE our breath the way God told us to. As it says in Psalm 150:6: "Let everything that has breath praise the LORD."

As it says in Genesis 2:7, when God created man, it says He "breathed into man the BREATH of life," and he became a living soul. You have the very breath of God in you. Use it to give glory and praise back to Him. Don't waste your breath on bitter words and wounds toward others. Don't waste your breath on complaints that no one wants to hear; or will do much about. Use your breath the way it was created—to give God praise.

And when I say, "Don't hold your breath," I also want to bring attention to the age-old remedy for overcoming stress and tension—BREATHE! Take a few deep breaths! This isn't just a figure of speech. It works. Medical research shows that deep breathing is an incredibly healthy physical exercise. It also allows us to calm negative emotions and return to our God-given place of peace. Just as there's a rhythm to the tides' rising and ebbing, our bodies also have a rhythm. It may sound overly simple, but deep breathing helps you find that rhythm, and get you in the present moment.

We need to realize what a powerful force breathing really is. Throughout the book of Psalms, there is a little word often tucked in between the verses: *"selah."* It means to pause, to think about what you just read. Breathe in the words and let them change you. As it says in 2 Timothy 3:16, the Scriptures are "God-breathed," the very breath of God. As you meditate on the words of the Bible, you are literally breathing in the life that God has always intended for you—the satisfied life!

7. *Be Grateful.* When we live in gratitude, we live in the moment and experience true contentment, while a thankless attitude is the

continued

source of emotional pain. So let's get rid of "stinkin' thinkin'," those mentalities of failure that ignore the gifts present in our lives. Isn't it true that we count our blessings all too rarely until something goes *wrong*: a loved one gets sick, we lose a job, our child gets hurt. Suddenly, with regret, we look back at our abundant past with appreciation and count ourselves blessed *after* the crisis has passed or been resolved. Let's do it NOW—in this moment. I can tell you that *gratitude is the prayer of the enlightened*. We appreciate what's right in front of us and don't allow anything to spoil it. It's not that we're settling for less than we deserve or that we don't have future goals and ambitions. Not at all. God wants the best for us—and designed life to get better and better. But right here, right now, God is good—and life is good, just as it is because God is *present* (with you, in the now)! Knowing this is the only true liberation.

And above all...

8. *Celebrate!* The Bible is a book filled with over 130 verses that include the word "celebrate," and hundreds of others that talk about feasts and festive occasions. Celebrations abound from Passover to Pentecost, from the Feast of Tabernacles to the Feast of Booths. There's even a passage in Scripture that says, "Seven days you shall celebrate a feast to the LORD..." (Deut. 16:15). Notice, this celebration was supposed to last an entire week! God is commanding us to live in the now, celebrating what He has already done, forgetting about yesterday, and not being bombarded with tomorrow. So, yes, be joyful—for living in the now is, at its essence, our ability to rejoice in each moment. While joy is an attitude, celebration is the behavior that we need to partake of.

Use your hands to praise and your feet to dance. Thank and praise God for what He has *already* done in your life. Praise the fact that you're alive—you made it another day! You have a job, a family, the abundance of food, and shelter. Praise God—and before you know it, midnight will pass and morning will come. And, friends, don't be singing praises *under your breath;* praise so somebody can hear you! In a word, part of praising is *appreciating,* feeling grateful for what you already have in your life. Focus on being satisfied with the life you have and, believe me, more will come.

If you've ever been to Italy, aside from of the great art, monuments, and architecture, there's something even better there—the amazing people! They always seem to find a reason to celebrate "the now." Every dinner is a gathering of family and friends, filled with laughter and love. Every night is a celebration! I've never seen people who better exemplify living in the now. It's their ability to capture the moment and bottle it— I'm not talking about the wine!—that makes it such a unique culture. Sure, people there also have their ups and downs, times of sadness and sorrow. But my observation is that they know how to live in the present. So can we.

My friends, **we can flow through life rather than struggle through it.** We can enjoy each step along the way, instead of dragging our feet, weighed down by worry, regret, fear, and anxiety. Certainly, acknowledge those emotions as only human—and then replace them with positive emotions and mentalities of success. Instead of letting worry choke out the joy and satisfaction that God has promised, look out—and look up!

Remember: the power of this moment is that *all things are possible* because you are not limited by your past—or confined by a predefined future. He wants you to be happy *now.* So take a deep breath and *relax,* for the satisfied and invincible life is waiting for you. It's here right NOW—in the present moment!

And remember that in this moment, we're never in lack of *anything;* because our hope, our expectation, and our trust is in Him who is *omnipresent, not omnipast.* God is with you right now.

Secret #16

Leave Your Country
FOR THE LAND OF ULTIMATE OPPORTUNITY

Far better is it to dare mighty things, to win glorious triumphs, even though checkered by failure, than to take rank with those poor spirits who neither enjoy much nor suffer much, because they live in the gray twilight that knows not victory nor defeat.

— THEODORE ROOSEVELT

In the 1890s, at the height of the immigration boom, millions left behind everything familiar, not only their homelands but members of their own families, too, for what they hoped would be a better life in America.

During the strenuous crossing of the Atlantic (which could take from forty days to as long as six months), these brave souls were crowded into the bottom of the ship, and given a meager diet, risking serious illness and death. Still, they endured it all for something greater!

And as their ships pulled into New York Harbor, the Statue of Liberty emerged into view. With tears streaming down their faces, their hearts pounding, these precious souls disembarked on Ellis Island with hope and the courage to begin again. At last they had reached the "Golden Land."

Yes, they were exhausted. True, they had little money and few possessions—and, of course, no knowledge of the English language. But they carried with them something priceless—the God-given faith that they could create a new life for themselves.

So in leaving their native lands, they had opened their arms—and their hearts—to a brand-new country with endless opportunity, freedom, and the promise of the satisfied life.

LEAVING THE LAND OF "NOT ENOUGH"

And now it's time for you and me to push beyond our native boundaries, to leave our "country"—the emotional home we've known—for a place much better. For anyone who has ever felt that their past has *hindered* them, this is your day—and your chapter!

"Leave your country"—sounds a little strange, right? After all, why would anyone want to *leave their country*—the familiar and comfortable place they call home, the upbringing and mind-sets that they're most accustomed to—for something unknown?

Yet, just as our immigrant ancestors found a better life in America, leaving your "country," in the way I mean it, is going to open up a whole new world for you as well. I can tell you that doing it revolutionized my life, just as I trust it will revolutionize yours.

In the early part of my life I lacked any sort of confidence in myself or any belief that I could accomplish something significant. I always felt like an outcast, a loner. The guys I called my best friends would party with me one day, and the next day we were one degree of temper away from killing each other. My emotional makeup was anything but normal! One day I would be enraged at someone or something; the next day I would be depressed and suicidal. I felt schizophrenic—*and so did I.*

> Our potential is limited when we allow our upbringing to "stamp" an impression upon us that hems us into a predictable and mediocre existence.

It would be easy to blame my family background or my parents for all this, but I really don't. We all have some baggage. But our potential is limited when we allow our upbringing to "stamp" an impression upon us that hems us into a predictable and mediocre existence.

Still, I knew that if I didn't break away from the mentalities I grew up with, I would never achieve a satisfied life. I needed to leave *my* country! And so might you.

So what do I really mean by this? Am I saying to pull out your passport, get on a plane, and pitch your tent in France or Argentina, Mexico or Iceland? No — (though a vacation would be nice). Sure, there are times in life when we'd all like to get away and permanently escape our problems, starting all over again.

But as soon as you get in the car to drive off to a new destination, guess what? Your problems, your mind-sets, and the roots to your dissatisfied life jump in the trunk and ride along with you! So you can change your geography, and transplant yourself to a new place, but wherever you go, you take "you" with you! There's just no escape.

Folks, **leaving your country means permanently putting behind the land of your old habits and mentalities — the patterns, expectations, and limitations of the "place you've grown" accustomed to.** This is the fresh start that God wants you to have, the one you deserve. It's a perpetual escape from the old way of looking at things, replaced by a genuine change and a renewed spirit.

> Aren't you ready to graduate from mediocrity to the next level of success, maturity, wisdom, and favor?

We're talking about leaving the life that was "handed down" to us by our upbringing, our parents, and our past. Sometimes, doesn't it almost seem as if we're preprogrammed to live the life we've always known? We sleepwalk through life on automatic, doing the same thing in the same way, just as we were taught to, repeating the same mistakes and mentalities of those who raised us.

Granted, you may have had a tremendous upbringing. But if you're like most of us, **there are inherited limitations and mind-sets that fence us in and keep us trapped in a mediocre existence.** As we've seen throughout this book, God has something much better in store for you than that!

As we saw in the "Be Expectant" chapter, few people would willingly admit that they settle for an average or below-average life, but our resulting behaviors say otherwise. We drag ourselves along, demonstrating minimal effort, sometimes feeling: *What's the point?* We don't aspire toward greatness. It's not us! It's our mind-sets that are keeping us defeated, from graduating to something better.

But aren't you ready to move from mediocrity to greatness? From lack to prosperity? From uncertainty to confidence? As we learned in *Discover the Greatness in You,* **you must *believe* that you were created for something special,** that you have incredible and unique gifts that only await your command.

This is not conceit, arrogance, or pride. You really *do* have an invincible future, no matter how old or young you may be. To believe this is actually a sign of humility. Why? Because you are accepting what God thinks about you, and rejecting anything less.

God told Abraham, "I will make you great, and I will make your name great." This is not something to boast about, but something to believe in with every fiber in your being.

Remember, Abraham began life as a wandering nomad, living, as his relatives had, by taking advantage of *someone else's* harvest. He started out as a "taker," the kind of person we talked about in "Be on the Giving Side," someone with no land of his own and no future. He was destined to repeat the same pattern of failure until he learned the profound secret of Genesis 12:1, when God told him, **"Leave your country, your kindred, and your father's house, to a land I will show you."** *That's* when everything began to change for Abraham.

And so it will for you!

We're going to leave behind the country of our limitations and weaknesses, those invisible fences that hold us back from growth and realizing our potential. After all, *someone* has to be the one who stops the "curse" that is so often passed down from one generation to another. Abraham was the one who did it in his lifetime. You can do it in yours.

What do I mean by *curse*? I'm referring to our tendency to carry the same habits, addictions, diseases, prejudices, and limitations that we inherited from our parents (who inherited it from theirs)!

Again, you may have had a great upbringing, and if you did, thank God and build upon it. But many of us are weighed down by our unwanted *inheritance*. I'm talking about the temper of your mother, the stubbornness of your father, the heart disease of your grandfather, the diabetes of your grandmother, etc.

Isn't it true that when you fill out an insurance form, you're always asked for a medical history of the diseases that "run" in your family? I don't know about you, but I'm running *away* from those things rather than letting them run *through* me and *into* my children! And it's the same thing with inherited patterns of thinking. I'm *disinheriting* them!

So often, of course, we automatically assume that limitation, lack, or mediocrity is woven into our DNA—so we're bound to inherit it! If our parents were poor, barely making ends meet, that becomes the ceiling that we expect for ourselves. If they had a lackluster marriage, we assume we won't find much better.

Several years ago a magnificent young tiger was imported from India and shipped to a local zoo in the States. A beautiful and expansive habitat was being built for him, complete with a waterfall, trees, rocks, valleys, and caves. While the construction was under way, the tiger was housed in a small temporary cage, thirty by thirty feet. He spent his days continuously pacing the cage from one end to the other. Although this enclosure was originally intended to house the tiger for only a few weeks, the construction took longer than expected and the tiger remained in the cage for several months.

When the habitat was finally completed, the cage was lowered into it, opened, and the tiger set free. But almost immediately, he resumed his pacing. But you can guess what happened. He kept pacing thirty feet forward and thirty feet back! Sure, he was now able to roam at will, no longer confined by that small cage. But he would move no farther. Why? Because the cage that once imprisoned the tiger had actually been *transplanted* into his mind.

The moral of the story is that the limitations imposed on us (or that we impose on ourselves) can be so habit-forming that even when we *have* the freedom to move beyond them and change our lives for the better, we don't! Why? Because we're not much different from that caged tiger, trapped in our old "country," the culture and impressions of our past that keep us confined to a limited existence.

Although the door to the cage is wide open, we're fearful of leaving the familiar "confines" of our own expectations, when, in reality, there's so much more that God has in mind for us. Yet we are prevented from enjoying it, trapped by the invisible cage in our minds.

Not anymore! You're about to break free and live the life that you deserve.

LEARN TO DANCE

Have you ever seen the movie *Take the Lead*? Based on a person's true story, Antonio Banderas plays the part of a dance instructor who sees a teenager vandalizing the car of the director of a public school. The next day, instead of turning in the culprit, he shows up in the principal's office, volunteering to teach ballroom dancing (and good manners) to inner-city students.

At first, the principal just laughs at him, as do the students. But he sees something in *them* that they cannot see in *themselves*—talent and the potential to move *beyond* their perceived limitations to a better life.

So over the course of the movie, Banderas's character becomes a blessing, patiently taming his rebellious students, and ultimately teaching them self-respect, dignity, and confidence. In the end he turns the formerly rowdy delinquents into fantastic dancers, their redemption complete by the time they enter a ballroom dance contest.

Each of us can learn to dance—a new way of moving, new habits, and a refreshed way of *thinking* that will transform our lives.

So today—yes, today!—we're *leaving*, for good, the country of our old habits, old relationships, prejudices, and mind-sets to a new land. We're leaving behind the land of "not enough" and the land of "just barely enough," and crossing over to the land of "more than enough," one flowing with milk and honey.

So, tell me, have you ever felt that *you* needed to leave your country? What would you change in your life—if you could?

Would you lose weight? Begin an exercise program? Improve a strained relationship? Control your anger? Overcome a fear? Get organized? Grow spiritually? Find a better job? Increase your finances? Break free from a habit or addiction?

The good news, as we've seen throughout the book, is that you can change any of these things. The Bible says, *"I can do all things through Christ who strengthens me"* Phil. 4:13). There are some simple steps you can take that will result in lasting change and lead you to the life that God intends for you—a truly satisfied life.

But in order to accomplish this, we can't just paint over our past, putting a fresh layer of new paint over the old ones. We need to strip away all the layers of paint from year's past, then resurface, prime, and put a new coat to produce a new finish.

I like to think of Luke 5:36, which says: " 'No one tears a piece of cloth from a new garment and puts it on an old garment; otherwise he will both tear the new, and the piece from the new, will not match the old.' "

Yes, folks, **we cannot put new actions onto old mind-sets.** For example, you can't put on the garment of "giving" because you want someone else to give back to you. That's the wrong mind-set. It's not giving—it's trading. As we saw in "Be on the Giving Side," we need to give with an open, compassionate heart, which begins on the inside. But the reason why so many people don't create lasting change in their lives is because they're trying to change it on the *outside*—trying to control their external behavior.

But, as we've seen right from the start of the book, change doesn't happen from the *outside in*. We can't keep thinking the same thoughts and somehow believe that we can change our behavior.

When we deal with what is wrong with our thinking, we *are* dealing with what is wrong in our lives. And as you change "from the inside out," you'll uncover the treasure that God has put in you, and you'll enter into His destiny for your life.

To do this, we need to cultivate an attitude of rebellion. What do I mean? We have all had at least a little rebellion in us, growing up, when we defied our parents (and wore clothes we wouldn't be caught dead in today)! But I'm not talking about disregard and disrespect for authority in our lives. I'm talking about "rebelling" against what was wrong in how we grew up—beginning today!

For example, if you were taught all your life not to trust "black folks" or that the "white man" was against you, you need to "rebel" against that way of thinking. If the people you grew up with (or currently spend time with) are negative thinkers or doubters, you need to rebel against that and—most likely—those relationships.

In other words, before you *settle* into the course you're setting for your life, you need to first "unsettle" the things you grew up with, shaking off the patterns and values and beliefs that have shaped a life of dissatisfaction.

More often than not, I've found that **most people are dissatisfied because they passively *accept* the life they inherit.** We do this because we're fearful of breaking away from comfortable behaviors that define and limit us. Even though they hem us in, they provide a level of security and comfort.

Friends, as we've already said earlier, it's time to get *uncomfortable and insecure,* so you can meet the new you.

For starters, look into the mirror—not your bathroom mirror! The Bible calls itself the mirror of the Word of God. The problem is that so many of us have learned to read the Bible as a book of commands or rules. This is not what God intended. It's called the mirror of freedom (James 1:25). It was written for us to discover who God said we are; who He made us to be. It's a new way of looking at things and a new way of looking at ourselves—and others.

Remember in *Snow White and the Seven Dwarfs* when the wicked queen looks into that magical mirror and asks, "Mirror, mirror, on the wall, who's the fairest of them all?" The Mirror always replies, "Why, YOU are!" While that was a lie, the Bible is not a lie. It always tells us how truly beautiful and lovely we are in God's eyes. Understanding it will shape the image that we have of ourselves—our sense of value and our expectations of what we can accomplish in life. It has for me, and it will for you. But first you have to look into it, and let it speak to you. As I like to say, "Mirror, mirror, in this book, tell me how I truly look!"

Many times we don't see ourselves as we truly are. The image in the mirror is distorted, like one of those crazy mirrors at a carnival, where we look like we're nine feet tall and three feet wide! We see ourselves as one thing, though we're really another.

I like the story of the man who found an eagle's egg and put it into the nest of a prairie chicken. The eaglet hatched with the brood of chicks and grew up believing he was one of them, behaving just as the other prairie chickens did. He scratched in the dirt for seeds and insects to eat. He clucked and cackled. And he flew in a brief thrashing of wings and flurry of feathers no more than a few feet off the ground. Why? Because that was his "country."

Years passed, and one day, in his old age, the eagle saw a magnificent bird far above him in the cloudless sky. Soaring with graceful majesty on a powerful current of wind, this bird flew effortlessly with scarcely a beat of its strong wings.

"What a beautiful bird!" said the eagle to his chicken neighbor. "What is it?"

"That's an *eagle*—the chief of the birds," the neighbor clucked. "But don't give it a second thought. You could *never* be like him."

So the eagle never gave it another thought. And he died thinking he was a prairie chicken!

This does not have to happen to us. We must see ourselves as we *can* be, as we were meant to be by God—soaring above, fulfilling our potential.

LEAVE YOUR COUNTRY

FOR THE LAND OF ULTIMATE OPPORTUNITY

Part Two

PARDON THE INTERRUPTION

In our quest to reside in a brand-new "country," let's circle back for a moment to the momentous passage in the Bible where God tells Abraham to leave *his* country, just as that eagle who needed to leave that chicken farm.

Abraham expected to follow in the footsteps of his parents and grandparents, all nomads in the city of Ur, where they worshipped idols instead of God. But as we know, Abraham experienced what I would call a *divine interruption,* when God turned around the status quo, thereby disrupting the mind-sets of his inferior life.

Likewise, in order to live the passionate, satisfied life that God wants for you, you have to be willing to be *interrupted*!

As God said to Abraham: "Leave your country, your fathers' home for a land that I will show you. I will make you a great nation and bless you...and bless those who bless you..."

Your own blessing starts with the mandate of leaving your country—exchanging your old mind-sets for new ones. Of course, you have to be willing to LET GO of what you're holding on to so that God can give you what *He's* holding on to.

There was a little girl who saved her allowance money in order to buy a strand of fake pearls that she saw in a jewelry store window while shopping with her mother. Although the pearls were only costume jewelry, they were precious to her, so she treasured them as genuine. In fact, she became so attached to the pearls that she slept with them under her pillow. One night her adoring father came into her room and asked her — "Do you love me, darling?"

"Of course, I do, Daddy. You know I love you."

"Would you give me your pearls?"

"Daddy, I'll give you anything — but please don't ask for my pearls."

"Okay, sweetheart. That's all right." The father, though, made the same request of her for the next three nights. Each time she declined to give away her pearls.

On the following night, before he could even ask, with tears streaming down her cheeks, the little girl tenderly placed her fake pearls in her father's hands, saying, "Daddy, I love you more than anything in this world, including my pearls."

Immediately her father pulled out a velvet box that contained a genuine pearl necklace, glistening almost as much as the face of the surprised and overwhelmed little girl!

All those nights the father was trying to give her the *real* thing, while she was afraid to let go of the substitute.

Friends, **God has something genuinely precious for you as well, but you have to be willing to let go of the familiar, the life you've become accustomed to.**

Hold nothing back from God, and He will hold nothing back from you.

TAKING EVERY THOUGHT CAPTIVE

So, are you ready to leave your "country"? You're about to make a permanent escape from those old mind-sets that hold you back, that leave you defeated and discouraged. You know them well:

God is mad at me.
I don't have enough.

That's just the way I am.
There's nothing I can do about my situation.
It's too late.
I feel guilty.

We're going to systematically eliminate wrong thinking from our daily diet and start putting new thoughts into it. As you'll see below, **your success on the "fast" from wrong thinking depends upon challenging every thought, *rebelling* against the status quo, and forever *letting go* of it.**

Let's leave these "countries" behind us, beginning with the few I have listed that you should leave right now:

• *I Can't.* We're all familiar with this one: *I can't change. I can't believe that. I can't go on. I can't make it. I can't forgive. I can't recover. I can't get it done. I can't find a job. I can't find a spouse. I can't go back to college. I can't pay the bills. I can't figure this out.* (This song will never be sung on *American Idol!*) This is a mentality that sets us up to fail, to quit, and to live a negative existence. It is a poison that we must no longer eat or drink. From this day forward, we're replacing this thought with: **"I can."** As it says in Philippians 4:13 says: "I can do all things through Christ which strengthens me." Say it over and over again, "I can," until it becomes just as automatic as "I can't." Trust me, if you believe you can, you will.

• *I'm Overwhelemed.* Feeling that we're at the end of our rope, that we can't handle everything all at once, can be a paralyzing mind-set. *This will take forever. I've got too much to do. This is too much for me to take. There isn't enough time. I can't endure it anymore.* These thoughts have to go! Let me tell you how. Most people don't understand what Jesus meant when He said, "Take My yoke upon you..." A yoke is a harness placed upon *two* oxen. It causes them to plow together, so that when one gets weak or overwhelmed, the other can take over. Likewise, when we feel overwhelmed, we need to remember that God is attached to *us,* and will help carry our load. Of course, He ends up doing most of the work. So, folks, cast your cares upon *Him*. Tell Him what's wrong. Ask Him to carry it for you. And believe that He will. In truth, you can handle *anything*. As it says in Mark 9:23, "All things are possible for those who believe."

• *Something Bad Is Going to Happen*. Say *"Hasta la vista, baby!"* to this damaging mind-set. Beginning today, we're fasting from the thought of impending doom and suffering. Of course, when something bad happens in the news, it's easy for fear to creep in, and to think we're open game, sitting ducks for twisted people to strike us down. After 9/11, thousands sought counseling for their anticipated fear of what terror would happen next. DO NOT open the door to the expectation of evil. Keep it locked. Of course, we offer compassion, prayer, and practical support for those who have suffered, but we can't allow a dangerous world to create our own expectations of the future. Remember that Job continually thought that something bad might happen to his family. And it did. He said, "What I feared has come upon me" (Job 3:25). Instead, BELIEVE God's promise, as in Psalm 91:10: "No evil will befall you, nor will any plague come near your tent." Expect something good to happen in your life, in your family—and it will!

• *My Life Is Not As Good As Yours*. When you *compare,* you *despair*. (*I'm not as well off, pretty, or successful. My life is not as easy or fun. Things seem to work out for them better than me*.) STOP THIS! You have the life that God gave you, and nobody can live it better than you. So give up the temptation to compare your body, money, marriage, children, car, or job to somebody else's. Remember: *Royalty destroys inferiority*. What I mean is that you are in God's Royal Family, inferior to *no one*. As it says in Romans 5:17, "…through the gift of righteousness, we reign as kings in this life." Realize that God has reserved a special gift and *portion* for you that no one can take. And as we saw in "Be Healed," stop thinking *backward* (looking at what you *don't* have) and start thinking *forward* (looking at what you *do* have). *Gratitude* is the secret to vanquishing inferiority for good. Declare this aloud: "I am secure. I am grateful. I have a special gift and treasure that God has given me. I lack nothing and therefore I am not jealous or envious of what *anyone* else has!"

• *That's Just the Way I Am.* What keeps us limited and defeated isn't usually our circumstances but rather our *opinion* of ourselves. This shapes our estimation of what we're capable of. (*I'm shy. I'm stubborn. I'm incapable of a relationship. I'll always be average—or overweight.*) But hear this: You are NOT a fixed, unchangeable being. You've only been *conditioned* to believe these self-imposed expectations; and remain hidden behind them out of fear. That may have been the way you *were,* but that's not the way you *are.* The Bible says God is the potter and we are the clay. God is working on you, to make you what He wants you to be. Trust the Artist to make a masterpiece. Be flexible and adaptable. See yourself as a good work in progress. **You may not quite be where you want to be, but thank God you're not where you used to be!**

• *Don't Get Your Hopes Up.* This mind-set has subtly found its way into our heads as a way of protecting us from the fear of rejection or failure. In *advance,* we let ourselves off the hook, so we don't have to succeed. Our hopes aren't up—they're down! We have been trained by doubt and *un*belief to lower our expectations—to brace ourselves for mediocrity and the status quo. But to hope, is to look *up*—to have expectation! To hope, is to live. Hope is like oxygen. It's like light in a dark and negative world. Proverbs 13:12 says: "Hope deferred makes the heart sick." And indeed it does. Tell yourself: *My hopes are UP!—and I'm keeping them up! I expect God's promises to come to pass in my life today—in my family, home, church, job, relationships, in my body and in my finances.*

• *I'm a Victim.* This is one of the handiest excuses we make to stay the same. IT'S NOT MY FAULT! (*My mother did it to me; the boss doesn't like me; I didn't get the right breaks; it's the government; my brother got all the attention; I didn't get the right education,* on and on. In this mind-set, the way our life turns out is always somebody *else's* fault—or fate itself is to blame.) Viktor Frankl, who does not view himself as a victim, survived the Nazi death camp at Auschwitz by defining ultimate freedom as the ability "to choose one's attitude in any given set of circumstances, to choose one's own way." I can tell you that **the worst prison is the one we put ourselves into**. It strips us of the power God has given us to rule our lives in victory. **Other people may have had something to do with how you got *into* the situation, but no one can keep you *in* it except you.** Eliminate excuse making: *No one helps me; no one understands; no one gives me a break. I was just meant to suffer in this way.* In John 5:7, the lame man told God, "I have no one to help me." The truth is he didn't need anybody else. **Stop making excuses.** It's not what surrounds you, but what's inside you that produces success! Friends, **we must accept total responsibility for our attitude and direction in life—to become victors, not victims.** Do something *now* to make things better. Don't let life dictate to you that "this is all there is." As it says in Deuteronomy 30:15, "See, I have set before you this day, life and prosperity and death and adversity...so choose life, that both you and your descendants might LIVE"—the victorious, abundant life you deserve.

• *It's Too Late.* This is what you say when you feel the party is definitely over! (*I'm all washed up, that chance is gone forever, it's never going to be the same again.*) We talk in *absolutes* as if we weren't still alive! We are so "time conscious," allowing that ticking clock to limit and define what we're capable of, or what God can do in our lives. Friends, it's never too late to change, to start a new career, to save your marriage, to recover from a tragedy or mistake, to take better care of yourself, to start saving, to be forgiven, to recover from an addiction, to apologize, or to get a second chance. And most important, **it's never too late to change the way you see *yourself*. UN-DECIDE that it's too late for these things to change.** *Un*-decide that you can't recover! *Un*-decide that the damage is irreversible. Tell yourself: *I believe that it is not too late for things to improve in my life, and radically turn around. I believe in the God of second chances. I can recover and there is nothing that God can't turn around in my life.*

• *It's Not Working.* So often, people think: *I'm trying, but I'm not really changing. My marriage is not working. Prayer is not working. My budget is not working. The Word of God is not working. Tithing is not working.* Keep sowing the right seeds. As it says in Galatians 6:9: "And let us not be weary in well doing: for in due season we shall reap, if we faint not." We need to believe that if we don't give up, we will get our harvest.

And so, my friends, beginning today, you hold in your hand the ticket to a wonderful voyage. As we escape from the mind-sets that have kept us living below our God-given destiny and privileges, we will enter into the new country, the land of more than enough.

Perhaps this book is *your* "divine interruption." I certainly hope that it is, that I have interrupted the pattern of your previous limitations, past expectations, and preconditioned boundaries.

What we believe *in* and what we stand *for*—the purpose for which we are living—needs to be elevated. It must not be based on the culture we grew up in or on what's familiar or popular.

Beginning today, I want you to think above, not below. Lift your head high and look up. Appreciate the love of God present in your life right now—and see everything from His point of view. Live in the moment and surrender being enslaved to the past or consumed by future worries.

You are bigger than those worries or your so-called "problems." You are bigger than your fears; and bigger than any mountain you may be facing today.

If you're willing to trust God and follow Him—even in unfamiliar territory, even when no one else is going with you, and even when it's "safer" to stay where you are—you can and will summon an invincible spirit.

This inner resolve gives us the strength *to find our calling in our conquering,* to persist and to prevail—leading us to the satisfied life that we long for.

So identify—as we have done in the past pages—the perils of familiarity that are excluding you from the greatness for which you have been born.

Endure the pain of leaving the familiar. And remember, you leave it first in your *mind.*

So *forgive yourself* for the past. *Believe* in the future. And be *expectant* to *discover the greatness within.* When you allow yourself *to be still*—and to hear God's voice—expect the darkness to turn to light. Expect your pain to be healed.

You will be amazed at the transformation that happens on the outside—because of what you have allowed to happen on the inside.

And there, awaiting you in all its splendor and glory is God's magnificent promise—**THE SATISFIED LIFE**.

Notes

Introduction/ Gateway to the Satisfied Life

Page xviii: "More Than Half of Americans 'Very Satisfied' with Personal Life," January 3, 2007, http://www.gallup.com/poll/26032/More-Than-Half-Americans-Very-Satisfied-Personal-Life.aspx.

Secret #1

Page 13: "He's Still Working on Me," Joel Hemphill © 1980 Bridge Building Music, Inc, /Friends & Family Music (BMI) (admin by Brentwood-Benson Music Publishing, Inc.

Secret #2

Pages 18 and 19: Associated Press, April 14, 1982, cited on http://www.straightdope. com/columns/read/2636/supermom.

Pages 19 and 20: Gordon Bellows, "It's Never Too Late to Be Successful, Age Is Not an Excuse," http://www.smallbusinessbrief.com/articles/inspiration/003327.html.

Secret #3

Page 41: Benson, Herbert; Friedman, Richard, "Harnessing the Power of the Placebo Effect and Renaming It 'Remembered Wellness,'" Annual Review of Medicine 47: 193–199. 10.1146/annurev.med.47.1.193.

Secret #4

Page 51: "CDC: Antidepressants most prescribed drugs in U.S.," http://www.cnn.com/2007/HEALTH/07/09/antidepressants/index.html.

Steven Grinstead, "Multidisciplinary Chronic Pain Treatment—Part I," http://www.recoverytoday.net/September_2008/grinstead.html.

Page 53: U.S. Department of Health and Human Services, http://www.hhs.gov/asl/testify/t060517.html.

Secret #5

Page 68: Guy Harris, "Listen More, Speak Less—5 Steps to Better Listening," http://www.insideindianabusiness.com/contributors.asp?id=718.

Page 70: American Psychological Association, "Stress a major health problem in the U.S., warns APA," http://www.apa.org/releases/stressproblem.html.

Secret #7

Page 100: Harvard Medical School, "Sharp Rise in Eating Disorders in Fiji Follows Arrival of TV," http://forums.studentdoctor.net/archive/index.php/t-501920.html.

Secret #8

Page 115: Jerry D. Locke, "Forgiving One's Self? It May Not Be a Big Deal, But...," http://www.tbaptist.com/aab/forgivingself.htm.

Page 117: U.S. Department of Health and Human Services, "Heart Disease is the Number One Cause of Death," http://www.cdc.gov/DHDSP/announcements/american_heart_month.htm.

"Heart Disease Facts and Statistics," http://www.cdc.gov/heartdisease/statistics.htm.

Page 118: MayoClinic.Com, "Forgiveness: How to let go of grudges and bitterness," http://www.mayoclinic.com/health/forgiveness/MH00131.

Secret #9

Page 130: "Individual Temperament as a Predictor of Health or Premature Disease," John Hopkins Medical Journal, http://www.ncbi.nlm.nih.gov/pubmed/430948, cited in *Reader's Digest,* November, 1979.

Secret #10

Page 147: Jocelyn Voo, "Drudgery Report: In a City of Frantic Multi-Taskers, for Many Workers Tedium Is Enemy No. 1," February 18, 2008, http://www.nypost.com/seven/02182008/jobs/drudgery_report_98176.htm.

Pages 152 and 153: Ellen Degeneres, http://www.the-top-tens.com/lists/the-funniest-stand-up-comedians.asp.

Secret #11

Page 170: "*Que Sera, Sera* (Whatever Will Be, Will Be)," Jay Livingston, Ray Evan, 1956.

Page 171: Peter Libby, M.D., *New York Times*, June 23, 2008,

Secret #13

Pages 193 and 194: "Rejected Orphan Hears, 'I Want This Child.'" http://www.preachingtoday.com/illustrations/weekly/02-07-29/13779.html.

Page 196: Bernard Rimland, "The Altruism Paradox," *Psychological Reports* 51, 1982: 521-522, cited on http://net.bible.org/illustration.php?topic=697.

Page 202: "Affluent Americans: Priorities of the Prosperous," February 8, 2005, http://www.gallup.com/poll/14857/Affluent-Americans-Priorities-Prosperous.aspx

Page 203: Harvard University, "Money Spent on Others Can Buy Happiness," April 17, 2008, http://www.news.harvard.edu/gazette/2008/04.17/31-happiness.html.

Secret #15

Page 233: "Health Benefits of Deep Breathing," http://www.healthmad.com/Health/Health-Benefits-of-Deep-Breathing.51144.

"Try Deep Breathing To Ease Tension, Boost Metabolism," http://path2healthyliving.com/breathing.html.

About the Author

PASTOR GREGORY DICKOW is the founder of the Chicago-based Life Changers International Church. He is the popular host of *Changing Your Life*, an international television ministry, as well as the highly rated *Ask the Pastor* radio program heard during the afternoon drive-time in a number of cities across the country. Pastor Dickow has been pastoring and counseling people for nearly two decades.

Ministry Contact Info

Gregory Dickow Ministries
PO Box 7000
Chicago, IL 60680

www.gregorydickow.org

800-763-9070